Also by Helen Franks

PRIME TIME
GOODBYE TARZAN: Men After Feminism
REMARRIAGE: What Makes It, What Breaks It

Edited by Helen Franks
WHAT EVERY WOMAN SHOULD KNOW ABOUT RETIREMENT

MUMMY DOESN'T LIVE

HELEN FRANKS

mummy doesn't live here any more

Doubleday

LONDON · NEW YORK · TORONTO · SYDNEY · AUCKLAND

TRANSWORLD PUBLISHERS LTD
61–63 Uxbridge Road, London W5 5SA

TRANSWORLD PUBLISHERS (AUSTRALIA) PTY LTD
15–23 Helles Avenue, Moorebank, NSW 2170

TRANSWORLD PUBLISHERS (NZ) LTD
Cnr Moselle and Waipareira Aves,
Henderson, Auckland

DOUBLEDAY CANADA LTD
105 Bond Street, Toronto, Ontario M5B 1Y3

Published 1990 by Doubleday
a division of Transworld Publishers Ltd
Copyright © Helen Franks, 1990

The right of Helen Franks to be identified
as author of this work has been asserted in accordance
with sections 77 and 78 of the Copyright Designs and Patents
Act 1988.

British Library Cataloguing in Publication Data
Franks, Helen
   Mummy doesn't live here anymore : why women leave their
   children.
   1. Society. Role of women
   I. Title
   305.42

ISBN 0–385–26905–6

Printed in Great Britain by
Mackays of Chatham, Chatham, Kent

Acknowledgements

My most grateful thanks go to the women who allowed me to interview them, and also to the 'children' who talked to me (most of them now adults), who were left without their mothers. Names are changed in almost all instances. Thank you also to the following organizations and individuals: the Anna Freud Clinic, Fiona Burtt, Daphne Carter, CAST (Creative and Support Trust for Women Prisoners), Susanna Cheal of the Child Psychotherapy Trust, the Children's Society, Child Guidance Training Centre, Wally K. Daly, Gingerbread, Mary Michaels of One Parent Families, MATCH (Mothers Apart From Their Children), National Children's Bureau, NORCAP (National Organisation for Counselling Adoptees and their Parents), the late Christine Orton, the Post-Adoption Centre, Rights of Women, Yorkshire Television (*First Tuesday*).

Contents

MUMMY DOESN'T LIVE HERE ANYMORE

Introduction

US AND THEM

This is a book about women who have children and, for the most part, expect to live with them and look after them during the years of childhood and adolescence. And yet, either through choice or force of circumstance, or a combination of both, they find themselves living apart from their children, sometimes far away, sometimes in a situation of love, often in one of great pain and conflict.

This is also a book about the rest of us, the people who do not leave their children, the ones who judge and sometimes misjudge, who are hostile or shocked or disturbed by the breaking of preciously-guarded rules concerning mother-love and who because of these attitudes inflict further pain on the breakers of those rules.

'It doesn't seem natural' is the way one man summed it up, and the sentiment rings true for many others, men and women alike. 'How could she?' . . . 'I can't imagine anyone doing it' . . . are the kinds of responses women give to the idea of mothers wilfully living apart from their children, though we are all very familiar with men doing so.

I embarked on this book as one entering unknown territory. I wanted to know: who are these women? why do they break the rules? what happens to them afterwards? do they really love their children? If I, too, started out half-expecting unnatural women committing unnatural acts, I finished up with something far more complex, often heartrending and sometimes exceedingly disturbing.

There is, of course, nothing new about women leaving their children or handing them over to other people, and what seems acceptable to one society might appal another. The Greeks and Romans left their unwanted babies on mountainsides to be devoured by wolves or picked up by some softhearted shepherd, a custom which seems horrific today. In the Bible, one of the most famous examples meets with modern approval. The mother of Moses sent her baby into the bulrushes to be found by the princess so that he should escape the fate of his fellow Jews at the hands of the Egyptian taskmasters. She sent her adolescent daughter too, to keep an eye on things, and one might imagine her agony and also perhaps the criticism of her neighbours who did not abandon their babies, even to royalty.

During times of war and political unrest, children are sent away to relatives or strangers in the safety of the countryside. This happened when children were evacuated to escape the London bombings during the Second World War. It happened to Jewish children spirited out of Europe to escape the Holocaust. Economic policies and the demand for cheap labour also part mothers from their children. In Britain, women from the West Indies or West Africa or the Philippines, even Spain and Portugal, work for years in low-paid jobs to send money home in order to educate their children.

But what of the women who put a cause or career first? We accept that the duties of the Royal Family must make them part from their children for affairs of State: Queen Elizabeth left Prince Charles and Princess Anne when they were four and two for a six-month tour of Australia, and her children were brought up by nannies, just as she was as a child. However, the Queen's daughter-in-law, the Duchess of York, received criticism from the media for leaving her new baby in 1988, presumably because her presence on a Royal tour was not considered to be of such great use to the country.

Commoners, even when working for the public good, are likely to be awarded both brickbats and bouquets for leaving their children. Elizabeth Fry, Quaker minister and prison reformer, led an active public life in the early 1800s, travelling and campaigning. She was much criticized at the time, since she also managed to fit in the births of eleven children of whom she saw very little. But to many she was a national heroine, as she would be today.

Ulrike Meinhof, of the Baader-Meinhof group, was not working for the public good in most people's estimation. But she was so convinced of her ideals that she not only left her children in order to be part of the terrorist group, but later had them secretly removed to Sicily from Germany, en route to a Palestinian orphanage camp. (Stefan Aust, author of the book *The Baader-Meinhof Group*, intercepted and restored the children to their father.) Her actions may have lacked wisdom or an appropriate sense of what would be best for her children, but her letters to them from prison show that she cared deeply for them.

Among the women who have sat out their vigil at Greenham Common were some who left their children at home. They too showed deep maternal concern and would say they were trying to make a better world for future generations. Were they sacrificing their children to their own needs or were they making sacrifices for the sake of their children? So much, it seems, is in the eye of the beholder and the mind of the protagonist.

There are no clear statistics about how many women are living apart from their children. A figure given by MATCH (the organization Mothers Apart from their Children), for which no source is available, is 80,000 in Britain. Other pointers include the fact that one family in eight in Great Britain is a one-parent family; around 10% to 15% of fathers get custody of children on divorcing; an estimated 200,000 children live with their fathers. There are also over 72,500 children in the care of local authorities in England and Wales. In America, figures suggest that the numbers of women living apart from their children are rising rapidly. A 'conservative' estimate gave the figure of 565,000 women in 1982, and this was double that of 1970.

All this suggests that what may seem unnatural to some is a reality for a large number of women and their children too. These women leave in many different ways and for many different reasons. Yet the general assumption is that they disappear without trace. They are not simply non-custodial mothers, they are *abandoning* mothers, wicked creatures who feed our fantasy world like the villains we love to hiss at in Victorian melodrama.

The reality is quite different. Most women living apart from their children, like many men, seek to retain contact, try to contribute towards their children's upkeep, and continue to offer care and love as best they can.

Their problems, however, are unlike those of men. Mothers are valued and devalued in special ways in our society. The intense disapproval they receive when they are seen to renege on their role colours their self-attitude, their relations with their children and their hopes for personal fulfilment. They misjudge and misunderstand themselves because they are judged and misunderstood by others. They take on the guilt and the shame, or they adopt an attitude of denial so that peace of mind eludes them and they fail to resolve their difficulties, or those of their children.

Most of the women – certainly those in this book – care deeply for their children. But motherhood is highly demanding. It requires patience, forbearance, tolerance, generosity, endurance. It does not thrive on poverty, poor housing or an unhappy marital relationship. Nor can it flourish with ease when there is a history of deprived childhood or mental instability. It is threatened by the

quest for romantic fulfilment and by women's economic dependence within marriage. It is also threatened by changed aspirations
among women regarding work or career, the low status of motherhood and the high standards of self-sacrifice expected of mothers.
Any, and sometimes all of these factors can contribute towards a
situation in which a mother lives apart from her children.

There is one group of women who come near to confirming
prejudices about selfish or irresponsible mothers. These women
are ones who choose to put their careers or their personal freedom
first in their priorities, though they could provide a comfortable
home and support their children. Their work might take them
many miles away so that contact is slight. They may have a deep
conviction that they must give priority to their talent or potential ability.

Even so, there is another way to look at their situation.
Sociologist Maggie O'Brien, in a study of lone fathers, found that
significantly more professionally trained wives came to a relatively amicable agreement with their ex-husbands over the future
of the children, than full-time housewives. She surmised that their
'financial, occupational and educational resources' increased the
variety of options open to these women and created a 'personal
psychological state whereby they could "allow" their husbands to
become the custodial parent'. She also suggested that some women
were prepared to go through the motions of legal proceedings to
retain custody of their child so as not to be perceived as a rejecting
mother. And as will be seen in this book, some twist themselves
into strange psychological knots in order to deny to themselves the
socially unacceptable truth that they cannot, for whatever reason,
live comfortably full-time with their children.

Here at last is the unnatural act, deeply disturbing because it
upsets what we take to be the God-given order of things. Can we
have been wrong about this natural order? On what grounds can
it be claimed that it is more unforgivable for a woman to leave a
child than it is for a man to do so? What are the circumstances
that drive a woman to this action?

The women who speak in this book help to provide some
answers. Though circumstances differ, a pattern did emerge,
particularly among women who left their marriages and their
children for their own self-development.

These seekers of liberation can be identified sometimes as
women who married young, perhaps because marriage provided
an escape from the pressures of their own family life. Their
husbands were traditional, mature – often quite a bit older
than themselves – and sometimes devoutly religious. Sex was
disappointing, babies were born too soon, and life appeared

predictable and unrewarding. The marriages were set against a backcloth of the sixties, that decade of new-found entitlement to an enriching sex life, and the seventies with their promises and consciousness-raising messages for women.

And then came the eighties, and exhortations of a free enterprise culture. The new materialism has brought a justification for leaving children that goes beyond a woman saying that she is not able to support them. Now she might say, as one American woman did (in the American magazine *New Woman*) when she voluntarily relinquished her sons to their father, 'Face it, these are the kids of the eighties. They want fifty-dollar sneakers and fantastic bikes. I couldn't deliver. We all would have been miserable.' Sad enough that those values were her children's, worse that they were hers too.

Materialism is however only one part of the contemporary message. Together with the build-up from the earlier decades, the overall effect of modern values has been to make some women want to be free as men are free, to find self-fulfilment, to seek social and career status, to eschew motherhood if need be.

The trend reaches its logical development in a new outlook among some women, one that makes motherhood an option rather than a lifelong commitment, rather in the way that modern marriage is an option – if it works, fine, if it does not satisfy, then consider something else. There are women – and at least one appears in this book – who undertake motherhood in this manner. They claim a right to make a new life for themselves without their children, taking advantage perhaps of a greater willingness among some fathers to keep the family together.

This lack of commitment could be seen as an anti-mothering element in society. The wealthy have always delegated responsibility for child-rearing to servants and used boarding-schools to rid the home of their freedom-restricting offspring if they felt so inclined. While other women have passively accepted the narrowness of their choices, the privileged could indulge in prolonged cultural tours abroad while nanny looked after the children. They could even elope with a lover, leaving the household to cope quite adequately without them. Both the Duchess of York and her sister-in-law, the Princess of Wales, experienced eloping mothers during their otherwise privileged childhoods. (That they have come to no conspicuous harm suggests that money and mother substitutes have their compensations, thought it might be said that they themselves did make somewhat singular marriages – ones which are strongly bound by convention and strict rules.)

Today it is not only the wealthy who question the sacrificial role of mothering. The widespread desire for greater liberation amongst women in general has led to a very real fear of being overwhelmed by motherhood. Women have come to understand that mothering qualities – being passive and making sacrifices – leaves them vulnerable to exploitation. They have a great fear today of becoming victims.

Despite the joys of motherhood, the price it exacts is high and the choices limited in a society where the vast majority of women must make their own arrangements for childcare, where there is no statutory parental leave when children are sick, where child benefits have been frozen, where out-of-school and holiday care barely exist in most areas, where returners to work are often limited to jobs at a lower level than they had before they gave up work to start a family.

It is impossible to separate the personal from the political when looking at reasons why women leave their children. The firsthand accounts here by women from very different walks of life are all deeply personal, but their individual circumstances alone do not sufficiently explain their present position.

I did not set out to do a statistical survey but it is interesting to note that out of twenty-three mothers interviewed (not all are included in this book), six women who gave up or left their children were themselves brought up by someone who was not their mother. They were either adopted or their mother died or moved away for some reason. Four in this category tell their stories in this book, and they suggest that early loss of a mother may affect subsequent maternal feelings in some cases. Perhaps the most significant aspect is that they were for the most part illegitimate and were adopted because of this. They were then denied proper access to information about their background because of the stigma associated with illegitimacy. (In addition, at least two 'children' – people whose mothers had left them, and whose experiences are also recorded in these pages – refer to their own mothers as having been adopted.)

Research by Dr Eva Frommer in 1973 suggested that women separated from either parent before the age of eleven found it difficult to cope with their own babies. More recent work from Tirril Harris, George Brown and Antonia Bifulco showed that loss of a mother before the age of seventeen, whether through adoption, death or separation lasting at least a year, was linked with depression in adult women. The quality of substitute care did seem to make a substantial difference, however.

Research in America by Patricia Paskowitz revealed that one-third of 100 non-custodial mothers had been raised in whole or in part by someone other than their natural mother. This is not far from my own figure.

But the majority of women in this book, as in the survey, do not slot into this category. Their backgrounds do not fit so neatly with a history of loss. Nor is it true to say that all are liberated, empowered through feminism to make sweeping choices. As will be seen, most appear to live in a state of siege, or in a kind of limbo.

The children in this book who experienced their childhood without their mothers again do not fit into easy categories. Some show surprising tolerance and understanding, others immense forbearance. Through the children who were adopted, in Section II, there is an exploration into who is the real mother: the woman who gave birth or the woman who nurtured and consoled and dealt with everyday needs.

The final section on the browbeaten and battered women who lost custody or had their children taken into care or fought to get them back looks at the way society treats mothers who don't quite fit into the norm or are of a minority ethnic background, or who simply can't beat the system.

The accounts throughout this book raise many questions about the status of motherhood and fatherhood. What is our idea of a good mother? Who determines it? What do children feel about mothers they have never seen or who have gone away? How much is feminism or our 'selfish' culture responsible for loosening the ties of motherhood? Are we in danger of becoming a non-nurturing society in which childcare is a service, to be paid for, and will we lose the knack or the need or the willingness to care for our own children, as we have to some extent already done with our elderly?

Are there still different rules for rich and poor? Do health professionals set unreasonable standards for mothers? How culpable is the media, with its stereotypes of supermother and super careerwoman combined? And how, in all this, can the best interests of the child truly be determined?

Though the majority of women would not dream of choosing to be apart from their children, the ones who do and who feature in this book, tell a story that has significance for every woman who has been or hopes to be a mother.

7

SECTION I

When a Woman Leaves
a Marriage

Chapter 1

LEAVING FOR A LOVER

Women have been conditioned to make sacrifices in the name of love. If that statement is true of their relations with their children, it is also true of their relations with men. And when a woman has to choose between maternal and sexual love, she may be very torn.

This chapter looks at women who voluntarily leave their children because they want to leave their husbands to be with another man. They do not necessarily want to leave their children, but they may feel that they have to make a choice. They are women who have either given up everything for love or have seen a love affair as a way out of an unsatisfactory marriage.

A great love, a passion that moves mountains, is not to be ignored. We may disapprove of the woman who follows her heart, but somehow we also understand her and sometimes envy her for the life of intensity that she has chosen. The hint that she may have *been chosen* rather than made choices does not diminish her allure, nor does an awareness that it was her beauty or some passive quality and no particular achievement that brought her special attention. Helen of Troy's beauty was sufficient to launch a thousand ships, so the flattering legend goes. In truth, it is highly likely that the woman was used as an excuse for the Greeks to extend their territory. But she appears to have been compelled in the name of love, she sacrificed security and reputation for that love and she derives her status and notoriety from her ability to inspire men to heroic deeds.

The romantic tradition for men is quite different. Here the great aspiration is self-expression, and the sacrifices are remarkably complementary to those of women. 'The true artist,' said George Bernard Shaw, 'will let his wife starve, his children go barefoot, his mother drudge for his living at seventy, sooner than work at anything but his art.' Men who subscribe to such thinking expect women to love them without reservation, thus leaving them free to pursue their own creative talent. Indeed, who but women primed for sacrifice could love them at all?

Of course, there are compensations for women too. Those who live in a great man's shadow rub shoulders with the great man's peers. They live vicariously, coming into their own when fighting off the great man's camp followers and writing their memoirs after the great man's death. What they lose during their liaison is autonomy. They are not even allowed to be mothers of children, for the great man sets himself up as the one and only child.

That gentle and humane painter Marc Chagall persuaded his mistress to send away her daughter to boarding-school rather than live with them. Several years later this daughter wrote to her mother, 'I feel that Marc ruled your emotions to the extent that your maternal instinct was diverted, otherwise how can one account for the discrepancy between your nurturing and devotion to him and your displacement of me?'

Frieda von Richthofen left her daughters to elope with D. H. Lawrence. William Walton's widow has spoken of having an abortion because she felt her husband would not be able to tolerate a child coming between them. Gala Dali rejected her daughter by Paul Eluard for her life as Salvador Dali's muse. Perhaps one should amend the saying – behind every great man there is a motherless child.

Could a modern, liberated woman give up everything for love, including her children? One who has done so speaks later in the pages of this book. The man in question is not eminent, but he meets her passion and intensity with his own, though very much on his terms. Most women, given the choice between being with their children or being with a man they love passionately, will opt for the children. Most men in a similar position will as easily opt for their lover. Maternal love is thought to be stronger than sexual love; the same cannot usually be said of paternal love. It is likely that the most passionate sexual love a woman can feel is one that embraces and absorbs maternal love too, as the daughter of Chagall's mistress so aptly states.

Leaving for a lover may not necessarily involve a great man or a great passion. A love affair which offers promise of security may seem to be the only way out of an unsatisfying marriage for a woman who has no obvious means of supporting herself. Lack of money can easily lead to lack of nerve, and it is another reason why a woman might choose to leave a marriage and the children with it. If a husband agrees to move out of the marital home, then the wife on her own with the children at least has a roof over her head, even when her earning power is limited or non-existent. If he does not agree to move out, then she is trapped in the marriage

12

and may feel that her only hope is to throw herself onto the mercies of a new partner who may not have reckoned with taking on her children too.

And then there is a certain guilt-ridden compassion that makes a woman leave her children behind. Such a woman might feel that she is breaking up the marriage, destroying family life for a good, solid, faithful man who loves her and is a caring, loving father. 'I'm going myself, I can't take the children from him too', is the way she might express this.

She might also weigh up what is best for the children and decide that they will be less disturbed, their lives less disrupted, if they stay with their father while she leaves. Those convinced that the presence of a mother, any mother, is more advantageous to a child than her absence, will find this decision suspect, but in real life it may well be the best one for some families. More under-standable to the cynical but harder to express for a woman filled with guilt is a very real fear, a panic, about coping with children alone, perhaps not too far removed from the feelings of those who succumb to post-natal depression. And there is another fear for some women who left their parents' home for marriage: they have never lived on their own and they dread the isolation. They need a new partner before leaving a marriage.

The accounts here illustrate some of these motives of women who leave their marriages to go to another man.

* * *

'You get to the age when you think, I've done so much for my children . . . I just feel I need some time to myself'

Heather is thirty-eight, a very attractive, soft-spoken, gentle woman with grey-blonde wavy hair. She has a sad look, her tribulations show. Altogether she has four children, two boys and a girl, aged eighteen, sixteen and fifteen from her marriage, and a daughter of three from a subsequent relationship. Her large thirties-style semi has an unfinished feel. There is a curtain half-drawn, obscuring the light. It covers a broken plate glass window, smashed by one of the sons of the man she intends to marry.

'I had a good marriage lasting fifteen years. My husband was good to me, a good dad, but we drifted apart. He was in the decorating business, and sports mad. I worked part-time with handicapped people, and I was glad when he went out a lot because of sport. I would rather be alone. I'd had one brief affair earlier but I decided my marriage was too good to lose. But then Alex came along. Well, he was a charmer. We met professionally so we had things in common. I couldn't cope with the guilt so it came out within three weeks. I left home to live with Alex, and

13

I left my children behind because I felt my husband wasn't the guilty party, and they were in the marital home which they'd always known. It felt less disruptive for them. My youngest was nine at the time. It sounds very easy but believe me it was the hardest thing I've ever done. My son said, "Mum, make up your mind what you want because you are no good to us if you are going to be moping around."

'I moved into a flat with Alex. My daughter was allowed to visit once a week. My sons refused to see me. I went through hell. Alex had no conception of what I was feeling. He didn't have children. He suggested we start a family and I said no. He'd been married twice before and his second marriage lasted only six months. I should have taken points from there, but you don't, do you?

'A few months after we got together, we had a phone call. My husband had dumped my daughter at my brother's. She'd got very upset and he said, well if you can't cope you'll have to go and live with your mother, I'm renting out your room. So she came and lived with me and she has lived with me ever since. She sees him once or twice a week regularly, but I didn't see my boys for four years. One Christmas I went knocking at the door of their house and they went out the back. They didn't want to see me, full stop. They still haven't really forgiven me. My husband is still very bitter. I offered money and I sent cheques but he would tear them up and send them back in an envelope. I was even denied supporting the boys, which would have helped me.'

Heather did eventually agree to have a child with Alex, and their daughter, Fiona, was born. Six months later the relationship ended. 'He couldn't understand my loss of my children. He didn't get on with my daughter from my marriage. He saw her as a threat, and he didn't want her there. He was beginning to show violence towards me.' Heather was given homeless accommodation with her two girls and continued working full time alongside Alex. He persuaded her to move back into the flat, but after a few months he himself left.

'I really loved him and I went on loving him after we broke up. I felt it was important for him to see Fiona. He did for a few months, but it was very spasmodic. He wouldn't come to see her really, he'd come to argue with me. It was a terrible six months, but within another six months he was remarried and had another baby. My ex-husband was fantastic, marvellous. He offered for us to go back. I guess he still loves me and it is very sad. I just wish I could turn everything back and love him, but I don't. I've not ever regretted leaving.'

There is something about Heather's gentleness, honesty, lack of guile or any sense of power, that sets her up to be the perfect victim. And people take advantage of it.

'**I had so many people criticize me, particularly my family. I lost contact with our friends. My parents thought I was the worst person on earth**, and they were not supportive until I left Alex. My boys started seeing me again when I left. They always said they would.'

The link with Alex is now very tenuous. He pays regular monthly maintenance for his daughter, but wrote to say that he did not wish to see her, which makes Heather feel very bitter: 'I would do everything in my power to stop him doing so now, even if he wanted to. In any case, Fiona has got another dad now, and at the age of three she cannot remember Alex.' This other dad is Steve, whom Heather also met at work, and with whom she began a relationship two months after she was completely free of Alex.

'Steve has three boys aged ten, fifteen and twenty-one. They live with him because his wife left three years ago and lives in Canada. We decided to marry a few months after we met. We bought this house together. He is not divorced yet, and I don't know about marrying. It is very difficult mixing two families. He gets on very well with Fiona, but we've brought up our children very differently.'

At present, the house is very full. Heather is there with her daughters and one of her sons because their father is converting the former marital home into flats. Her older son was staying with her too but left after a family row. Steve has his two younger sons in the house. The mix makes for all sorts of temporary alliances that cause friction, anguish, violence.

'Both Steve's children and my boys have been brought up in male households. When we went on holiday and left the house to my oldest son and Steve's middle one, they left it in a terrible mess. When I told my son off about it, he left. I think he has used me an awful lot, and my younger son too. It's difficult to define whether they are using you or just being difficult teenagers.

'But I've got a different feeling for them now. Whether you get it from getting older, I don't know. I mean, I still love my boys as much as my girls, but I love them differently. Perhaps I am being quite hard on them, but they hurt me a lot. I've made lots of advances. I've had cards, money, presents thrown back at me. One particular year Alex and I bought the boys a computer, and on Christmas morning my eldest put a note through my door which I've still got, which said we're keeping this computer. You were selfish, we want a computer, so we're keeping it.'

Though Heather could be seen to be trying to buy love, this rejection must surely be the bitterest twist. One can say her sons were hurt, angry and wanted to hurt her. But they were also greedy enough and selfish enough to take what was given, and then to hurt more. When does the punishing stop? Whatever the answer, Heather accepts her guilt.

'My ex feels very much that I was selfish. He says I can understand why you left me but I can't understand why you left your kids. But basically, I left my children because they were in the more settled atmosphere, in a house they knew with a father they loved. I did care about him and I did trust him. I would never have left a child with Alex. I take the blame completely.

'**My children are very important to me, and if I didn't have them I would almost die, but I have changed. I know it sounds silly, but now my children are the most important thing after me.** It actually got to the stage where I was more important, and that has kept with me. I think most women get to an age when they think, well, I don't like my life. I've spoken to a lot of women who feel this. You get to the age when you think, I've done so much for my children. I've given up so much, so much time. I've worked part time which perhaps I didn't want to do, because my children were at home. I know it was my choice. All my children were planned. But I just feel I need some time to myself.'

This is probably the most significant statement about modern motherhood in this book, and it gets to the crux of a problem which will be discussed in detail in a later chapter, on women who really do leave as mothers to make a life on their own. In this case, Heather is aware that she made sacrifices as a choice, expecting no more reward than the pleasure of loving her children. But she has at times been denied that pleasure in circumstances that must have driven her to the edge of sanity. To hold herself together, she had to make a new choice, realizing that the time for sacrifice was over. But she is not truly hardened, nor truly resolved in her attitude.

'My fifteen-year-old daughter is having problems with Steve's ten-year-old. He teases her and he can be spiteful. There was an enormous blow-up last night, and at the back of my mind is the thought that when her father gets his place together she is going to leave and go and live with him. I couldn't cope with that. If she feels driven out of this house through circumstances, then I would go with her because as much as this relationship is important to me, she's been through enough, and I am not going to forfeit my children's happiness any more.

'Last night I said I did not think I could go on. I'd been out for a couple of hours to see a friend. I came back to find my older daughter crying. There had been a row because Steve's son had hit Fiona. He got very violent. Both of his younger sons have a temper on them – that window out there, one of them did that. Last night a door was smashed, cement fell off the wall. Steve said I hadn't handled his son right.

'I feel increasingly that there is no place for me in this house, however much I care for Steve. We get on marvellously, but living here is living a lie. If I stay, I'm going to have a breakdown. I think living apart is the only way we can go on together.'

* * *

'I did not want to take my daughter because I thought I stood a better chance of Eric coming to live with me if I was on my own'

Denise is forty-two and has a son of twenty-two and a daughter of thirteen. She is a compact, energetic-looking woman with prematurely greying hair and a strong, sensual face. Three years ago she left her family and chose to live alone in the hope that the man she loved would leave his wife for her. She still lives alone and the affair continues.

'I was nineteen and three months' pregnant when I got married. I grew up in the north of England and my parents were strict Catholics. I was the eldest of four. We used to kneel down and say prayers every night. There was a lot of fuss about the right boyfriends – my parents didn't want me to go out with the farmers' sons. A cousin came to stay and brought his best friend who was in computing, very sophisticated in those days. I fell for him and of course my parents forbade me to see him. So I finished my A levels on the Friday, left home on the Saturday and went to Oxford with Raymond and started work the following Monday. Cleaning work. Then I got pregnant, and I had to get the bishop's permission to marry a non-Catholic.

'It was a hand to mouth existence. I never had any fun, never went to any dances. We were weighed down with responsibilities.'

Denise took her son to a childminder and started work in a bank. She took exams in order to gain promotion, and after several years had a second child, Joanna. Then she was offered a better job that meant moving to another town, and the whole family moved.

'We'd always said we'd go wherever a career move produced the most benefit, but Raymond began to resent my position. My job was definitely more prestigious that his. But I really wanted to make a go of the marriage and I worked hard at sharing his interests instead of following my own.'

17

By this time, Denise had become a bank manager and was also deeply involved in local politics. The couple gradually grew apart, pursuing their separate interests.

'And then I met the guy next door. Eric had always been an awful flirt and it was nice because he made a fuss of me. We kept saying this is just a bit of fun, neither of us are going to let it affect our marriages. That was about five years ago. The relationship increased proportionately with my marriage decreasing. Eric is fifteen years older than me, he has two grown-up daughters.

'I developed an ulcer and was admitted to a private hospital suffering from stress and a suspected minor stroke. So I had a complete rest and told the specialist everything, and he said you have to make a decision. The family came to visit once on the Sunday and Raymond brought work with him. To me it was saying, I'm the worker, you're cracking up. Eric came to see me every day. I was thirty-seven. I said to Raymond, that's it, I've decided to leave you and the sooner I go, the better. And he said, thank God you've made the decision. It was a relief all round. He did not know about Eric, by the way, and as far as I know still doesn't, though they still live next door to each other.'

Denise moved into her present flat which belongs to the bank and is about twenty miles from the family home. She volunteered to pay maintenance for her daughter, then aged ten, and continues to do so. Within six weeks of the divorce her ex-husband remarried.

'I didn't want to take the children with me. Definitely no. My son was happy where he was – he has now moved out. I did not want to take Joanna, and this is the bit where I have to be totally honest which I haven't been so far. Normally, I say she elected to stay with her father. I did not want to take her because I thought I stood a better chance of Eric coming to live with me if I was on my own. I did not see how I could tear myself in little pieces as I had done as a wife and mother. I wanted to concentrate on one person and one person only, and that was Eric.

'**It's quite difficult to actually admit this, and it's probably doing me a lot of good, but I'm not a very maternal person. I really wanted an abortion when I was expecting Joanna**. Having her seemed to be threatening everything in my life. I was still working on the Friday and Joanna was born on the Monday, and on Tuesday morning I was on the telephone clearing up the work that was on my desk. I went back to work when she was nine weeks old. My next-door neighbour was a childminder. Maybe I didn't have a chance to develop any maternal feelings. I didn't have a good relationship with my mother. She was happy with my father, but running a home was a strain for her and the children were in the way.

18

'Yes, I do feel guilty. You can imagine what the tabbies in the village made of it. It made a lovely bit of scandal. Nobody knew that Eric was involved. He kept saying you are making the right decision, with or without me. I generally see Joanna once a week and I speak to my son once a week too. He rents a house with a friend and comes round fairly often. Joanna and I get on ever so well, we really do. Maybe it's because she is now older and it's children I don't like. She comes here in her holidays and helps me with my local political activities. We're far more friends now than I imagined a mother and daughter could be. I'm not allowed to choose her clothes or anything. Her stepmother does it all. She gets on well with her. My ex-husband won't have my name mentioned in the house. He does not encourage Joanna to contact my mother, her grandmother. He has gone off me, but it's not too bad.

'I didn't tell her I was going. She overheard Raymond and I quarrelling. All he said to me was just do one thing, teach her the facts of life. So I sat down with her and we had a fairly heavy botanical briefing. She is allowed one phone call to me a week. I could ring her but I know Daddy would get cross.

'Eric and Joanna get on terribly well. I've never discussed him with Joanna, never with either of the children. At the time, I was ashamed actually. I was ashamed to admit that the marriage was failing, that they were going to lose out. Ashamed for all sorts of reasons. So I couldn't say anything. How can you say anything when you are so ashamed? I felt I was a total failure, I was saying look everybody, my marriage is a wipe-out, and I'm not a good mother either. Maybe my job has been my prop. When I first moved out I'd go in at weekends and at seven in the morning. I could wrap the job round me and feel I was being of use. It was lovely.

'It took Eric about eighteen months before he made up his mind that he definitely wasn't going to leave his wife. He has to go round the country a lot, sometimes one day every week, so I take that day off and spend the time with him. He has a flat in Italy and I go and stay in a hotel opposite. We have a complicated system of different coloured towels over the balcony meaning different messages that we work out beforehand. You see, though his wife knows about me, she doesn't know I'm there. It would drive her mad. We work everything out beforehand about what times of day I'm allowed into the town or on the beach. I was willing to lie on a beach the whole afternoon and read a book, and I'd be on a certain part of the beach so Eric would come down for a lunchtime swim and an evening swim. It was very pleasant.'

19

This somewhat extraordinary state of affairs is clearly acceptable to Denise, who seems to enjoy the elaborate clandestine rules – in stark contrast to the religious rules imposed on her in her childhood. Here she can experience the excitement of disobedience. She can also lead a life that is far from mundane. A situation that would be intolerable to many has its compensations.

'Yes, I know I've done all the giving and none of the taking. I have changed my name by deed poll to Eric's. I wanted to belong to him. Every night we meet after work and we go home together to my place and have supper. Then he goes home to his wife and I get on with the washing-up. His wife hasn't cooked for him for years. If he needs buttons sewn on or shoes polished, it's me who does it.

'He never did promise to come and live with me. He nearly went out of his mind with what he should do. In the end he said "I can't leave my wife. She has never done anything specific that would cause me to walk out on her." It's bad enough that she knows and has to put up with him getting home late in the evening, and if he has trouble with her he will expect me to understand. And I do, I sympathize with him. We've thought of the three of us living together, but she won't have it. And again that's quite understandable. We've discussed the question of him living on his own and seeing the two of us. We had a fantastic fortnight when he stayed with me for the week and went home for the weekend. But she couldn't cope with that and she was causing him a lot of grief. Of the three of us, I am the strongest, the one in the best position to give and take. So I'm the one who has to continually make the concessions, but I make the concessions because I still get something out of it.'

There is no doubt about the sacrifice Denise is making, or her comparative disregard for the possibly unexpressed needs of her daughter. The intensity of the relationship with Eric makes everything else pale to what is perhaps a frightening degree. Eric is her father, mother, child, her total life.

'At weekends I see him when I take Joanna home. He goes down to his garage and I pop in and say hello, a quick kiss, and then I'm off again.

'There's no problem for Joanna. She knows we see each other. There's no problem because no one asks about Mummy at home. She knows about me changing my name and when we're out together she will ask, is my surname X or Y tonight?

'It's three years this week since I left home, nearly five and a half years since the affair started. And it is always an absolute pain when we have to be parted . . . When he goes to Italy for more than seven days we make an arrangement beforehand that he will phone me at certain times, like as soon as he gets to the airport and again at another appointed time, say Monday between nine and ten, and as soon as he rings me on Monday morning, I say when are you next going to ring? I know I just measure out my time till the next call. Eric spends more and more of his time trying to manipulate his life to fit with me. He phones me first thing in the morning, at about ten past seven, then I phone him when I get to work. I phone him at ten past one, then he phones me when he gets home to say he has got home safely, and then he phones me to say goodnight. And occasionally he might phone in between. And at weekends it will be four or five times on a Saturday or Sunday.

'**Is it an obsession?** *Yes, I suppose it is.* Are you telling me off about it? I suppose I expect to be told off. I have been to a counsellor on my own and with my ex-husband, and whoever I've spoken to, people have not understood and they have disapproved. They think I should get out of it, maybe grow out of it, but does one have to?

'When Eric and I are together it's just like being two halves fitting each other. It's perfect. We occasionally have disagreements and he is super-critical of me which is good because I don't accept it from people very well, but I accept it from him and try and do something about it.

'You may say that there is no room in my life for anything but Eric, and that's true to some extent, but I am heavily involved with my political Party and those things happen after eight o'clock in the evening by which time Eric is home and I am then free to do that.

'Very occasionally, after I moved out, I'd see a woman out with a child of Joanna's age and I'd think I wish that was me. Not very often, probably when ovulating or something, but often enough to feel that I wasn't a totally inhuman person. I suppose I do think that of myself at times. Eric is considering retiring and might buy a large property in Italy. Of course he would buy something for me too and I'd live there. There is nothing to keep me here. I'd come back occasionally to see Joanna.'

* * *

'**There was no way I could take Greg . . . it was the close bond that had built up between him and his father and the fact that he was very much his father's boy**'

Catherine is forty-two. She has been married twice, the first time at nineteen, and there are two children of that marriage, now in their twenties. She remarried at twenty-six and had another child, now twelve, whom she left with his father when he was five. Since

21

*then she has been living with another partner and has a son by him,
who is five. She works full time as an administrator with a national
charity. Catherine tells of her experiences quietly, with an air that
suggests she has gone over them many times but still does not
quite make sense of them. She is dark-haired, good looking, with
no sign of the rebel she hints that she was in her youth. Catherine
was adopted as a child, and tells that part of her experience in
Chapter 8.*

'With hindsight, leaving my child had a great deal to do with the
fact that I was adopted – I was never settled about who I was in my
own mind, what I was doing. I was pregnant when I got married
the first time. We were both nineteen. The marriage broke up
when I fell in love with someone else. My husband was in the
army and I was bored and homesick. I had no excuse except that
this other man, Alan, was gentle and sweet. There was a lot of
sexual attraction between us. He said his father was wealthy and
would give us somewhere to live, but that was a lie. He borrowed
money from me and gave me cheques that bounced.'

The outcome of this was that Catherine found herself living
alone with her two children in a rural area where she'd had earlier
connections. She got a job in a local shop and was able to live
in the flat above. Her father died, and she felt overwhelmed by
problems, took a drug overdose and was taken to hospital. Shortly
after this she was told that she had been adopted.

'My confidence was gone. I felt I couldn't go back to working
in the shop. People in the village said there was an eligible man,
quite a bit older than me. He was good old George, the one who
had to transport everyone everywhere. We eventually met and
within about six weeks he said, "I'm going to marry you." I was
tired. He was like the rock of Gibraltar. I didn't fall in love with
him, but I did learn to love him. His mother did not approve. I
was blamed for taking him away. I had blonde dyed hair then and
false eyelashes. I must have been quite a shock as a daughter-in-
law. I felt very undermined by her, as if I wasn't a person in my
own right.'

After five years, Catherine had a son, Greg. She felt frustrated
and wanted to find an interesting job. The relationship deterio-
rated. There were sexual problems which Catherine attributes to
being torn and having stitches. Her daughter, then an adolescent,
was difficult to cope with. George's parents lived next door and
added to the family conflicts. There was a spell of family therapy
in an attempt to right things.

'The therapist suggested George should make some changes,
especially with his parents, but he wouldn't. The therapist said to
me, I think the best thing you can do is pack your bags and go.

You think the grass is greener somewhere else. You might find it is brown, but you've got to try it to see.'

Therapists are not usually quite so explicit as this, and it is possible that Catherine is seeking some justification for leaving by interpreting his advice in this manner. She might have been told, as Denise was by her physician, that it was time for some kind of decision to be made about commitments. In the event, Catherine did leave, but just as she had jumped into marriage with George as a kind of salvation, so she found a similar solution with someone else.

'Alan, the man who had in fact broken up my first marriage, phoned me up. He came down to see me, and he offered me a room in his house. My eldest son was already going to live nearby with his father, and it seemed a good idea. My daughter wanted to stay with her stepfather.

'There was no way I could take Greg. My way of looking at it was that it wasn't that I didn't want him. But I could not take him away from his happy, secure environment. The actual physical hurt and ache that you get from knowing your child is somewhere else, and you want to see that child, you want to see it in bed, you want to kiss it goodnight . . . It wasn't an easy decision. And it wasn't finances, not that. It was just the close bond that had built up between Greg and his father, and the fact that at five he was very much his father's boy. I could not take the child from that lifestyle among green fields to the life I knew I would lead. So I walked away from home.'

No matter how others may judge, to Catherine her act was a supreme sacrifice.

'I didn't get to see Greg more than once a month because I didn't have the money. I paid Alan rent, but after about five weeks we started to have an affair again and we lived together. I had a bit of savings and I lent a lot of it to Alan. I got a very lowly clerical job through a friend. I should have realised a lot of things about Alan. At one point I found a little packet of white powder. He said oh that's something somebody left. Throw it away. I found out later it was cocaine. I could not understand before where all the money was going.

'Then I got pregnant and had Timothy. That was five years ago, and I am still with Alan. Eventually it all came out about the cocaine. He has promised never to take drugs again, but I know he lies. I've more or less made up my mind that I will go back to the country with my young son.'

The telling is flat and factual, but it cannot totally hide the shock and disillusion and anguish that Catherine must have experienced during the last few years, nor what it must have cost her to come to her present decision. Of course she should have seen and known, but she needed somewhere to live, and she needed a partner.

'If I go back to George I'll have my own bedroom. I'll be there with Timothy and with Greg who is now twelve, and with my daughter. She is doing well at college. My oldest son is now married. And I am going to commute to London during the week because I want to keep on my job. It is very satisfying and important to me. I've told Alan this in temper, but he doesn't believe me. I will stay with my sister-in-law during the week. Timothy will be at school soon, and they are happy down there to look after him. My mother-in-law wants me back and George is happy about it. I never divorced him and he never wanted to remarry.

'Greg is always phoning me up. I thought he would forget me, but it is not at all like that. He says, why did you leave, Mum? is Dad that awful? and I say no, Dad isn't that awful, it's a lot to do with me. He doesn't yet know about my past and the fact that I found my real mother a couple of years ago.

'He does have a bad temper, and he has to be told exactly what time his father will be back and not to be late. There's a fear there that Dad will go too. Yes, definitely. But he is very sweet with Timothy. One would expect that a child whose mother has gone away and has had another baby, a boy too, would feel replaced, would not like his half-brother. But Greg is the most loving protective child you could possibly wish to have. And he is to me too. He has said to his father, it's all right Dad for you to have a girlfriend, but you're never to divorce Mum because she might want to come back one day.

'**I do feel that what I did was terribly terribly wrong. I left someone who needed me. I've never in my heart really been able to forgive myself**. And if Timothy had not happened, I think I would have gone back before. Not that one child replaces another, when you are longing for a child who's away and you can't have it in your arms and you've cried and cried. You want your child, but if you've got another one, it's not a substitute, but it is someone you can cuddle, a comfort.

'Quite honestly, I hate myself for what I did. But on the other hand it gives me insight about how it was possible for my own mother to have me till I was three months old and then to have me adopted. I realize that dilemma about what is best for the child. She did it for me, she got rid of me at three months and regretted it even when I found her again.'

And in many ways Catherine has repeated that. She too did what she thought was best for her child, and perhaps events have proved her right. Greg has remained in touch with his mother, he knows who he is, and he has been saved the disruption and possible damage of living in a very unstable environment. And now, what about Timothy?

'I feel all right about leaving him because I know it is not for all the time and because he will have lots of love around him. George is wonderful with him – that's another thing I don't understand. I don't know what Alan will feel about this. I've left two marriages and I've never asked for anything. I've never said to the children I don't like your father. But this time I feel a certain bitterness because Alan has gone through all my money, he has been on drugs, he can't pull himself together, and Timothy needs security.

'My choice this time is to share with another single parent who happens to be my husband and to make a family unit there. If I had to go to court, I would have to say that I don't think Alan is a fit father, though I am willing for him to have access.

'I feel I have at last pulled all the parts of my life together. George is happy now for me to be the way I am. His parents want me to come back. I can continue to work in London and can also enjoy the strong maternal feelings that I have.'

* * *

Accounts such as those above are inclined to provoke hostility and distrust. It is easy to be sceptical when a woman says she leaves a child because the family home provides a more stable environment, never mind whether it clearly does or not. Prove it, we say, and even when women do we still suspect them of other motives. The notion that 'it doesn't seem natural' remains obstinately dominant. We scrutinize a woman's words for guilt and remorse, and perhaps for signs that would reveal just how 'unnatural' in her emotions she really is.

Why?

One reason is the assumption that a mother who leaves her child cannot really love it; another is the assumption that the child itself must think the mother doesn't love it. These factors are accepted as enormously damaging to a child's future happiness, so it is to be expected that women will not want to admit their lack of love. This in turn means that any other motives they offer are automatically devalued, whether they make good sense or not.

We don't respond in this way to men, who may acceptably say they leave a child with its mother because that's where the stability and love will come from. Just as women are supposed to be super-loving with their children, men are assumed to be rather less important to them. And these being self-fulfilling prophecies, women and men tend to act out the parts. Mothers *are* supreme, fathers take second place. Any deviation from these modes evokes suspicion, which is useful for men who prefer to opt out of nurturing and reinforces the idea of the mother as the *only true and natural carer*.

If we believe this, then it is easier to regard women who leave their children as selfish, irresponsible and unnatural than to take into account the idea that they might leave but still love them and grieve for them. Once we accept that women can both love and leave, we are into very deep and uncharted waters.

Women who leave appear to be breaking a taboo. Their action arouses anxiety in women who cannot imagine leaving their children, though those same women may at times have felt trapped and even tempted. A common dream among new mothers is that they have forgotten their baby and subsequently cannot find it. This is an anxiety dream, part wishful thinking, part dread. The women who actually commit the act bring out that anxiety in the form of a condemnation.

For men, the anxieties are different. Women are the people with whom we entrust our children, equality notwithstanding. Like a captive, subservient, but utterly loyal sub group, they are relied upon to do the job of nurturing, and to do it well. If they are so ambivalent and imperfect, who instead should do it?

Commonsense would dictate that the person in the family best-suited to taking care of the child should take on the main nurturing role, and that there should be flexibility and choice and, ideally, sharing between parents. It is likely that women who leave their children in the family home move away knowing that their children are in the good and loving hands of their fathers (and often of their grandmothers), and that in many cases it is where the children want to be, though it goes without saying that they'd like their mothers to be there too.

This does not mean that these women have no other motives. One of the hardest things for a mother to do is to state – and admit even to herself – that she does not want her children with her, either because someone else assumes more importance in her life, or because she fears coping with them on her own. Whatever one might feel about Denise, it took a great deal of courage for her to say the things she did. It is something of an irony that she sees herself as an unmaternal figure when she exerts such energy on mothering her lover. Perhaps she is more honest than Catherine, whose plans yet again mean that she will miss out on quite a lot of her youngest son's upbringing.

Women who leave a marriage for a lover and take their children with them could be doing quite the wrong thing. If the children are unwanted by either party, they might be in danger of being neglected or possibly abused by a reluctant stepfather. Maya Angelou, in the first part of her autobiography, *I Know Why the Caged Bird Sings*, tells of being left with her grandmother and then joining her mother, only to be raped by the man her mother lived with. In nearly a third of sex abuse cases, people other than the child's parents are implicated, the most likely person being a stepfather or a man living with the child's mother.

The woman who decides it is best for her child to stay behind is expected to feel guilt and she is censured if she shows no guilt. But if she does feel guilt, then her judgement is affected. The moral strictures actually work against a woman thinking through what is best for the child, and they also prevent other people from seeing what's best.

Sadly, Heather's attitude seems the most acceptable merely because she has become the scapegoat. She may well feel that she deserves the ill treatment that she has received and that she does not deserve the love of her children. Indeed, her greatest punishment is the seeming loss of her sons' love. And these sons are relieved of the need to look into their own behaviour because they have righteous anger on their side.

Widely-held assumptions about mothering can be used as weapons against women and obstruct true understanding in a way that is detrimental to all concerned.

Chapter 2

OPINIONS AND JUDGEMENTS

When students and staff working in human development studies at a university in Texas were asked to assess which lifestyles received approval or disapproval from the population at large, the two that came in for most censure were non-custodial mothers and people living in homosexual co-habitation. Non-custodial fathers were accepted and slightly more approved of than single people, and even the voluntarily childless were granted a neutral tolerance. Researcher Judith Fischer said in her report of the survey in 1983, 'A decade ago, voluntary childlessness might have been included in the least-favoured group . . . On the other hand, mothers who voluntarily lived apart from their children were unheard of ten years ago.' The statement reflects academic interest in the subject rather than an accurate historical statement. It also reflects an acknowledgement that the phenomenon had become recognizable as a 'controversial lifestyle', an aspect of a social climate in which women were questioning their roles as the natural custodians of children.

Despite the negative view of this lifestyle, women who live apart from their children rarely abandon them any more than they wantonly give away their babies or consistently reject them. A survey from the American organization Parents Without Partners of nearly 1,200 lone fathers showed that 60% of their ex-wives visited their children at least once a month, the majority of them doing so on two or more occasions a month. Another 30% saw their children during holidays. One mother in ten (9.3% to be exact) was described as having no contact, which is a low percentage compared with that relating to non-custodial fathers but is possibly higher in this self-selected sample than in the population at large.

Surveys on the contact of non-custodial parents are rarely broken down by gender. But given that in the vast majority of cases the non-custodial parent is the father, the statistics are revealing: in Pennsylvania, a study by Furstenburg and Spanier showed that 50% of children in disrupted families had not seen the non-custodial parent in five years. In Britain, 40% of non-custodial parents, mainly fathers, have no contact two years after divorce. Though no proper comparisons can be made, it does look as though mothers without custody have a better track record.

Some pay maintenance for their children – only a small number in Britain, which may be more a reflection of women's limited earning power than their unwillingness to support financially. In America, increasing numbers of women do so, some because this is requested by the court, but others because they choose to, even if the sum involved is a mere token amount. Another survey from Parents Without Partners (entitled 'Mothers Without Custody and Child Support') showed that even this token amount gave women the feeling that they had a right to remain involved with their children. They were consulted more frequently by the father than were mothers not paying support.

Why after all this are we so unforgiving towards women who leave their children? One of the most basic of reasons is that we are primally linked with our mothers, not so much through love as through our origins. As will be seen later in this book, the 'real' mother is not necessarily the one who nourishes or protects us, but the one who gave birth to us. She is part of our naming of ourselves. She is the place from which we first became separate and unique human beings, the mother of the self.

There are many instant objections to this predetermined order. We can say that women are given the responsibilities of child-rearing with very little assistance from fathers, so that too much pressure is brought to bear on the role of mothering. We can say that there is no special case for the supremacy of the mother, that it is almost solely culturally conditioned and depends on the fact that women are the assigned care-givers. We can even say that it is conditioning that makes children expect the presence of a faithful, loving mother, and this contributes to their sense of deprivation when that mother is absent.

Psychoanalyst John Bowlby has likened mother love to vitamins, essential for a child's growth and development. His 'attachment theory' suggests that babies attach themselves to the mother figure for survival, and this person is the most important to them and must continue to perform the act of mothering. Others can help, and from the age of about two and a half a pre-school playgroup is acceptable. But the mother figure is at the top of a hierarchy of caring adults. Ideally, says Bowlby, this mother figure is the child's natural mother. Without such a constant caring person, a child is at risk of growing up disturbed, and the fact that 10% of the population spend some time in mental hospitals bears witness to this. These patients, and others who are treated by psychoanalysis or other therapies, often demonstrate during their treatment that the absence of a caring mother contributes to their problems.

One doesn't have to subscribe to the Bowlby theory to see the importance of constant loving figures in the life of a young child, though the key ingredients are surely the quality of the love and the consistency of the care which might well come from two parents sharing the nurturing, or from others for that matter.

Martin Richards of the University of Cambridge Child Care and Development Group has called Bowlby's theory 'a very simple view', pointing out that communication between mother and baby is reciprocal and bonds are subtle and complex. Some babies have been observed to cry more than others from the very moment of birth. Such demanding infants create a certain kind of relationship with their mothers, no matter how 'good' those mothers are. (Who has not felt disorientation and exhaustion from constantly interrupted sleep or an inability to let up for an instant?) Babies and small children respond well to a number of carers in day nurseries, as long as they are given reasonable attention and comfort should they need it. They do not forget their parents or show confusion about whom they belong to. Premature babies, who are cared for by a number of people in hospital, also still respond positively to their mothers.

Historically, mothers were not considered such a necessity to their children's well-being as they are today. Under English law, a father's rights over his legitimate children were seen as absolute and natural – as indeed they were over his wife – until the mid nineteenth century, so that if a wife wanted to leave a marriage, she had no choice but to do so without her children. One victim of this law was Caroline Norton, granddaughter of Richard Brinsley Sheridan. She married at nineteen, in 1827, and when the marriage foundered some seven or eight years later, her husband unsuccessfully sued for adultery. Despite vindication of her good name, and evidence of physical violence inflicted by her husband, Caroline Norton found herself barred from seeking a divorce and from seeing her children, aged six, four and two when the couple separated. She campaigned for changes in the law, and in her biographical writings noted the following:

'After the [adultery] trial was over, I consulted whether divorce "by reason of cruelty" might not be pleaded for me; and I laid before my lawyers the many instances of violence, injustice and ill-usage, of which the trial was but the crowning example . . . I learnt the LAW as to my children – that the right was with the father; that neither my innocence nor his guilt could alter it; that not even his giving them into the hands of his mistress would give me claim to their custody.' Caroline Norton was effective in helping to bring about the Infant Custody Act in 1839 which established visitation privileges and a procedure for women to solicit custody of children under seven. This was one of several piecemeal reforms in the nineteenth century which allowed married women certain rights in terms of claiming custody of their children.

It was not until 1925 that the Guardianship of Infants Act established the principle of the welfare of the child as the paramount consideration, so that mothers and fathers had equal rights of appeal for custody before a court. But even then, the common law rule was that parental rights were vested exclusively in the father. In 1973 the Guardianship of Minors Act finally gave mothers full equal rights with fathers in relation to custody and upbringing.

Under Muslim law, fathers still do have sole custody rights over their children, which is one reason why there are so many 'tug-of-love' and child kidnapping cases between a Muslim man and a non-Muslim woman when a marriage breaks down. In Muslim societies, a man with several wives may evict one who has fallen out of favour, but any child will be his, a valuable part of the family labour force.

There is a widely-held theory, based on a book by Philippe Ariès, *Centuries of Childhood*, that children were regarded as smaller, less effective adults before the sixteenth century, and that the concept of childhood as a stage of development requiring special protection did not emerge until comparatively recent times in Western society. Children were regarded as a man's property and he had the power to impose his values and ideas on their upbringing, though the practical work was of course delegated to women.

Male judgement has long dominated child-rearing practices. Galen, physician of the ancient world, declared that a baby taking milk from a woman who was not its mother would imbibe some of her characteristics at the same time. He also said that intercourse while lactating soured the milk, and was believed until the seventeenth century, according to Diana Dick in her book *Yesterday's Babies*. The philosopher Rousseau put forward his view in 1762 that no mother worthy of her name should lightly hand over her child to a hired nurse, and he set up a fashion for breastfeeding. Inexplicably, he consigned his own five children to a foundling hospital, explaining in his Confessions that 'if I did not boast of it publicly it was solely out of regard for their mother'. Most women would prefer a different kind of solicitude.

31

In this century there have been men like Truby King, Benjamin Spock and the aforesaid John Bowlby to promote their individual theories which women have followed, though the theories have not always fitted with a mother's own observations or needs, and support from society at large to implement their theories has not always been forthcoming.

Underlying these changing fashions in child-rearing are the practices that women resort to in real life. The notorious wet nurse (who seems to have existed from Roman times, if not before) not only took on the babies of the wealthy, sometimes to the detriment of her own child, but, in the nineteenth century, she would also take the babies of mothers forced to work in the mills. Wet nurses were often employed by charitable institutions and foundling hospitals, and some babies would remain with them until they were weaned. 'Baby farmers' also offered their own brand of childcare, sometimes taking children for an entire working week, or bringing up children in the country because their parents wanted to protect them from the disease-ridden city.

Feeding and nurturing were saleable commodities before artificial substitutes were established as a safe alternative. Elizabeth Badinter in her book *The Myth of Motherhood* records that nearly 80,000 babies in France were sent to wet nurses as late as 1907. There seems little doubt that the development of condensed and evaporated milks from the 1870s and the discovery of the need for vitamins to be added to the milk in 1906 put the wet nurse out of business. Will she make a comeback now that bottled feeds are getting a bad press, with stories of the milk containing high doses of aluminium? If so, one might expect to see interviews in magazines and newspapers with hard-working celebrity mothers on Why I Employed A Wet Nurse. The experts, of course, would grumble and much would be made of the possibility that AIDS can be transmitted through breast milk, but this would not stop the trend once it became fashionable. Perceived necessities are always the mother of invention, especially when some are willing to pay for them and others need the money.

The early twentieth century was a time of burgeoning knowledge about hygiene and nutrition – the two great advances that increased life expectancy. Women were taught that to be good mothers they needed to run clean homes and provide nutritious food, no easy task for the poor, living in perhaps a couple of rooms with no running water, to whom this advice was specifically addressed. During the Depression, when men were on the dole, all the weight of this new morality (cleanliness was deemed to be next to godliness) was felt by women. They were told that their children's welfare was literally in their own two hands. If the child did not thrive, it was obvious whose fault it was.

But when women were needed for the munitions factories and to work on the land during the Second World War, state nurseries were provided and were suddenly regarded by the experts as the ideal environment for the young child – a clear example of necessities and inventions. Once the war was over, the female work force was no longer needed. Was it coincidence then that John Bowlby's work was so widely accepted and promoted at this time?

The 1950s saw mothers confined in their nuclear families, in their semi-detached houses and high-rise council blocks, trapped with small children and their brand-new washing machines and food mixers, now totally in command of hygiene and nutrition, and cut off from the outside world. The nanny, at this time a scorned figure considered no substitute for Mother, took on a new guise in the form of the au pair girl who was presented as one of the family, thus very often providing dissatisfaction to all parties concerned. Somewhat more satisfying were the 'mothers' helps', who were presumed to have at least a little expertise, though never enough to erode Mother's natural authority. For the slightly older pre-school child, local playgroups and part-time private nurseries provided a minimal break for non-working mothers, as they still do.

In the late 1980s, the thoroughbred nanny came back into fashion, a necessity for the affluent working mother. (She was never out of fashion with the upper crust, who have always known that it was absurd to bring up children single-handed if you could afford to do otherwise.)

The non-affluent working mother has long depended on childminders, who take children into their homes – a situation reminiscent of the baby farmers. The alternative is the overcrowded, understaffed state nursery, often attempting to serve a small proportion of the most underprivileged of inner-city children.

It would be over-optimistic to say that today, perhaps for the first time, women are becoming powerful enough to influence government policies instead of having to find makeshift ways around them. However, if there is at last some pressure within Government to provide more nurseries, it is purely opportunistic: women need to be encouraged back to work to compensate for a drop in the numbers of school-leavers. The main initiative in providing nursery facilities is, significantly, coming from private industry. What really needs to be recognized is that rich or poor, mothers of young children need and often seek a regular break, whether they work at home or out of it, and regardless of how much they do or do not love their children or how great their sense of responsibility. Women do the mothering for the children, their husbands, their lovers, their elderly parents. But no one mothers the mothers.

In other cultures, parents reveal very different priorities in their child-rearing practices. In rural areas of Africa, mothers breastfeed their own children but there are strong expectations that other women share in the general care – older daughters, grandmothers, sisters. A young mother is likely to take her baby with her on her back while she works in the fields in some West African countries, like Sierra Leone, where women constitute up to 80% of the agricultural workforce. Mothers with larger families are too busy preparing food, often a long and laborious business with no electricity or gas or running water, to take much notice of a baby who cries. There is simply less time for the kind of relationship Western mothers are supposed to have with their children. And the children themselves are expected to perform domestic chores before and after school, which may induce them to fall asleep during lessons but nevertheless reinforces family loyalty and cooperation.

Fostering is a common occurrence in Kenya, where children from rural parts of the country go to relatives in more prosperous urban areas and receive board and lodging and an education in exchange for working in the house, possibly experiencing some exploitation at the same time if the blood tie is not a close one. Sometimes the traffic is the other way, and children from the towns go back to the country to relatives, either as toddlers because crowded domestic conditions are considered unsuitable for active infants, or when they are older, in order to learn tribal traditions. To send a child away for either reason is an act of love in the mother's eyes. There is no guilt involved, though there may well be pain. It is the benefit of the child that counts.

It is often for the benefit of their children that black women in South Africa work as domestic servants. A sample of 175 domestic workers, interviewed in *Maids and Madams*, revealed that in 102 cases no one else in the family was employed. Almost all had children whom they had to leave during a long working day well past school hours. Some lived and slept in their employers' homes. An in-depth sample of fifty of the workers showed that twenty-five of their children were cared for by a relative or older child; six were in a crèche; twelve had no one in charge of them. Many of the workers were expected to take an annual holiday away with their employers and to work on Christmas Day.

Whatever the experts say, mothers will work out their own solutions, often because no one else will address their real needs.

If they are poor and need to go out to work, then looking after their children may seem like a luxury. If they live in primitive conditions or have poor prospects for their children, it may be considered a privilege to have the opportunity to send them away. If they are wealthy enough to have choices, they will choose to pay for regular time for themselves.

* * *

Theories about mothering can also distance the experts when women look to them for help.

What kind of help do women who live apart from their children receive? The answer is very little. The organization MATCH, Mothers Apart From Their Children, is one group offering help in Great Britain, not only to mothers who choose to leave, but to those who have lost custody or whose children are in care. Many of the members are those who leave for a new relationship or in order to get away from an unhappy marriage.

MATCH was started in 1979 and is a loose-knit organization depending on donations and relying on members to set up local groups in each other's houses. Its strength lies in the sharing of experiences and emotions and in putting mothers in similar situations in touch with one another. Solidarity increases confidence and much is gained by talking through painful emotions concerning loss, criticism from friends and parents, feelings of guilt, the difficulty of telling people that you have left your children. The weakness of the organization is that it lacks input from psychotherapists or professionals who might be able to offer some guidance and who can give a useful outside view. However, since all too often the professionals only add to woman's problems, it is no wonder that their voices are not heard.

One kind of advice a mother might want is how to tell a child that she is leaving. Nicky Model, senior child psychotherapist at the Anna Freud Clinic, points out that children of different ages need different ways of telling. 'You don't say to a three-year-old that Mummy's got a lover. You might say, "Mummy isn't very happy and it's nothing to do with you. She still loves you, but she wants to go away and think things out for the present." If you are dealing with a twelve or thirteen-year-old, it's a different ball game. You can be open with them and say, "Mummy and Daddy aren't getting on well and Mummy would rather live with John." And it is important to say, "I still love you. We want to make arrangements so that you can still see me and still see me as Mummy and think of me as Mummy." '

But then comes the sting. 'Of course, that's words. It doesn't necessarily answer just how the children feel. They will feel deserted. I think they will feel that she doesn't love them. It is more than a young child can understand, that somebody leaves you but still loves you. You can say it to them, but I don't think they can take that in. If Mummy goes away, she goes away because she doesn't like me.'

A leading psychotherapist in child guidance, who chose not to be named, took an even more uncompromising view. 'Mothers who voluntarily leave their children aren't enjoying them in the way that other mothers are. The ordinary mother, whose relationship is going well, falls in love with them. She doesn't want to be away from them for perhaps more than a weekend break from time to time. It is a pain to be away and a pleasure to come home, and then the question of leaving them doesn't arise. When mothers want to go away and do something else, then you know the relationship with the child is unsatisfactory. In some way, the children are already missing out.'

The idea that a woman might tell her children that she loves them but they are better off with their father cuts no ice. 'What does love mean, if love means leaving? When love becomes a worthless coin, it is just a word. So often women want to deceive themselves that it is in the best interests of the child and they cannot acknowledge that the children are more than they want to cope with or that they put their profession first or whatever. They may feel that love can be conveyed by long-distance communication and that the child won't have to feel unloved because Mother has chosen not to look after him. But they do feel unloved, and they do feel it must be something about them which is unlovable, and they grow up without much self-esteem.'

Any mother who has not left her child is likely to perceive the instant truth of these words. They are what we have all been brought up on, what every woman knows about child-rearing. But where do the women of Kenya fit in, or those in South Africa? Or parents from the West Indies who came to Britain in the 1960s to earn money to send home for their children's education? Or indeed our own aristocracy, with its long commitment to nannies and boarding-schools? Should we be quite so complacent and set in our views?

Recent research is beginning to suggest that emotional disturbance and problem behaviour may not always be a result of upbringing. A gene has been found that is linked with schizophrenia; disruptive adolescents have responded to a switch in diet from processed foods with additives to fresh products with vitamins; some alcoholics may be suffering from an inherited predisposition. The 10% of people spending some time in mental

36

hospitals during their lifetime may do so for a variety of reasons not necessarily connected with inadequate parenting.

Even children who have been physically or sexually abused or neglected have surprised the experts. The assumption that they will grow up to be inadequate parents has not proved to be quite correct. Dr Edward Zigler and Joan Kaufman, pulling together all research on the subject, found that two-thirds of maltreated children turn into perfectly adequate parents, a group that tends to be ignored by researchers. The other third constitute no more than a minority of all inadequate parents. Factors affecting likelihood of abuse being transmitted across generations include health of the baby, extent of parents' social networks, the quality of the marital relationship, the number of stressful life events and whether the individual when growing up was abused by one parent or both.

Distressing life events may still trigger emotional disturbance, especially in those already vulnerable. So may distressing economic conditions. And so can pressures to conform in a way that does not fit basic emotional needs. When the pressures come from *everyone* in society – psychotherapists, husbands, teachers, social workers, counsellors, grandparents and children themselves, who must surely pick up a hint or two about the condemnation of mothers – they become an immense burden.

Those women who doubt their abilities or deviate feel they must pay a bitter price, as the ones who speak in this book demonstrate. Women who give children for adoption, the ones who experience post-natal depression, or who snatch their children in unwise attempts to prove their love, or want their children back with them even though they know they might be exposing them to battering or abuse, cannot fail to have been influenced by our cultural attitude towards mothering. Better to expose the children to abuse or insecurity or poverty than to admit to an equivocal kind of loving. And the mother who leaves the marital home must feel the pressures more acutely than all the rest. All the weight of disapproval is brought down upon her, including that of adolescent children who may have become knowing and sometimes manipulating, aided and abetted by their fathers.

It is far from ideal, from a child's point of view, to lose close contact with a beloved parent. It is far from ideal that marriages break up, that women, and men too, feel their only move towards happiness is to disrupt family life. Some mothers love more wisely than others or can put aside their personal needs with greater resolve than others, a point that is also true of fathers. Those who succumb may be weak or foolish or selfish or all three. But by stressing the crime of the errant mother, we lose sight of what is best for the child. If mothers leave, then fathers may have to be seen as best. A secure and loving home has to be seen as best.

With the oppression of received opinion lifted, women who leave may be able to see more clearly how to leave well, so that they say the right things about love and continuity, and are not silenced by their shame and inadequacy. They may be able to accept more stoically the withdrawal of a child's love and see it as something that time will heal, and not as a punishment. They will be able to be more true to themselves, and not resort to pseudo 'encouragement' from friends or doctors, who are used as ammunition to justify their decision to leave, as so many women in this book seem compelled to do. Once a woman has made a choice, the only way to make it work for everyone is for her to accept it with the minimum of guilt and the maximum of understanding.

The child psychotherapist quoted earlier stresses the importance of preparation. 'Giving children warning about going is important. They need time to talk, time to think. For women who find it impossible to talk, sometimes they might get together with a partner or a friend who is less involved and can help to support them while they are doing it. Because of course children don't want to hear either. If a parent embarks on an explanation, they may find the child pays no attention or asks to go for a walk. The temptation is not to persist and to feel that it really doesn't matter, the child's not bothered.'

Some parents think that if children don't ask, they don't want to know or have no feelings about the matter. But one only has to think about one's own inhibitions to realize that not asking and not thinking consciously about a topic does not mean one has nothing to say and has no underlying feeling about it. Sometimes questions and thoughts are too difficult for words unless someone else makes it easier for you to express them. Sometimes you don't say anything because you want to protect the other person, which is something that children do too.

The psychotherapist has some judgemental words to follow, but they have genuine value nevertheless.

'What we understand psychiatrically speaking is that children who know they have been rejected can tolerate pain and can grow up to create a better future for their own children . . . They can learn to tolerate and accept that they have a mother who prefers somebody else to them. Then the realities can be known and thought about. The child may be sad or angry, but they have a right to be. Then they can be prepared to give something better to their own children than the pretence that everything is all right, which is a bad preparation.'

A less rigid and punishmental attitude might allow for the idea that a child could learn to understand that its mother was unhappy enough to feel she had to make a choice, and that choice might seem like rejection but it is not what she, the mother, actually feels. A child might then learn that choices can be painful for those who make them as well as for those on the receiving end. He or she will learn more easily from a woman who does not carry within her the bleakness of the psychotherapist's message.

How far should a woman go to demonstrate her love and constancy once she has left? Some mothers choose to return to the family home every day to bath the children and put them to bed. Others have their children every weekend or for tea every day after school. (And others, through shame or self-fulfilling prophecy, keep away altogether.)

As the psychotherapist says, 'It depends a lot on the relationship between the two parents, and how the children experience it. There can be situations where the children feel very tantalized by brief visits. But if there are regular, reliable times, they can look forward to visits and not feel at the whim of people appearing and disappearing. Unpredictable visits are very disturbing and keep hope alive, so you can't settle down and get on with ordinary living. You have the constant repetitive pain of rejection as off she goes again. If a mother returns every night, even if only at the beginning, it is valuable if it is regular. There is time to share the day and talk. The mother might be doing a valuable job of bridging the gap.'

Nicky Model also sees the value of a regular routine, but she has other ideas if a stepmother arrives on the scene: 'A very small child cannot come to a resolution – ie, who is the important mummy – because if the natural mother has left and the stepmother comes in, it seems to me that the natural mother needs to be able to let the stepmother take over. And that means she has to make her visits rather occasional and discreet, which calls for a lot of maturity. Older children can cope more easily, though the people concerned have got to be aware of the child's tendency to stir things up between them all.'

Perhaps the greatest agony of all for a woman is to see her young children taken over by a stepmother, but it is an agony that must be borne in these circumstances. A woman who leaves her children has to take into account the fact that she will not be doing the 'motherly' things for them most of the time.

Few experts in the field of counselling and therapy have considered in any depth the emotional consequences for women who leave their children. Judith Fischer of Texas Technical College, quoted at the start of this chapter, is concerned that the subject be explored in any therapist-client relationship and suggests that whatever the processes by which a woman lives apart from her children, she will feel society's disapproval. She comments that the difficulties make a woman 'more vulnerable to psychological distress than the woman who has separated or divorced and who has the children living with her'. She may feel low self-esteem, and even if she has lost custody will blame herself for it. She may even experience a sense of guilt when she begins to find that she can live happily without her children.

There is a further point to consider: 'It is important that children, whether with mother or father, grow up believing in the value and capability of each parent, as parent and as person', says Fischer. Reason enough for counsellors and therapists to look more closely at the issues, and for everyone else to curb their condemnation.

Child psychologist Cora Lynn Goldsborough, in an article in the American *Single Parent* magazine, suggests ways in which non-custodial mothers can set up a new relationship with their children. If living accommodation is limited, she recommends that sleeping bags should be kept permanently for them in their mother's new home. They should be encouraged to leave some of their toys there too. And the moving-out works best in families where the father has already played an equal role in looking after the children.

Things are likely to go more smoothly when there has been some preparation for the split. The value of sitting down with the child and explaining the situation has already been stressed, but proper planning also means talking through the options before-hand with the other parent, and with the children too if they are old enough. Honesty is essential, and that means some straight thinking before the talking, perhaps with the help of counselling or divorce mediation services. Research shows that parents who continue to negotiate and remain friends provide an easier adjust-ment to divorce for themselves and their children than those who cannot resolve their differences.

A major area of adjustment for women is the loss of authority over the children. Some don't want to let go, and try to impose rules from afar which add to conflicts; others go overboard the other way and over-indulge on sweets and treats – just as some non-custodial fathers do. Christine Moore, writing in American *New Woman*, sees the answer in acquiring a sense of detachment over day-to-day management while finding other ways to imbue certain personal values. She gives the example of a mother taking her sons to tennis matches as a way of balancing their father's insistence on rougher sports. Another woman maintained contact with a daughter who was unwilling to speak to her by sitting it out and learning to listen without criticism or retaliation. The unbiased listening eventually gave way to greater trust and intimacy.

'Quality time', as this latter example surely is, does have a place in a relationship, especially when it's going wrong. But it can be overdone. There is an idea that it is necessary to work at a relationship in a conscious, structural way to compensate for the fact that it is based on intermittent contact. This might inspire a conscientious parent to listen constantly for clues and follow them up with high enthusiasm and energy, so that the child feels watched and becomes watchful. Quality time is difficult to quantify, but it must surely be composed of trust and relaxation, of allowing individuals to be spontaneous and natural. That can include allowing a child to withdraw into a quiet state, watch television, disappear down the road with friends. A mother intent on winning back her children's love (which she may never have lost, though she may fail to see it), needs to listen and wait and tolerate and resist rushing in to soothe her own sense of being rejected.

Of course there is the other trap of being passive and overpatient. A deep sense of guilt may make it difficult for a woman to exercise authority over a child or even to defend herself against unacceptable behaviour. Another false approach is to maintain the position of the optimist who prefers to ignore the warning signals and either does not see or refuses to acknowledge signs of a deep rift developing, a hostile or excluding wall of silence. It should go without saying that any of the pitfalls described above could apply to fathers as well as to mothers, but mothers receive and accept the raw edge of criticism far more acutely. What they need instead is greater understanding and tolerance. Only then can they begin to assess their behaviour and understand themselves.

Chapter 3

HOW FATHERS FIGURE

In the film *Kramer vs Kramer*, a mother leaves her marriage and her child, acknowledging that her husband was reasonable, her marriage acceptable, but because she suffered frustration and restraints on self-expression and personal growth, she owed it to herself to go. There is a court scene in which she fights to get her child back, knowing that he is settled in a secure and loving relationship with his father. Meryl Streep, playing the part of the mother, is said to have written the key speech on her motives herself. She tells the court that she left because she felt she was incapable of functioning normally. She would have been a bad influence on her child had she stayed, because she lacked self-esteem. Now, having developed as a whole human being, she knew she could be a good mother. She loved her child. She felt he needed her more than he needed his father. She should not be punished for leaving.

This is surely wacky thinking of the Hollywood variety. Any sensible response would have been that the child wasn't picky about whether his mother was a developed human being or not, and her desertion might have been at least as damaging to him as her depression. But the desire of the court to display liberal sentiments, while at the same time reinforcing the idea of the mother as the true carer, leads to her gaining custody. Only when she can actually claim her child does reason prevail and she leaves him happily where he is, in his father's home.

Fathers are not given a great deal of status or consideration as nurturers, a fact that hardly encourages them in that role. The psychotherapists' pronouncements on absent mothers in the previous chapter barely acknowledge the significance of a secure relationship with a father.

A poll conducted at Exeter University in 1987 showed that teenage children, fifteen- and sixteen-year-old daughters particularly, did not rate their fathers very highly. Friends and siblings supplanted fathers as people they got on well with: only 7.5% named their fathers, while 37.7% named their mothers. Among sons, only 12.3% got on best with their fathers. Few of the children shared their problems with fathers, most of them turning to mothers, siblings or friends. Even on career problems, less than one in five consulted their fathers.

An American survey from the National Association of Social Workers indicated another area where fathers are seemingly redundant. Mothers bringing up children alone found that the absence of men made the home more peaceful, and enhanced family harmony. They felt that being without a partner had made them more independent, given them confidence, stamina and the ability to enjoy a closer relationship with their children than other women could achieve.

There has been much anger within the women's movement about the way men have neglected their role as fathers, and some of it comes out in the attitude above. But men are beginning to respond to the invitation to be in there taking a greater share in the joys and responsibilities of parenthood. They are also, some of them, feeling anger about female independence and hitting out by fighting to keep their children after divorce. Both of these trends have resulted in growing numbers of men being granted custody.

Between 85 and 90% of divorcing mothers get custody of their children, but that still leaves an estimated 95,000 fathers as single parents in the UK. Some of them will have won custody; others will have taken over the parenting because the children's mother chose to leave them. In many instances, the mothers could only contemplate leaving because they knew they had the option of a dependable father who would look after the children. Traditionally, the option of leaving without the children was presented by the availability of a grandmother. Increasingly, it is presented by the loyalty of the father, albeit quite often with a grandmother nearby.

When it comes to fathers getting custody, one of the biggest shifts in emphasis, pointed out by sociologist Lorna McKee, is the move from 'paternal rights and the issue of control, toward paternal duties and the issue of responsibility'. Judges are expected to make decisions with the best interests of the child in mind. If a father can demonstrate competence and the ability to make satisfactory child-care arrangements, he now stands some chance of gaining custody. Inevitably, this can give fathers an unfair advantage, since they are more likely than working mothers to be able to afford satisfactory child care. Also, men remarry more quickly than do women, so they may appear to offer a more conventional lifestyle to the courts. (But Families Need Fathers, the self-help organization for men, points out that there is still a great bias against paternal custody, and a mother who leaves and then later decides she wants her children back still stands a good chance of retrieving them.)

The bias against fathers can make life complicated for those trying to break the mould. A particularly gruesome finding from American researchers Thomas Draper and Tom Gordon is that some men experience anxiety when they see other men displaying love and affection to children. The researchers presented two versions of a story to two groups of men aged between eighteen and twenty-six. The story concerned a young man babysitting. In one version he behaved in a 'nurturant' manner, reading to the child, having him on his lap, singing to him when putting him to bed, and giving him a goodnight kiss. In the other version the babysitter did none of these things. The men rated the affection-ate babysitter higher in 'goodness' and 'obedience' but they saw him as less masculine and active. Men who nurtured were assessed as unlikely to have future success, as being less powerful and as exhibiting less sexually appropriate behaviour. Unfortunately, in-creasing publicity about child abuse may be driving men into less demonstrative nurturing than ever.

Toity Deave, a British health visitor, sent a questionnaire to fellow health visitors to explore experiences of single fathers. Their greatest problem was society's attitude that women were the natural homemakers, and their second was the lack of support they received in their role as the caring parent. If mothers get little outside help, the situation is even worse for fathers. There were few opportunities for them to meet other lone fathers and they experienced great isolation, with little sympathy from friends and bosses. Health visitors themselves perceived men as needing more practical help than women, but some feared there might be sexual abuse where fathers were left with their children, especially in the case of daughters.

It would not be true to say that all fathers welcome being left holding the baby when their wives leave. Geoffrey Greif, of the University of Maryland School of Social Work, found that the majority of fathers who keep their children do not want the marriage to end. Some keep the children through mutual consent with their wives. Those who had their children foisted onto them felt the least happy about it. In a survey based on 1,100 replies to a questionnaire in the American magazine *Single Parent*, one out of three fathers had taken over the children through mutual consent and had actively participated in the decision. One in six had the children because the wife had chosen to live on her own, and one in six fathers got custody after a battle. A frequent reason given for having the children was that they preferred to live with their father.

As a rule, the fathers in this survey said they were viewed with admiration by society, unlike their British counterparts above, but they felt a conflict between going out and socializing, and staying home with the children. Most felt their greatest satisfaction lay in their relationship with their children, but a few felt the arrangement was a mistake and that their careers were damaged. Child-rearing responsibilities were not considered problematical, but handling loneliness and maintaining a social life were. Greif concluded that the rarity of the family structure made its members more appreciative of each other and there were special attempts to 'get along'. But most of the results sound as if they could have come as easily from lone mothers.

A British survey of fathers with custody reveals some similar strands. Sociologist Maggie O'Brien isolated different categories of lone fathers, according to the way the marriages had ended. One category she called 'conciliatory negotiators', men who had ended their marriages by mutual consent and, despite conflict or anger towards their partner, managed to negotiate over the needs and welfare of the children. They took on relatively high levels of responsibility for child care before separation, some even restructuring their work life. A number said they felt closer to the children than did their wives. As O'Brien points out, the blurring of gender roles can make conventional solutions inappropriate.

Her second category were the 'hostile seekers' who sought custody against their wives' wishes when the wives asked for a separation. With greater hostility, the welfare of the children became subsumed under the marital conflict. Many of the fathers were morally outraged, especially when their wives were leaving for a lover, and the custody fight was a way of administering punishment. The predicament of women who lose custody is discussed in Chapter 17.

The third group of fathers as single parents were the 'passive acceptors', who appeared to have been taken by surprise by the break-up of their marriages. Communication between the partners had been poor, so that the separation often seemed sudden and abrupt, even though there might have been a long period of unhappiness beforehand. Again, a third party was often involved, but the moral outrage was absent. Some men claimed that their wives showed little interest in the custody arrangements and even avoided court appearances – O'Brien suggests that the reason for this may have been embarrassment at having to state publicly that they did not want custody, but another characteristic of the wives in this group was the fact that there was little or no contact in the 'post departure' period, in one case for an entire year. The rejection of a way of life, combined with shame and guilt, and the inability to communicate with the ex-partner may well have been further determining factors. In this group, it was a sense of duty, loyalty and responsibility that often persuaded the fathers to keep the family together rather than a close loving bond with their children.

Though fathers complain that they have few support networks, they are not totally without resources. Gingerbread, the single parent self-help group, welcomes fathers as well as mothers, and one Meet-a-Mum network in Yorkshire changed its name to Meet-a-Parent because so many fathers turned up. Families Need Fathers campaigns for men to be given greater recognition as fathers and has self-help branches in many parts of the country.

A 'dads' group' in a deprived area of Birmingham, run by health visitor Anne Willis, invited lone fathers to meet together at a health centre. Many were found to keep their children clean and well-fed, but they lacked ideas about stimulating them or taking them on outings. The group created a network, so that the fathers could help each other out with babysitting and shopping. Anne Willis concluded that their needs reflected a working-class problem, and though middle-class men may feel isolated, they do know where to go for help and can usually pay for it. The fathers tended to be a bit suspicious of the team at the centre at first, but gradually they talked, revealing a strong need for advice and support.

None of this sounds remarkably unfamiliar. On the contrary, young and inexperienced mothers often have similar needs and problems. Men, like women, have to feel their way into parenting. Women feel motherly because they look after their babies and develop an intimacy with them from infancy, which may be more important than the influences of pregnancy and bonding. Men, too, have demonstrated the ability to develop intimacy with their children.

But men are far more hindered by their circumstances and environment and the attitudes of those around them. Fathers traditionally have been remote from child-rearing, and their expectations from an early age have been geared to achievement outside the home. They pass on to their sons a sense of awkwardness concerning nurturing and intimacy. Many have difficulty communicating with other men on a personal level, and their occupations traditionally demand an impersonal approach that denies warmth and vulnerability.

Women have at least had a model in their own mothers on how to nurture (and those who haven't may be more liable to leave their children). Even today their education gears them in a more 'homely' direction: an Equal Opportunities Commission report on six Welsh schools in October 1988 revealed that all denied or greatly discouraged girls' access to craft activities, woodwork and metalwork, while boys were equally denied opportunities to study home economics and needlecraft. There is as much need to encourage men into nurturing roles as there is to encourage women to be engineers. If women today are prepared to leave their children, the men who take over must be able to do so with warmth and involvement. If men could share more actively in parenting, then perhaps fewer women would feel driven to leave.

Chapter 4

MOTHERS WHO GO ALONE

It is a strange irony that theatre-goers are cheered at the sight of Ibsen's Nora leaving her oppressive doll's house, but fail to show the same understanding for mothers today who, like her, choose to leave the family home in order to find themselves. Of course we can view Nora's plight with hindsight, and our sympathies go out to her without reservation, so that we feel with her the loss of her children, and accept that her own needs are paramount. Critics of modern Noras would say that women today are not constrained or humiliated as she was. Mothers can legally take their children with them and even get some state benefits as single parents.

Nevertheless, the modern phenomenon of leaving the family home not for a lover, but for oneself, has antecedents. Nora, like contemporary women, saw the opportunities for self-fulfilment and in opting for them began to grow up.

Not all women who choose to leave their children are quite as clear about their needs or motives. With so much guilt and public condemnation loaded upon them, they may find it very difficult to discover their real reasons for departing. They may feel that they love their children, even if they are told that they don't. They may say that they cannot any longer be martyrs to motherhood, but few will listen to them or try to understand what they are saying. They may use feminism as a defence, in that they feel they have a right to decide their own destiny, but they will be told that feminism is therefore devaluing family life.

Whether or not one has sympathy for mothers who decide to leave their children to follow the path of self-fulfilment, their action overturns many conventions about mothering and they force us to question the role of women as mothers today, their status and expectations.

There is no doubt that the subject of mothering and child-rearing troubles modern society greatly. Television presenter Esther Rantzen told a conference of teachers in 1988 that Britain was a nation of child-haters, and Germaine Greer in her book *Sex and Destiny* went further with the same accusation and included the whole of the Anglo-Saxon Western world. Women, she said, didn't deserve to be mothers.

However, not only might some be more deserving than others, the experts aren't always sure which exactly are which. When runner Paula Fudge announced that she would not participate in the 1988 Olympics because her four-year-old daughter pleaded with her to stay at home, child-care expert Penelope Leach was reported in *The Times* as saying 'Such a huge disappointment from the mother could put a major burden on their future relationship . . . bitterness can creep in later.' (*Are mothers never right?*) She added that four-year-olds tend to play power games and if they win that could cause problems too. A few days later in the same newspaper, psychiatrists Dora Black and Elizabeth Arbiter of the Royal Free Hospital responded with: 'a twelve-day absence for a four-year-old who has already had one traumatic separation might be experienced as a devastating and bewildering abandonment and risk affecting her trust in adults.' (The 'traumatic' earlier separation had been reported as 'Fudge remembering how miserable the child had been when she was away last time'.) A correspondent who had worked as a counsellor put yet another view: she could only think that the child would suffer from guilt for many years to come for having deprived her mother of a well-earned Olympic place.

Further passion greeted a woman who wrote a humorous self-deprecating article in the *Sunday Times* describing her life as a mum, washing and cooking and cleaning and looking for lost socks while the menfolk and the children lounged around. It brought in much protesting correspondence from readers ordering her to tell them to get their act together and to stop being a martyr before she ended up as a coronary victim. (*Wrong again, Mother.*)

But perhaps the two most interesting media subjects in connection with this issue are the young Royal mothers, the Princess of Wales and the Duchess of York, both, it may be remembered, children of mothers who left the family home for a new marriage. In 1988, the Princess of Wales spoke at a Barnardo's conference on the vital elements of family life: commitment, togetherness and the need to nurture and prepare children to become stable and confident adults. She expressed fears as a modern mother about bringing up children in a society plagued with 'prostitution, drug addiction and divorce'.

49

Meanwhile, her sister-in-law, the Duchess of York, was receiving criticism from the media for going off and leaving her ten-week-old baby for an extended tour in Australia. While some columnists called her self-centred and irresponsible, others pointed out that royalty had always felt free to leave children for prestigious foreign tours. The duties of ordinary mothers did not apply to royalty.

Today, royalty is not so remote. The two daughters-in-law of the Queen may be seen as symbols of contemporary motherhood. The Princess of Wales speaks for the traditionals, the constant mothers who are a bastion against the uncertainties of a world in which values are changing. The Duchess of York was acting as many young women feel it is their right to act today: to choose the life they want to lead, whether it is to travel with their husbands, to pursue their careers, even to go off on an adventure alone.

The problem for most women embarking on motherhood today is that they have been brought up in an environment that expects them to be both constant mothers and people who can seek fulfilment for themselves. They want to love their children, but they want freedom for self-expression too. They are even, within reason, encouraged by child experts to keep up interests outside the home, if only to stop them from getting depressed and possessive when the children grow up. (*Oh yes, still doing things for the wrong reasons.*)

This conflict is at the heart of the matter for at least some of the women who choose to leave their children, whether or not they also display emotional immaturity or seem unduly frustrated because of their marital circumstances. The three case histories here invite so much comment individually that they are discussed separately.

* * *

'I have to recognize in myself that I am not the sort of person who is happy in the home all the time'

Samantha is forty-one. She has a son of eighteen from a previous marriage and a daughter of nine. When her son was two years old she left the family home to live alone in a bedsitter. She is a pretty blonde woman, thoughtful and composed, living in a comfortable suburban Edwardian house with her second husband, and working as a freelance public relations consultant.

'I was twenty when I married the first time, and my husband was ten years older. I am quite sure that was very significant. I was too young, my husband very much wanted a child and didn't want to wait. I was very ambivalent about it. I didn't protest strongly enough, or perhaps I should say that I didn't listen to my own feelings.

'By the time my son was born I had realized that my marriage was a mistake. A perhaps unusual feature is the way religion, in this case orthodox Jewish religion, played a part in all this. My husband was extremely orthodox. I thought I wanted that. I came from a mixed marriage. My father was Jewish, my mother wasn't. I am an only child and my parents' marriage was not good. They did not offer each other companionship and they were fairly old, in their late thirties, when they had me. I grew up fairly isolated, no other young children, not even cousins.

'I think I may be saying that my mother did not feel rewarded by me. I'm not saying she wasn't a good mother, I was quite close to her. But I wasn't enough for her either in that she wanted to go out to work. She always worked part time, which was quite unusual in those days. In many ways I've repeated what she did in needing to work outside the home. I don't blame her for that. I don't in all honesty think there is tremendous virtue in a woman forcing herself to stay at home with the kids. I feel it is the quality of the time, not the quantity.'

Samantha could not be accepted as an orthodox Jew because her mother was not Jewish (the religion is matrilineal) so she went through an official conversion, a very demanding process requiring commitment to strict dietary and other religious laws.

'It was what I thought I wanted. His mother was average, middle-of-the-road Jewish. She did not want an orthodox daughter-in-law. But he wanted it more and more. I was the opportunity for him. I was a virgin when we married and he wasn't far off.

'**I was very unhappy after Martin was born. It could have been post-natal depression, but it is hard to separate from the unhappiness in my marriage**. I was very lonely, very frightened of the responsibility of a child. I can remember this enormous nostalgia for the rush hour. All those people going off into the real world, and here am I not even being able to look forward to my husband coming home.

'When Martin was five or six months old I was offered a part-time job. It was a couple of mornings a week, an absolute lifeline. It gradually became more important in my life than anything else. I felt enormously guilty. I did love my son, but I never had a sense of falling in love with him. My husband was extremely involved. It felt as though he was much more his child than mine. He was an extremely good father, but not only the child's father, he was also my father. He took over the role, the dictatorial father, with me as well.

'I had a reliable woman in to look after Martin. I felt torn in two about wanting to work and feeling guilty about enjoying it. It got to the stage when I started to realize that I couldn't spend the rest of my life like this. My husband didn't want to acknowledge that there was anything seriously wrong, but I had to keep on impressing on him my desperate unhappiness. Finally he brought his mother down from Manchester and we came to an arrangement that I would go away for three months and try to sort myself out. It was very good of her. She was a widow, very possessive, and he was a devoted son. My husband has red hair and it was always assumed that our baby would have it, and he did. I was upset about that because if he had not, it would have made him much more mine. It was a claiming. He was his father's child.'

Samantha found a bedsitter, left her part-time job for a full-time one as a secretary and was able to support herself. She was persuaded by her family to go to marriage guidance counselling which only confirmed her desire to stay on her own. She found her job exciting, and was gradually dropping her strict observance of Judaism. However, she did agree to return to the family home 'out of guilt, though I knew it was a waste of time'. She left finally after a few months when a colleague at work offered her a room in her flat.

'**It was amazing how Martin appeared on the surface to cope with it**. He was around twenty months when I went back, and he must have got used to his grandmother because he was more disturbed with us both there. His sleep pattern was disturbed. He settled down more when she went to her own home for Christmas. There was obviously something about both of us being there that upset him. But he was a very contained child. He had been from the start. And he is a contained adult.

'My husband was extremely angry and extremely hurt. There was no way he would consider Martin being brought up except as an orthodox Jew. When the subject of custody came up there were a lot of implied threats which I was not mature or strong enough to fight. And to be absolutely honest now, I probably wasn't motivated enough to fight. If he had turned round and said, right, you take the child and cope on your own, I'd have been terrified. Maybe I would have coped much better with him on my own. I just don't know.

'Leaving the second time when Martin was two was more difficult because I knew it was final. I sat up one night for hours after he'd slept, thinking about it. And it was then that it really sank in that I was leaving him. I thought of all the things I was going to miss. I realize that I am a person with no affinity with babies as such. The older my children get, the more I enjoy them. They

52

bring different problems of course, but I am not someone who takes to young children.

'My husband warned me not to expect any help from him, but I had kept my job open. I gave up all rights to the house. The only support I got was him paying for the servicing of an old banger of a car. I know I did all the rejecting, a pretty awful experience for him. We had joint custody and arranged regular access. I used to go over on a Sunday when Martin was very small. Later I would take him to my parents. When he started nursery, I'd see him in the holidays. Life slipped into a pattern and I don't recall any problems. I've never, even to this day, been able to get very much out of him about how he felt. I think he buried it. Perhaps he hasn't had the need to resurrect it.'

Both Samantha and her husband remarried within two or three years. For her son, it meant a stepmother instead of his grandmother looking after him, followed by a half-brother and sister. Samantha also had a second child, a daughter, when her son was seven.

'I'm afraid it meant a different set of problems for Martin. It sounds awful to say it, but his stepmother was absolutely abominable to him. And for me it was difficult, with another woman becoming the mother. But I felt it was hard for her, taking over somebody else's child, and I wrote suggesting we met. It didn't go down well. When I came to collect Martin the next time, she gave me an absolute mouthful, saying who did I think I was and why didn't I just get out and stay out, all in front of my son, who was then about five, sitting there mute. I felt I didn't care, so long as she was OK with him. I couldn't get him to talk about it though.

'**It wasn't until he was about twelve or thirteen that I realized how unhappy he was**. He took himself off to a counsellor at school and asked me to see her. Then I heard things like how his stepmother would not do his washing, how he was treated differently from the other children in certain ways. I was still seeing him at weekends. Now he started bringing over things for me to wash. The counsellor saw his father and stepmother and she suggested I should stop seeing Martin as it was upsetting everything. I could not understand how a counsellor could suggest that.

'My son was beginning to turn to me more and more. It was beginning to occur to me that we should have him with us. My second husband, Mark, had said almost from the word go that Martin would end up coming to live with us and that he would give up orthodox Judaism. He'd always had his own bedroom in our house and I more or less kept a kosher home for him. Mark is Jewish too, but we are far more relaxed about it.

'Then a couple of years ago Martin had to have his appendix out, and because his father was away he came back to us to recuperate. And he never went back. It just happened. Gradually his possessions began to creep over.

'He settled in easily. I'd say he is a normal teenager. He gets on well with his half-brother and sister as far as I know, and he is OK with my daughter Susan. He is less orthodox and is more physical than academic. He is thinking of becoming a professional golfer of all things. Perhaps there is something of the loner in him that may be a reflection of his earlier experience.

'I expect you want to know something about how I felt when my daughter was born. I was actually terrified before I had her. I was seriously contemplating an abortion. Mark wanted a child very much and I felt it was something I should give him. But he was great. He didn't pressurize me in any way. He said it has to be your decision. I went back to the counsellor I had seen before. I realized I would go ahead but it brought back the unhappiness when Martin was tiny. I must say I didn't enjoy Susan as a baby particularly, but she was much easier and the whole circumstances were very different. I enjoy her very much now, but I did have the same need to get out when she was born. In that sense I haven't changed very much although I wasn't depressed. But I felt trapped again being at home. I have to recognize in myself that I am not the sort of person who is happy in the house all the time with a small child.'

* * *

Samantha is a woman who has seen many rapid changes in society in her adult life. She married a traditionally-minded man who offered her stability, security, an ordered future. He was the father figure she appeared to need, and Jewish orthodoxy provided the framework. For the young woman who was bored or restless or unhappy at home, early marriage and motherhood were not only a salvation but also a conventionally acceptable answer. There were the pressures to conform. The older husband of course wanted a child, and life was heavily determined by what husbands wanted.

But the times were changing. People were expecting more satisfaction sexually. Women were wanting to explore non-traditional roles and rejecting marriages which they felt imprisoned them. Mothering itself for some seemed equated with male oppression. It was becoming fashionable, and later acceptable for women to say they did not want to have children.

For Samantha, the rejection of her husband extended to rejection of her son, the child with red hair, his father's child. She is able to say now that she had 'no affinity with babies', because it is socially acceptable to do so. At the time, she guiltily admitted that she did not fall in love with her baby, possibly because of post-natal depression or unhappiness over her marriage, or because the child was 'contained' as she put it. She did not behave in an emotionally disturbed or psychotic manner – which perhaps would have been acceptable. But inevitably she subscribed to the high standard demanded of mothers. She was imperfect, and so she removed herself, knowing her son would be well cared-for in his father's structured religious household.

And in the end, the relationship with her son mended. Her second marriage gave her a second chance to be an acceptable wife and mother, but in a less traditional way. Over the years, she was able to put the needs of her son in the forefront of her mind and to come to his aid when she saw the problems he had with his stepmother. Sadly, the counsellor still kept the stigma in mind: a mother who leaves is a disturbing force and has no moral claims. It was an easy option to suggest Samantha kept away. Had Samantha taken her advice, would she be enjoying the relationship that she has today with her son?

* * *

'I felt I did have some talent and I felt I had a duty to it'

Jane is thirty-nine and has two sons of twelve and nine whom she left with their father three years ago. She is an extremely attractive woman, looking younger than her years, with a slight air of petulance, a kind of artful innocence. Her voice is low, modulated, husky. Her home is a tiny cottage, one up, one down, in a rural village in Suffolk where she works as an illustrator and writer of children's books.

'I was married at nineteen to a social worker who was ten years older than me. My parents were Catholic and I was a practising Catholic. He was from a Nonconformist background. I was a virgin on my wedding night, and he was a bit of a father figure. My parental home at the time was in turmoil. My parents are mercurial and eccentric and very nice. My mother was having a late baby – my brother is only eighteen now. My father's business had gone bust and we were very poor. I felt displaced because my sister, five years younger than me, seemed to be livelier and prettier than me. We went to private schools, though there was never enough money. My father was a small-town businessman though he had wanted to be an actor. I wanted to study art, but my parents seemed to think I ought to go out and earn my keep at sixteen. Neither of them had any formal education, my mother had been dragged from school to school. I think they expected me

55

to be a bank clerk or something. I was a girl, so there wasn't any expectation.

'I did manage to get into a local art college for two years in the nearest main town to our village. My mother was pregnant and she wanted me to give up at college to help her at home. It was my final year. My parents said they wouldn't be able to support me. It seemed very important to me to get my qualification, so I did something which looked terrible at the time. I left home to live near the college. Just as I was finishing the course I met Matthew.'

Jane got a very junior job in the art department of a woman's magazine which took her to London. She was lonely, sharing a 'grotty little bedsitter with a girl from home'. The two did not get on, and when Matthew came up to London from his job in Sussex, she was happy to see him.

'It was just before the permissive time got going. My room-mate got pregnant and was so ignorant she didn't even know how it had happened. I remained a virgin at that time for the simple reason that I was not attracted to Matthew at all physically, but feeling adrift as I was, I agreed to marry him.

'There is a special reason though, about the sexual thing. When I was twelve I had a crush on a priest from a seminary in his late twenties who was known to my parents. He suggested to my mother that he babysat occasionally. I may have looked old for my age, but I was totally innocent. I hadn't even been told the facts of life. One day he grabbed me and gave me a kiss. It was obviously a sexual kiss, though I did not recognize it as that. All I knew was that it wasn't like the kiss that uncles gave me. I was absolutely revolted, plus – the classic thing – I felt guilty. One day when my mother went shopping he threw me on the bed and pressed down on me and there was heavy breathing. I was terrified, absolutely terrified. I screamed get off, get off, but because I'd had a crush on him I thought it was my fault.

'I never told my parents. I didn't let him anywhere near me after that and I used to leave the room when he came in. My parents could never understand why I was so rude to him.

'He was found out by my grandmother when she was staying. My mother had just come out of hospital with yet another gynie thing – it was always happening, from having babies. I've got this weak bladder which I think is from having babies too, by the way. Anyway, he was there, and he started interfering with my sister. Because she was so much younger she said, oh Simon kept putting a hand on my leg. That was enough. My father said he felt like killing the guy. When they spoke to the head of the seminary I was accused of being a maladjusted child and making things up. But luckily it was found out that he had done similar things to other children and he was eventually excommunicated.

'**At the time I was so ashamed, and the result was that I was terrified of every single man I met**. If there were boys on the train when I went home from college I would go to a different compartment and absolutely shake.

'And then I met Matthew who came from a puritanical Non-conformist background and respected my need to remain a virgin. He posed no sexual threat whatsoever. He was a nice man who solved my social, work, economic and family problems. But he was prudish and didn't show emotions, and he was unfrivolous. Our first married night was fairly disastrous since we both were virgins. I had gone dead for so many years. I should have found out what lust was when I was in my teens. But we were told so often that to show sexual desire or to sleep around would make us be seen as cheap. No one would want us. They'd take advantage but wouldn't marry us. And marriage was the ultimate aim.'

Jane got a part-time job in a local crafts college and was promoted very quickly to a senior full-time position. She also met a man at the college . . .

'I was twenty-three and it knocked me absolutely sideways. We didn't have an affair, but I actually lusted after somebody for the first time. I felt I had to be honest so I told my husband and he was very shaken though the whole thing died out eventually. That delayed us having children, but my husband was an only child and he wanted children. A couple of years later he was offered a job in a fairly remote part of the country. I had the choice of giving up my job or giving up my husband. But I was young and frightened of being alone so I went with him. I couldn't find a job so I gritted my teeth and became pregnant. It was a terrible time. We were renovating a house that had rats in it. I'd left behind my work, friends and colleagues, all my contacts. Though my parents weren't too far away, my mother never helped. She'd spent too many years bringing up her own children. She couldn't appreciate my problems of being isolated. I hardly saw my husband. Even in the evenings he was studying.

'When the baby was born I felt he was wonderful, but there was no one to support me. My husband was busy furthering his career. I started an Open University degree and got good grades, but then I gave it up. I didn't know it, but I was getting depressed. When my son was two, I had an affair. It was sheer desperation. I just wanted someone to take some notice of me. It wasn't very successful, and I hated myself for it – sleazy, horrible.

'I did love my son, but he was difficult, hyperactive even, partly because I wasn't in tune. Again I told my husband about the affair. He said he'd divorce me, but we papered over the cracks though I was totally sexually frustrated. I was married to someone I was not physically attracted to. I suppose having another child was a way of making it up to him. That birth was so easy, whereas the first was difficult and traumatic. He was a lovely child, all calm and gorgeous. He still is whereas the other one has remained hyperactive and restless.'

There followed several years of 'fairly isolated pram pushing', then another uprooting for the family when Jane's husband was again offered promotion in another part of the country. She was again depressed at the move, though the new house was 'lovely' and she now had use of a car. The children were at school and nursery, and Jane began to write short stories. She sold one or two and then got a couple of commissions.

'**I began to think, what do I want to do with my life. I'd never thought about it before. And I opened a cupboard full of skeletons because I had buried what I was feeling**. Unfortunately, I also knew what I didn't want, and that was my husband. The beautiful house, the lovely furniture didn't mean anything to me because the person inside it didn't mean anything to me. Once I realized that my world fell apart. Gradually, I withdrew from Matthew. I began to think about leaving. I made it clear I wasn't satisfied sexually, but then I'd back off and say it was my fault. I maintained Matthew's ego by saying it was my fault, I'm the one in the wrong.'

It does not seem to have occurred to Jane that the responsibility might have been shared, which might have eliminated this hint of martyrdom, but perhaps martyrdom was what she was seeking. In any case, their lives were about to change. The house was proving too expensive and the family moved to a smaller one. Jane's share from the sale would have given her enough to buy a small property, but not one that she felt could accommodate the children.

'I couldn't bring myself to bring up the children in a damp house with plants coming out of the ceiling, because that was the only kind of house you could get for the price I could pay. So the day we moved as a family to our new house I decided: I'll get this house straight for the children, and then I'll go. I stayed for eighteen months and removed myself from the marital bed.

'The children were around seven and ten when I left. First I stayed with a friend a few miles away. The talk was that I had left for another man, which I think people found easier to understand. I started off going back to the house to stay three nights a week. Then I bought this place and I went on seeing the children every weekend and after school once a week. Matthew asked me to go over and sort out the house at weekends, which I did, and in the week he was relying on a sixth-former to collect the children from school.

'I was subject to a lot of pressure over the divorce. We sold the second house and I got a lump sum and a small amount to live on – £180 a month, it's always in arrears. At the court hearing, Matthew was very generous. He said, my wife is a superb mother but she has a career to start, and it was on that basis that I was given maintenance payment and joint custody. I have a small mortgage on this house. My only regular income is from a tiny teaching job, part time. I have to live very carefully.

'**When I was leaving, we were going to present the situation to the children together**, saying that Mummy and Daddy wouldn't be living together any more but they would be in a nice new home near their school and it would be much more exciting than village life. But Matthew sat there in silence and I had to tell them on my own. I had to sit with my arms round my children and tell them I wasn't going to live with them any more. They responded the way children do. Things like who's going to have the TV and stereo.

'I was doing very well at work and considering coming up to London. I had overcome so many obstacles. I felt I did have some talent and I felt I had a duty to it. I had a duty not to kill it. My ex-husband feels anti careers for women. I think he feels I should be working in a wine bar or something like that in order to support myself.

'A few months after I left, Matthew's mother sold up her house to come and live with him. He was beginning to find his job suffered, but with him there was no problem of which came first. Then he met his new lady, a divorced woman of forty with no children. And after that he would start dumping the children on me at the weekends, so he'd have the time clear for courting. So I was alone all week and sitting in on a Saturday night. I felt I was never going to meet anyone again.

'Last year friends said why not make it every other weekend. The children could stay from Friday to Sunday instead of one afternoon to the following afternoon, and I could see each child separately once a week for tea. So that is the arrangement now.

'My children are very proud of me. We are very fond, there is a strong bond. My mother-in-law accused me of taking Matthew's money and being able to come and go as I please while he was tied with the children. No one worried when it was me who was the one who was tied.'

Eventually, Jane made a new social life for herself and gained a kind of independence, though there were disillusions.

'**There were two or three boyfriends but they were absolute shits. They didn't want me as part of their social life. They just**

wanted a mistress tucked away in a cottage. So I decided that life is best if you live it like a man. I joined a sailing club and I concentrated on my work. My toes didn't touch the ground. I was getting things published, getting commissions. People were cooking for me. I had a marvellous social life. It was a revelation.

'Then I met Robin. He is widowed and has a daughter aged nine. He chased me because I didn't need a bloke by then. But he cooked for me, took me around. He said you need to spend more time with your kids, so we all took a villa abroad for a month, him and his daughter and me and my sons. It was marvellous. After that Robin said come and live here and sell your house. He says he wants to marry me, but I see difficulties. One is that his daughter is holding him back in his job. He has to rely on friends to pick her up at school most of the time. He is putting a little pressure on me at the moment, not to be a mother, but to help solve the problem. I know that he feels I grudge doing it. He goes away on business occasionally, and he will expect me to cook for her and look after her then.

'I suppose it is a bit Freudian, her and me competing for him. I'd have to be there in the mornings to take her to school and pick her up when he is away. It would be painful for me. It would bring home to me the fact that I'm not doing it for my own children. I must admit I don't want to. I do like the freedom to come and go as I please – a dubious freedom perhaps, but I have it. I don't want to be a stepmother, I suppose that's it. But he is making my boys welcome – it's the trade-off.

'I was totally blocked by the family situation and that is why I need my independence. Going with Robin would be the thin end of the wedge. Before you know it, you're in the old situation again.'

It was at this point in the interview that I asked Jane: why do you see motherhood as such a threat? There was a moment of recognition before she answered, as the layers of self-justification and rationalization fell away. She nodded and wept and then replied:

'Because in my marriage I always was the one taking the kids to the doctor, things like that. I always made the sacrifices. My mother said, "You'd feel more for the children if you felt more for their father." They would have felt less of a responsibility if I had loved my husband. My mother's life has been one of complete subservience. She has spent a lifetime bringing up children, so she had unknowable ideals. She was on anti-depressants for eighteen years after my brother was born, and I was the one who always mothered her.'

* * *

60

Jane's story has some similarities to Samantha's. Both married young to men quite a lot older who were sexually inexperienced, religiously observing and responsible. But the recurring themes through Jane's life are deprivation and martyrdom. Her father was a redundant businessman who wanted to be an actor. Her mother missed out on proper schooling. Jane herself was expected to find paid work and not study. She missed out on burgeoning adolescent sexuality because of her dreadful experience, and she also felt she was missing out on the permissive society.

Her marriage as she tells it is a catalogue of sacrifices: moving to a strange area because of her husband's job, having to give up her own job, having children because her husband wanted them. And then there was what seemed to her the supreme sacrifice, the overburdening responsibility of motherhood. Her own mother is seen as a sacrificial victim, having suffered depression and gynaecological problems (and Jane hints that she herself suffers a weak bladder through childbirth). Jane's response to her mother's needs as a teenager was to escape when her brother was born, though she felt this to be a terrible act, a betrayal, perhaps because she saw herself as chosen to be the mother in her family when the real mother couldn't cope. This may be why she says at the end of her story that she has always mothered her mother. She did it in her fashion, which was to leave but to feel guilty. She still appears to want to escape being a mother, fearful of taking on a stepchild or becoming absorbed in family life. But she still also feels the guilt and the responsibility, struggling to keep her children as part of her life.

Many women would not see Jane's marriage as sacrifice. She followed her husband, just as women are supposed to do. She could have lived a pleasant life and been well-provided for. She could even have developed her talent within the bosom of the family. Her feminist stance on the need for self-realization could be just as much a masking of immaturity as the puritan ethic was a masking of sexual problems.

But to explain Jane's behaviour solely as immature (or as feminist for that matter) reduces its significance. She experienced a childhood in which she did see a woman making many sacrifices. She herself was expected to continue in that tradition, accepting the loneliness and isolation of being a wife and mother, cut off from friends, from satisfying work and a familiar way of life. Another woman might have felt less sorry for herself, but there would still have been sacrifices, and no one to help soften them.

Undoubtedly, men make sacrifices too, but at least they have choices when they decide to change location to fit in with their

61

work, or spend long hours away from their family to further their career. Any dissent on their wife's part is often construed as lack of loyalty and wifely support. Often, the best a concerned husband can or will do is encourage an 'outside interest', though nothing that might threaten a woman's traditional role in family life.

With so much feeding her sense of martyrdom, it is not surprising that Jane developed a defensive attitude towards her 'talent', though it is not very different from Shaw's dictum quoted in Chapter 1, which puts a man's art above his family. She is not in touch with her children's needs – how can she be when her own are so pressing? Her urge to escape and her guilt led her into the spurious preparation she gave to her children when she spoke of their future without her: the talk of the 'nice new home' in an 'exciting' place, so sadly distanced from the true emotions that both sides were experiencing. Such a false approach denies feeling and creates distance between a parent and children.

Jane used friends to strengthen her argument on the need to curtail visits – another evasion from which no one seems to have been able to save her. She talks of a 'strong bond' and the pride that her children have for her, almost as if she needs their admiration and approval, and even their understanding.

In her new relationship, Jane shows clearly her need to be nurtured. Robin cooks for her, a real source of pleasure. And why not? Men accept nurturing for themselves as a matter of course. Women get little enough of it once they are adult. But Jane is a woman who feels she never was nurtured, a feeling learned partly from an understanding that her mother too in her time was never nurtured, partly because she felt displaced by her 'livelier and prettier' sister and then her brother. She has a hungry need that is never satisfied, that makes her ungenerous to others. Like many a man, she has used success in her work as compensation, and she has used her prettiness to attract men and to protect herself from the thing that she finds the most difficult to do, which is to become a parent instead of a child.

* * *

Tania is slim, sharp, intense-looking, a poised woman of forty-nine. Her elegant, one-bedroomed flat is in a converted Victorian warehouse – 'very yuppie land' she says. Tania first married when she was a student, and married again when she was thirty-seven. Two years ago she left this second marriage to live alone and work in London. Her two children were aged five and seven.

'I still am rejected by the children. It is an upward fight each time I see them'

'I am from Australia, and I had been living in London for seven years, teaching. I decided to move to Somerset where I had some friends and to take a job there, and through them I met this bloke. We got married and because of my age I said look, if you want to have a family we have to start fairly smartish. So we didn't have much of a courtship. Most of the courtship – if that's the word – was spent decorating the house.

'We married because he was being pushed out of the nest at the age of thirty-one. I was getting rather alone in the world. I had come through a long and very painful relationship with someone who was a homosexual and a transvestite. I had wanted to put some distance between us, so it was a kind of rebound. I was feeling vulnerable, in a new place. I didn't see any point in waiting, so we got married within six months of meeting.

'Within two months I was pregnant. I did not expect that. Both of us were only children and had no experience of child-rearing. I had no family of my own, and his mother, who actually lived next door to us, was a walking caricature of a mother-in-law. I sympathize with her a bit, chucking him out at thirty-one.

'I never felt if I don't have a child I will never be fulfilled. If anything, I felt vaguely equivocal. If I missed it, I missed it. But it was a bit of now or never.

'It was a difficult birth. The child was born in the dead of winter when there was nothing to do but peer out at the snow and cuddle something nice and warm. That euphoria lasted certainly through six months of breast-feeding, but by that stage I was getting a bit jittery that suddenly life was all baby shit and nothing else. Having both been only children we felt it was grossly unfair not to have another child. So we took a deep breath and decided to go in for siege number two, by which time I was thirty-nine.'

Tania's son arrived a week before her fortieth birthday. He was a big baby, weighing 10lb. She found the birth difficult and her memories are still vivid and intense. 'There were stitches, episiotomy, haemorrhoids, all sorts of rubbish – ugh. And it was late. Which was not nice.

'He was the ugliest baby anybody would ever set eyes on. Rolls of fat, horrible. Oh boy, was he grim. He is (pointing to a recent photograph) smashing now. And he was outraged at the whole experience, very hungry, terribly demanding. The eldest child, with whom I'd been very close, now had a strong regression to babyhood, just when I wanted her to be understanding. I was at a low ebb. She was only a titch of two and a half, but . . .

'I was still in a state of siege. The first year was spent being pregnant, very tired, and decorating the house we had bought. It needed enormous renovation. So the first year was being spent in

63

siege of the pregnancy. The second year was spent in the siege of baby and decorating, then there was a kind of six-month lull, and then I got pregnant again. And then this demanding baby.

'I was miserable, and I hadn't yet put it down to the marriage. I just wasn't having any fun. My husband never wanted to go anywhere. He kept saying we had to save. He is a surveyor. I had no income, though he was making a very good income. We put money away for school fees and converted a house as an investment.

'**My husband used to complain because I was not the good housewife that he wanted**. But he more or less ignored the children and was never there except at weekends. He could never understand that you had to watch the children every second because they might fall down steps or on a rock in the garden. So I had to do it. You couldn't read a book or anything. One never had a moment off. When the children were two and four, I said to my husband, look, I'm going to end up completely crazy if we don't get someone to come in and have the children so I can do something else.

'So we got a young girl and she came in for the afternoons. I started classes in restoring broken china and ceramics, and gradually I even got some paid work doing it. It was something that I could do rather than just being a domestic person.

'My husband had been totally inexperienced sexually when we married. I had given him books which he did not read. I had to endure sex with him. There was not a firm basis sexually, intellectually or spiritually, because we disagreed on religious grounds even before we got married. I was atheist, he was an observing Christian. I agreed that the children would be brought up in the Church.

'We should never have married. If we had met and married five years earlier we would not have had children so quickly, and we would have split in a couple of years. If he had not had this thing about virginity before marriage, we might have had an affair and that would have been the end of it. Before our marriage, there was nothing more than hugs and cuddles and I accepted that because when I married my first husband I was a virgin and had been harassed over it. He was very frustrated on the sexual side, and, I learned later, disappointed.

'I was so pent-up and frustrated by then that I was letting it out on the children. I knew what I was doing was wrong but I couldn't stop myself. A friend heard me shouting at the children. She said this is wrong, and read me the riot act. I suppose I had been afraid to face it. There was something desperate going on. I said but my husband would never go to marriage guidance. We knew the people who ran it, as you do in small places. Before I decided to force him to go to counselling, I had to grapple with the implications if at the end of it he wasn't going to change or was unwilling to change or if in fact it was going to drive him further away.'

This pre-planned negative attitude to counselling was to be another aspect of Tania's siege-philosophy to life. There was no straightforward way for her to cope with her difficulties. All she could do was to plan alibis in advance, using marriage guidance, her GP, and a psychiatrist to set up a pattern of defence. This helped her to avoid painful self-examination and to make way for her ultimate aim, which was revealed through fairly tortuous reasoning:

'I thought, what would I do. Am I employable at this stage? Because one of the things in this particular marriage was the meanness of the man. I knew that if I and the children were dependent on him for a cheque every month, it was the quickest way to have a heart attack. You would never know whether the money was going to come. I knew how difficult it was to get a job locally. I knew I didn't want to teach. In the end, I got a job part time with a small antique shop specializing in books, and this was going on when we were having the counselling.

'Anyway, I had faced the alternatives before I started counselling. It was impossible to be dependent on him maintaining me. We did have another place which we had bought as an investment, but it would have meant the children changing schools, which would have been upsetting. [*The children at this stage were aged five and seven.*] I didn't know if I could get a job in London. Then I saw an ad for a manager of an antiquarian bookshop in London, and as I had studied art history and knew a bit about antiques I was able to get the job. It didn't take me any time to find that the salary offered didn't match up to what was needed for accommodation for me and a room for each child and a nannie.

'I went to pieces in my GP's surgery. I said I'm contemplating taking a job in London because my marriage is going to pieces and if I go where there's a job, I can't afford to have the children. He said are you feeling guilty about it, and I said yes of course, because after all I knew it would do them a great deal of damage, and he suggested I saw a psychiatrist. I had an appointment within two weeks.

'**The psychiatrist said what kind of a mother do you think you've been? and I said pretty lousy**. He asked why. I said because I feel so frustrated, I'm angry all the time. He said, do you think that is normal? I said I thought so, though I don't have many yardsticks. He asked me if I battered them and of course I said no. My tongue is my weapon – but just as hurtful. He asked which do you think would be more damaging to them, you being a mother as you are, or for them to have no mother? I said no no no. I didn't come here to answer the questions. I came here to ask you the questions. He said well, you've made the decision, and I said yes. I made the decision but I'm trying to learn to live with it.

'At that point, I still hoped our joint marriage counselling might sort things out. But we had both aired our views and why we were disappointed in the relationship, and at a very few points did they meet. All I asked for was tolerance. I wasn't going off with any other man. I was so off men, it never occurred to me. But his response was negative. I said look, I'm taking a job in London. It will give us both space to simmer down. He wasn't outwardly angry. I was though. I decided to come back every weekend, though I did fall apart physically. I didn't want to upset the children. I didn't tell the children I am leaving your father.'

Tania was not happy in London at first. Her job was not a success and she was dismissed after three months. She lived in cheap accommodation with a former flatmate. She had made contact with her transvestite friend but the meetings were not satisfactory. She appears to have had doubts about her sexual identity, feeling an intense dislike for and rejection of men. 'I was so disappointed, I was on the verge of lesbianism, if anything.' Her husband wanted to remortgage the family house in order to release money for investment. Tania refused to sign away her rights. She, inevitably, was protecting her assets should there be a divorce. Perhaps he was trying to do likewise, though Tania appears not to think so.

'He got hysterical over the phone, and said I was trying to ruin him financially. Of course, he had no idea that I was probably not coming back to the marriage. The nanny had been there three years and the children were fine. At first I went down every weekend. I was so relieved to walk out of the house every Sunday night. It was a horrendous trip. I had no car and I had to get local buses from the nearest station and would arrive about midnight on a Friday. I stayed in the marital bed because if it came to the crunch he couldn't do me for desertion. I studied the marital laws. I didn't want to be thrown out before I made the decision. I wanted to plan things coolly. There were moments when I could have cheerfully murdered the man. On the other hand, I could see the immediate consequences of that would be that I would be left alone with the children, and how on earth would I manage? Not well.'

After a period of unemployment, which she did not reveal to her husband, Tania got a part-time teaching job in London and then 'fell into' management consultancy. Suddenly she had a good salary and excellent prospects. There was a showdown with her husband – she had been away nearly a year by then.

'He said you're not taking any interest in the house or family, blah blah blah . . . He wanted to make me the great ogre who had gone off career-hunting. I felt it had been survival. We agreed to go for a quick divorce, with me applying for it and giving him custody of the children. He had become a good parent – his mother had cracked the whip and seen to that.

'**I thought he would become a good father when I went, and if I went back he would revert to being as he had been before**. Now he takes them to school and he's home by about six to relieve the nanny. They are seven and nine now, so you don't have to watch them so closely. Now he doesn't want me to come more than once a month. That's been agreed through a conciliation arrangement.

'Friends at the organization MATCH counselled me to get the access spelled out as soon as possible. So it has been arranged that I have the children for a fortnight every summer, and every other year I have them for a week at Easter or Christmas. Last year it was Easter – very difficult because their father and grandmother had poisoned them against London and they didn't want to come. He drove them up and the scene was dreadful, just dreadful. One of the children went hysterical and didn't want to leave him. I still am rejected by the children. It is an upward fight each time I see them. They are very aggressive towards me. I've only had them here that one time.

'I had really planned and plotted that visit like a military siege. It's true I don't have a lot of room here for them, but they shared a bed which they were still young enough to do, and they liked that because they have separate rooms at home. I slept on the sofa bed in the living room. I would like to get a two-bedroomed flat but my husband sees that as a threat – that I might possibly be trying to take them away. Perhaps he fears the glamour of London. And children are very mercenary little souls, God knows they are. They say why don't you make as much money as Daddy? Why can't you afford to buy us an inflatable dinghy? And why does Daddy have to give you some money? Of course they overhear snatches of conversation and say it's Daddy's house. The oldest child is able to articulate, which hurts but is wonderful. The younger can't quite yet, so he tries to thump me and call me things. That's how his aggression comes out. The mothers at MATCH say don't worry, they will start to question when they get to a certain age. The nice thing about the women there is that you find they are normal people, and you do feel you are a monster to leave your children.'

Tania took the children on her own to a holiday cottage. Again the children resisted and asked to telephone their father and grandmother every evening, and again she planned amusements and games that did not appease them.

'It was excruciatingly awful. But I don't think it would be right if I never saw them at all because they feel I have rejected them as it is. I have left them, so I have to keep proving to them again and again and again that I have not left them, that I still do care for them, that I am concerned for them, that I am interested in what they are doing, that I want to know. I find it very difficult to write to them because I have nothing to tell them about. I can't say look, I'm doing really well in my job, because that points to everything Daddy has said – that Mummy left to have a wonderful career. I can't write and say I've been to the theatre, I've done this or that, because they'll say if you have the money to do this why don't you go out and buy us a wonderful dinghy?

'I am having them this Christmas, and I am dreading it. They will come just after some really heavy work and the idea of them coming will be very stressful. I'll take them to see the lights because they'll want to go, but it will be awful – crowds, traffic. But I have to do something with them.

'My husband and I are not divorced yet, and I have no certain future, no pension or anything like that. The only thing I have is this flat and another small flat in London which is my investment, my pension really. I don't know what the settlement will be, but it will be a battle.'

*   *   *

Life is an immense battle for Tania, who emerges as a highly manipulative person, desperately trying to escape from reality. She is so deep into her manipulations that she may be living in a fantasy world which could be seen as a distorted version of current values and attitudes.

The values of feminism, of child-rearing, of counselling, are all drawn in to add substance to Tania's fragile wall of self-deception. She could not be a good mother because she had 'no experience of child-rearing'. She 'needed to gain independence, to find her real self'. The marriage faltered because 'there was no time for courtship'.

Somewhere in Tania's background is the spectre of a mother-less child, seeking understanding from her own 'titch of two and a half' and being challenged by parenthood beyond her endurance.

When a woman fails to meet the challenge as she has failed, the sense of defeat must also be beyond endurance. And so Tania has to seek someone to blame and invent obstacles in order to avoid admitting even to herself that she finds motherhood intolerable.

Why did this woman choose a sexually inexperienced man as a husband and agree to have children? There are hints that her own sexual identity troubles her or is uncertain. Perhaps she wanted to prove her 'normality' or even her humanity, she who refers to herself as a monster and an ogre. She has absorbed these labels that the rest of us so easily give to her, and all they do is increase her shame and lock her in her agony.

Again and again throughout this book women cite friends, GPs, shrinks, anyone who appears to be giving them support for leaving or giving up their children. Tania's anger at her psychotherapist is due to the fact that he would not play her game. Perhaps if she had been able to feel less guilty about her anger – and even hate – towards her children, she would have been able to express it more openly, and to have come to terms with it. She might have communicated this to her husband, instead of turning her hate on to him too. But women are not supposed to hate their children, or want to live away from them. Tania is having to deal with a hate that dare not show its name.

She refers to her children as 'these children', creatures who are not part of her. The burdens of looking after them are real enough for her, but they also cloak an unspeakable truth: that there is no pleasure or reward in being with 'these children'. They are merely a source of threat and frustration.

Tania is punishing herself for such ideas, and punishing others too. For of course she saw her children as well as her husband as part of her oppression. If she is brave about acknowledging her children's rejection of her - and this surely must be the thing a mother fears most - it is because here she has the opportunity to demonstrate that she is not in the wrong. It is all their fault; they are the monsters; she is not rejecting them. In truth, their rejection is part of a logical and inevitable progression, but Tania's only defence is to twist the argument to suit her emotional needs, which her children probably sense.

A man who has made Tania's choices, with a carefully set-up bachelor pad conveniently located a long way from home, might have the courage of his predilections and give up seeing his children altogether. Why doesn't Tania do that, and so put everyone out of their misery? The reasons must be a cocktail of self-punishment, guilt, pride, fear of condemnation, fear of jeopardizing the divorce settlement. The chief ingredient might be to prove to herself that she is lovable and that her children are not. Such motives might seem alien and unnecessary to many men.

Whatever the reasons for Tania's persistence, here is a tortured woman who cannot trust anyone but who craves reassurance. We all practise manipulation to some extent, but few of us become quite so clever at it or so dominated by it. In the end, the person most manipulated is Tania, a victim of her own self-deception. Her need for such self-deception must come at least in part from the deep sense of failure to live up to society's expectations of selfless motherhood, of nurturing, of loving femininity.

There is, however, one modern concept that helps bolster Tania's move into a new life alone. Motherhood is no longer an unavoidable fate. Choice, not destiny, rules. If having children is seen as one choice, one career path to be pursued, then it is not perhaps so surprising that some women would choose to put it aside if it proves unsatisfactory. Tania's foray into motherhood proved a failure, so she removed herself into another career path that is more rewarding, less threatening.

This is indeed a worrying development, though a logical one, once it is accepted that some women do not find satisfaction through their children and do not want to live with them. It is a most unpalatable idea for most of us to accept, especially those of us who love our children and can understand the stress they would experience if we followed this path ourselves. We are tempted to cry out to these women: don't you see what a precious thing you have thrown away? But how could our voices be heard above the clamour of pain and the fashionable rationalizations? We are dealing with women who cannot live with their children, and cannot live with themselves.

Chapter 5

WHAT THE CHILDREN SAY

Child psychotherapists usually provide a gloomy prognosis for children whose mothers go away. In this chapter we listen to individuals in different age groups who look back on a childhood marred by the fact that their mothers left them and their fathers to live a new life with a new partner. They were left, inevitably, with a huge burden of unhappy messages and assumptions concerning their mothers. They did, however, make a new, and sometimes better relationship with them in later life.

* * *

'I felt I had driven my mother away, because I wanted her to go.'

Mandy is twenty-six and works in radio. She has two younger sisters, one adopted. She was twelve years old when her mother left and her sisters were ten and five.

'My family don't talk about things. The whole history of this is what I can put together and remember. My mother never said anything at the time and still hasn't. How it happened was that I came home from school one day and my younger sister had been kept home by my mother. My little sister was at home anyway. She had told both of them that she was going. She'd kept my sister home from school to do that, but she had let me go to school, and when I came home, my sister told me she'd gone. I think she did it like that because I was at an age when we had a very difficult relationship. But I wish she hadn't done it like that. It's the one aspect I cannot forgive her for. Everything else I can understand. But doing it that way, basically making me feel that I would not even be interested in the fact that she was going . . . I think that's what she felt. She didn't really owe me an explanation because she thought I didn't really care.

'I was a lot more confident and independent at that stage than I am now, so what I did was laugh. I swear that I felt relieved. I was glad she had gone on one level. I felt guilty about

71

being relieved. My middle sister told a friend that I had done that, and she was quite appalled. I felt I had driven my mother away because I wanted her to go. Feeling relieved was a way of helping myself. It was my way of coping with it. There had been tension between me and my mother and also between my mother and father. One came from the other. I took my father's side. My parents' marriage had been very bad for at least a year, and I was very much a daddy's girl always.

'I think she was very disturbed at the time. I'm sure adolescent daughters are a lot to handle when you are under a lot of stress. I think at times she did hate me. I think mothers should be allowed to, well, hate is too emotional, dislike their children.

'I didn't tell any of my friends at school. I don't know if anybody else ever told my teachers. I didn't. My father didn't, so we pretended nothing had happened. My father found it difficult at home, but I was happy at school and with my friends. That aspect of my life carried on as normal.

'I think the first difficulties came about two years later when my grandmother died. She was my father's mother and she looked after us quite a lot. She'd looked after me before then at times because my mother had had two nervous breakdowns from the time when I was five and my middle sister was starting nursery school. She wasn't happy being a married mother and it was when she was doing some work in an adoption agency that she ended up adopting my younger sister because she was coloured and at that time hard to adopt. Anyway, when my grandmother died, I wanted my mother. It was the first time I thought, well, I miss her. I missed having an adult woman. My sisters saw her, but not me, for the first eighteen months.

'She was with a man whom she left to go to and subsequently married. She is still with him and very happy. My father hadn't told me that because he might have felt it was bad for me to know, but when I found out I was glad. I was glad she wasn't lonely. I have never blamed her for going because had she stayed it would have been worse and worse for her.

'When I saw her again we had an argument about something quite unrelated – the IRA in fact. I was about fourteen. Politics were something my parents had always argued about. It was one of their differences and in this case I was taking a strident viewpoint against her. So it wasn't a success. We didn't speak again for over a year. There were two periods like that in my teenage years when we didn't speak for eighteen months. I'm sure she was more willing to speak to me than I was to speak to her. She didn't get in touch in those times because I think she felt the arguments were indicative of my attitude towards her – angry and taking sides with my father. I was completely unforgiving and she didn't know how to handle that. She felt I had rejected her. She used to send presents, and I knew where she was.

'Then I calmed down a bit and I was seeing her more when I was sixteen on a more polite and civilized basis. I'd meet her in a department-store coffee shop and we'd go shopping, and later I went and stayed the night. Now we have a reasonably good relationship although it is not as honest as it should be.

'I've no doubt that she loves me and she worries about us more than other mothers I know. Because she hasn't been there to watch us grow up she has a tendency to be over-protective. It is something to do with guilt, I suppose.

'My mother had been left by her mother when she was small. So my grandfather brought her and her sisters up, and an aunt did a lot of the mothering. My mother does not talk about this. I find it a bit worrying for my own future. I don't feel ready to have children. My mother had me when she was twenty-seven. I feel if you have been in a family where there is a divorce, whichever parent goes, you are either very against marriage or very romantic. I can be either, depending on mood. If you've never seen the reality of people making a marriage work, you don't have the knowledge. Children in intact marriages learn that you are allowed to fail. You can make mistakes but go on and try again. I suppose my mother did mother me, but in a way she wasn't there for me because she was ill a lot, basically unable to cope. So I spent a lot of time away, and maybe I haven't learned about proper mothering because I didn't experience it.'

* * *

'I have never felt bitter that my mother came between me and other women'
Carl is fifty-seven, a teacher who took early retirement. He has been married for nineteen years and though he has no children of his own, has brought up his wife's two sons from her previous marriage.

'My mother was German, my father too. But he was Jewish. They came here in 1933 but my mother was very unhappy in England, and she went back to Germany during the war, leaving me with my father. I was about seven.

'You can view it from different perspectives. I on the whole rather shared my mother's view of it – you could say that was because of my mother's dominance. She was aware that she was leaving me, but her view was that she couldn't take me back to Germany. She had a strong relationship with a man there who

73

was very keen to bring me over, but she said there was no way she would have a half-Jewish child in Germany.

'I was in a little private boarding-school and very happy there. I made friends with the three teachers who ran it. They were sisters, and as I got older and went to another school, I would come back to them and stay with them in the holidays. My mother came once a year to visit me. My father was living in a boarding-house and he visited me.

'My mother knew I would never live with my father because he was someone who could not relate to children. I did not get on well with him. He was very sarcastic when I was young and I was very much in awe of him. He brought quite a lot of money out of Germany, and I was educated privately, but he was very anxious about money, and if I lost anything he made a great thing of it. He was a very bright academic who wrote books that I learned later were considered quite original, a bit out of the ordinary. He knew he had a lot of talent, but for a while here he was very unfulfilled.

'Inevitably, as a teenager I wanted to rebel against my father, which was impossible because to have a confrontation was beyond me in the face of his sarcasm. In my own way I did rebel. A crucial point was when, after a row, he said you talk just like your mother. And I knew then that I'd rather be with her. After the war she had asked me to come, but I didn't then. But when he said that I suddenly thought, I must go and see her. I was twenty-two.

'**We got on like a house on fire from the word go. We had a lot to say to each other, and a great affinity**. There was a strong relationship between us till the day she died. We spent a long time talking about the negative influences of my father on both of us. We compared notes about his anxiety about money. It could have been my mother influencing me, but we found we had similar experiences. I saw how both her father and her husband had the same kind of approach to her. They would both say you're no good, you'll never get anywhere, you'll end up in the gutter. And there was no doubt, my mother could never have done certain things in her life if she had stayed married to my father. He would never have given her the scope for it. In business, employing people. She knew she couldn't do that in England. Though she went back to another man, she eventually got on her own. She needed to do that. In Germany, during the war, she started a business and she was a great success. She had lots of men and did all kinds of things. I accept that she had to have that fulfilment, which she couldn't have with me as a half-Jewish child in Germany. I have always thought that I had to pay that price for her. She went through a period of psychoanalysis and after that she felt she could stand on her own two feet, she could break free of dependence on men.

'I understand what she had to do. Perhaps from a Jewish point of view it was an obscene choice, going back to Nazi Germany, but she had to go back to her home.

'I did not marry until I was thirty-eight. Any girl I met wasn't good enough for me according to my mother. We had rows, and I got fed up with her dominance, but she was a good influence on me and she introduced me to all sorts of worlds that I would not have known without her. I have never felt bitter that my mother came between me and other women. Yes, she did put me off women, but I honestly felt they were wrong for me. In the end I met my wife and I told her I was getting married. She was a bit appalled and there was a strong resentment, but my wife has a strong personality too. There was a time when we were having problems with my oldest stepson, and I was in a position between two strong women and not handling things too well. I was corresponding with my mother about my stepson and when my wife found out she was quite rightly enraged and I stopped. My wife very sensibly left me to work things out with my stepson. She said it was no good her dictating how we should do things, and we do have a very good relationship now.

'I'm not prepared to see everything through some Freudian theory about this, but I have to say, and my wife knows it, that I really did think that my mother was the most interesting woman I have ever met.'

* * *

'I've always felt that my mother didn't really care for us in the way a mother should'
Cecilia is thirty-five, a freelance editor, divorced with a son of seven and living in a stable relationship with another man. She is the second of four sisters, and her mother left the family home when she was sixteen.

'My parents had argued for years. They had the most terrible rows, so that we reached the point where us children were pleading for our parents to get divorced. I can remember almost petitioning them: for Christ's sake, will you get divorced. On one occasion my sister called the police in to stop them fighting. One can't tell how emotionally scarred one is by such things, but I must say I don't like raised voices at all.

'So when my mother decided to go off with somebody else we were pleased. She had asked my father to leave many times but he refused to go, and it was difficult for her because she was totally dependent on him financially. No job of her own. He'd

75

refused to allow her to work, even though she had been a dress designer and had had a very good business when she was young. She was an extremely talented person, and she does all sorts of things now. She had no option. If someone was going to go, then she had to.

'She went to stay with a friend at first. I don't know how she got any money. I think this boyfriend helped her out a bit. As soon as she could, she took my two younger sisters and put them in local schools, then she and the boyfriend set up house together, and they lived together for about ten years. I was at school doing my O levels, and obviously couldn't leave school, so she couldn't take me with her. My oldest sister, four years older than me, immediately saw that everybody was going, so she got up and went off to Paris to live. So I was left with my father, who I didn't get on with at all. It was a ghastly situation for me. He was quite elderly – he is dead now – and I was a headstrong teenage daughter, and he didn't understand me at all. We used to have vicious arguments about things like racial prejudice, and he was dreadful.

'Fortunately, a teacher at school spotted me and said I'm going to do something with her. I'm going to get her off to university. He picked me up and sort of trained me up when he saw the situation at home. Eventually he said you come and live with me. So I went to live with him and his family, and I stayed there for about a year and half till I went off to university.

'Meanwhile, my father was talking about selling the flat and retiring to Devon, and there was no talk about what I would do. When I went back to the flat he'd thrown everything of mine away. I was angry, but it was odd because the real awfulness of that situation has only really occurred to me in the last five or six years. You realize what a blow it was when you tell other people about it. I suppose as I had these parents who fought all the time it took me an awful long time to realize that people had happy families. But then I was so lucky living with the teacher and his family. They were such a lovely couple and I am still very close to them.

'I've always felt that my mother didn't really care for us in the way that a proper mother should, and that applies from when we were very small. Her mother died when she was three months old, and she was brought up by a housekeeper with her sister where no affection seemed to pass at all. She doesn't understand affection. I don't blame her for it. I mean, poor old Mum, it's terrible really. She obviously doesn't know what it's like to sit on someone's knee and have someone sit on your knee.

'**Now she's getting older I think she realizes what she missed out on with her children. She never cuddled us or anything**. She's

76

a bit more affectionate with my son, but she never sits him on her knee. Quite different from his other grandmother. Fortunately, I'm not like that. I'm an affectionate individual.

'When my marriage ended, because my husband was having an affair with someone else, I realized that I could not cope with that kind of uncertainty in my life. I knew I had to sort things out for myself, and I was able to find work so that I could keep the house and pay my ex-husband his share. I am very independent. It's something to do with a feeling of insecurity with people and having to be free. Because I have my own house, my own income, I can control my life and that makes me happier. My partner accepts this.

'My mother is a curious person, and I did find it very difficult when my husband and I parted because she actually went to dinner with him and his new mistress. I didn't expect her to be unpleasant to him, but I didn't expect her to embrace him as a poor old thing either. In the end she saw my point of view, but she obviously doesn't at all understand how people tick. There's something missing. She can't see the other side of it. Most peculiar. I've never talked to her about anything, and she doesn't know what I'm really like. I like her as a person, as an individual, but at arm's length. She's not like a mother would be at all. But I feel I have been extraordinarily lucky in my life. I may not sound lucky, but I've always had the most amazing escape routes. From living in a family at war, I was living in a very happy household. Somehow, something always turned up.'

* * *

The experience of losing a mother, even with the sense of relief if there had been rows, seems to allow for an empathy between mother and child in some cases, and an extraordinary generosity. Of course time and distance dull the anguish and anger and may obliterate the more traumatic memories. Mandy is ambiguous, with her comment on being 'totally unforgiving' followed by 'I have never blamed her'. Carl's terrible need is buried within his passionate involvement with his mother in later years. Cecilia acknowledges a compulsion to be in control, having been in a household that was disintegrating for years.

When time has not provided its mellowing influence, there is an enormous challenge for both mother and child to work through the anger. Two of the three remaining interviews in this chapter are with teenagers whose mothers have left them. Both are angry, and neither have come to terms with their feelings.

First is an interview with a mother who left her child, followed by one with her daughter, the only instance in this book where it was possible to match a mother with her own child. The pair were interviewed separately, with each other's permission.

* * *

'I would not have gone if I had not thought it was all right . . . But I sort of knew it would be in the end, even though we all had to suffer'

Cynthia is forty-seven. She was married at twenty-four, and remained married for twenty-one years. Two years ago, when her son was nineteen and her daughter fourteen, she left the marital home to live alone. She is a neat, precise woman, living in a modern converted flat which she rents. On the wall is an old photograph of her father. In one corner is a small carved Buddha. She is crisp, guarded, practical in her manner.

'I hadn't been thinking of going. In a marriage you try and make it work. I'm a tenacious person but when you're living with someone who won't or can't recognize that things haven't been right, you can't live with it. You try to push things out of your mind, perhaps with the greatest will in the world to do the right thing, but in the end something makes you stop and assess. I was very honest with myself, and I felt I wasn't in the right place.

'My ex-husband is a writer and he works at home. I helped him with the typing or did part-time work when the children were small. So I was practical support. But as the children got bigger, I was making forays into picture restoring. I didn't have to rush home. One can devote more time to work, and it was agreed that I should. Our house was small, and that made it good for one of us to be out of it. I wanted to earn money in order to give my husband more space to do creative work.

'What I didn't realize at the time was . . . well, my father died when I was seventeen, an absolutely stunning man, very calm, generous, self-educated. Just beautiful. We didn't see a lot of him because he was in the RAF, and when he was demobbed he had heart attacks and I was helping my mother in the house, giving her support. I have an older brother but he was not practical or capable. So I was used to looking after someone, and I think I looked after my husband, really.

'I had a very free upbringing. My mother trusted us. I knew London, went to parties, though I never did anything she would have disapproved of. When I met my husband, I assumed he was a man of the world. He was from the north of England, and he was quite unsophisticated in fact. I fell desperately in love with him. He is a very complicated man, desperately insecure and lacking in confidence and I think I was probably mothering him. I tended to push my own deep requirements to one side. I thought he was

78

being supportive, but in a way I was manipulated. I've always put other people first. This is the first time in my life I've not done that.

'I saw the changes in myself and that's why I had to make a decision, and I made this one, to go on my own. The most painful thing has been the fact that you cannot explain to children. You really can't.

'My ex-husband is a brilliant parent, brilliant with his daughter, so I didn't leave her, not in capital letters. I actually left the house with them living in it. That's how I consider it. She is well cared for. The sad thing is, she did miss me, I suppose. And I'm not there to put my arms round her, which I miss terribly. She coped well with it. She is a single-minded lady, always has been. My son had already left home and was sharing with someone, but he was terribly upset because the structure was gone. But he is very understanding. It was a big thing to do. I had no money, nowhere to live and no work. I did not want any support, I went on the dole. I would have liked some help, but I think it was good that I had to struggle and indeed I think it was right to give my husband time. But I do hope he will do the right thing now, otherwise I will have to get difficult. The property will have to be sold because I shall need some capital to buy myself something. But I shall bide my time whilst Anya is there. I am not a wicked, evil lady, but you have to respect your own life.

'People have asked, did I do enough to make my ex-husband understand. This is frightfully difficult to do. I think now he has had such a shock, but I wasn't trying to teach him something by going. For me, it was simply the end. If only he had listened, taken more from me of the way I am. We didn't row, but he could annihilate with words, evil wicked words. I felt very battered mentally, and I couldn't win, so I pushed it all to one side.

'I can't remember what I said to Anya when I went. I said things weren't quite right and I was going to stay with friends and I would never be far away and would ring every day. Vague things like that. She didn't actually say anything. She was obviously very confused and hurt and upset, I'm sure, and just didn't know what to think, but when I did try to give some sort of reason I could see she was frightened I was going to say something against her father. I wouldn't have done that, of course. It was nothing to do with her. It was between the two of us, nothing else. I could see she wouldn't listen, so I didn't bother any more. I'm a great believer in time healing.

'She comes to stay, and I encourage her to do so, but unfortunately she is very busy. We are very close; we do have a rapport. It's quite spiritual. I would not have gone if I had not thought it was all right, no way. But I sort of knew it would be in the end, even though we all had to suffer. There is no easy way, is there? I think I might subconsciously have fought against recognizing what I really felt, in order to survive a tricky situation I suppose . . . We did it all in a burst.

'I'm not at all jealous of the two of them together, not at all. I don't suffer from jealousy. We have a good relationship, and I love to be with her, but I don't need her. I feel her with me all the time, and I've told her I'm there all the time. I'd like to see her a lot more. I think it is important to give her my input which is hopefully of some value. We don't speak on the phone. She doesn't ring me very often, though I do ring her. But I always manage to do it when she's got friends round or is doing homework.

'She was with me for a week a couple of months ago when her father was away. We didn't do anything, we just had a lovely time. She went to school and came here in the evenings and it was very relaxed. There is the sadness that after all those early years of lovely things, one isn't there with what has been created. But honestly, I felt I've done that. That bit of my life is over. Let's get on with the next one.

'Of course in terms of work, I could have carried on in the marriage. I would probably have got as much work if I'd stayed. But I think I've done it better this way simply because there are no pressures at all. I am completely at peace. I've forgiven myself. I've forgiven him. I have become a Buddhist, and I believe in leading a good life and doing good things to help other people. That may sound a contradiction in terms, but I actually believe that in the end my ex-husband's life will be better. I don't think you can ever do anything differently. You have free will, but the free will makes you make a certain decision when you feel the time is right.

'I'm working as a temp at the moment, very boring, not the work I want to do. But I can support myself, and I do it. I can earn my rent and that's very important. So I go out happily each day and I come home happily each evening. Nothing dramatic, but I live a very fulfilled life – dinner with friends, theatre. No, not a man, unfortunately. But I went when there was still time, at forty-five. I don't know that age is relevant, but my mother married again at fifty-five and she's had twenty-five wonderful years.'

* * *

'She didn't want me to go with her, and she can't confide in me, so I feel it must be something I've done'

80

Anya is now sixteen, living with her father in the marital home.
'I see my mother maybe once a fortnight, once a month, lately
not so much. I get on very well with my dad, I was always closer
to him than to my mother. And my brother was always closer to
my mother. I can't really explain why. There has just been a bond
between us, between me and my father. My mother never asked
me to go with her. She came into my room one evening and just
said look, I think I should leave, I've had enough. And she said I
think it's best if you stay at home. But I feel that my dad needed
me more than my mother did. And I need him more. I was very
hurt when she said it though, because she never explained to me
why. She still hasn't explained why she left. So obviously I was
very hurt. But no more than my father.

'Yes, I am angry with her. I know he isn't, and I can understand
that. But I'm angry because she hasn't had the courage to tell me
exactly what happened. Yes, perhaps she doesn't know. But my
brother knows a lot more than I do. Perhaps that's because he is
older. My brother isn't angry. He's very understanding of her. He
hasn't taken sides at all though. I'm very close to my brother.

'We don't get together as a family, though we did once last
year. But the atmosphere was awful. Really false, like my parents
being very bright to each other. My brother and I, we just found
it very awkward and so we decided not to do that again. It was
not fair to any of us really. I was just getting over the pain, and
then that brought it back and it made me realize that things were
never going to get better between them. When it first happened,
I had a hope that maybe my mother would realize she needed to
be here with us as a family, but as time wore on I realized that
there's no way they could ever get together again. Though I'd still
like it very much.

'I was angry with her for hurting my father, because I could feel
he was so upset. I was angry with her for not telling me what had
happened, because when I have gone over it with her she has said
well, there are some things you will never know and I can never
tell you about it. Obviously it still hurts her but she doesn't seem
to see what this is doing to me still.

'I do think she is selfish. It seems to me she is thinking, well,
I can't be bothered with it any more. And she is selfish for not
telling me. If she did it would be a way of her showing me that
she loves me. I do feel she doesn't love me. I think she feels
guilty. She'll phone up sometimes and she'll say she didn't really
mean to hurt me, but she must have known beforehand if she can
say that now.

'I do in some way blame myself for her leaving. I'm not sure
why. Maybe I didn't love her enough. But she didn't want me to

go with her, and she can't confide in me, so I feel that it must be something I've done. I know that is a very common feeling, but it doesn't change anything.

'She lives very near, a twenty-minute bus ride away, but the fact is that I feel I can't talk to her. I've been there to stay for a weekend at her flat, and the atmosphere, it's like there's nothing to say to her because you've grown apart, which I didn't actually want to happen.

'I never did confide in her though. I always confided in my father. I think perhaps she was very unhappy. Apparently she was. I can see she doesn't communicate a lot. Whereas my father naturally does.

'I know I don't really hate her. I don't mean it. But I am angry enough to want her to show me that she can talk to me. I'm not going to go to her. The atmosphere in this house wasn't very pleasant when she was here and subconsciously I noticed that because it made me a very quiet person, and I was a bit of a loner when I was younger. But now just being with my father, I've got to know him so much better.

'It may get better as I get older, but at the moment I can't consider seeing her. When my mother left she said it's not good for me to stay here, I can't go on doing it. Basically I didn't seem to care. I was quite happy to stay at home with Dad. I know that he cried a lot. I saw him cry once, but I left him because I couldn't cry about it. I do sometimes, but mainly I can't. I don't know why. I was very bad at school when it happened. I didn't do any work. I regret that now because what I should have done is to have sat down and got on with it. But I didn't, and I was very rebellious. I did pass my O levels, and I'm doing A levels now, and I'm working hard.'

* * *

There is a sad discrepancy between these two accounts, as no doubt there would be between many of the other mothers and children in this book, had both been interviewed. What emerges is the destructiveness of self-deception. Cynthia has constructed a view of life that serves to block her sensitivity. Her new religion may have given her inner peace, but it has cost her the ability to face reality. She wanted to communicate with her daughter, but failed through what seems to be a lack of nerve. She could not trust herself to keep her anger towards her husband under control when talking to her daughter, so she gave up trying to talk. Sensing her daughter's unwillingness to listen – and it is as hard to hear the worst as well as to tell it – she backed off. A lifetime of serving others before herself has left her without an ability to understand her own potency. What Anya sees as selfishness, outsiders might see as fear of being swayed by 'annihilating words', of being persuaded by guilt to remain at home, or of being unable to admit, 'leaving for myself is part of my self-development, and it is something I want and need to do alone'.

In a more equal world, what Cynthia has done, given her feeling of being stifled in the marriage, would be seen as sensible and humane. She has left a loving father and fairly adult child in the marital home, perhaps giving the daughter the opportunity she missed, having lost a beloved invalid father at seventeen herself. But mother love is doubted in our society if it is not strongly sacrificial, a picture of selflessness. Anya as yet cannot see the love for the selfishness. Her father can cry and understand; her brother too. But she does not want to understand. She wants to be angry, and cannot do so face to face with the object of her rage, who refuses to see the anger for self-protective reasons, just as she refused to give her own anger expression. It is not necessary for a mother to show a child the anger she feels for that child's father, but it is a great mistake to close off communication and disallow the child's anger to her. Perhaps all Cynthia needs to do is to say 'I'm sorry. The most painful thing has been the fact that I couldn't explain to you', and then to listen and to cry with her daughter. Underneath the anger, all that Anya wants is to see her mother grieve, and to share the grief with her. But to do this, Cynthia would first have to admit to herself that her actions have hurt her daughter. A difficult thing to do, but a healing one.

* * *

'Mum is the one who's become the child, and we have to be grown-up to cope with Dad'

Paula is nineteen. She is an only child and lives with her father. Her mother left the family two years ago.

'I have been very angry with my mother, because I think she let my father down. But I can also see why she left. My father drinks a lot. When he starts he can't stop. My mum couldn't take it. Her own father was an alcoholic, and I think it really got to her when she realized Dad was going that way too. I don't know why he did. I know he lost his job, and then he went into business with someone, and that folded. He is still in a bad state, and I think it's very unfair that Mum went. I know she feels guilty, she said so. Dad said a lot of terrible things about her. He was sure she was having an affair with someone. I don't know. She says she hasn't and I wouldn't blame her if she had. But I don't see why she had to break up the family. She said she wanted me to go with her when she left, but she must have known that she could only do it

83

because I wanted to stay. I couldn't leave Dad, knowing the state he was in. And she didn't even have anywhere to live. She went to her mother at first, and now she's in a bedsitter. I don't know what she thinks we would have done together. She's the one who's become the child, and I'm the one having to cope with it.

'She's going to a counsellor at the moment, and this woman actually backed her up about leaving. It's all to do with her self-esteem she says. She has to develop and become a person in her own right.

'Of course she married very young – seventeen – I'd never have done that. It was terrible for her and she had a hard life. But my father accused her and all that because he felt so let down by her. He wants her to come back, and when he realizes she won't he gets drunk again. She says the only way she can be herself and not be dominated by my father is to get away, but she doesn't see the effect she has on him. It's her who's the stronger one really, and she doesn't see that. That's why I blame her.

'My grandma is a big help, and she comes up to be with Dad sometimes, but she is too old for it really. Mum should think of that too. I don't know what's going to happen. It worries me. I don't think Dad can be on his own.

'Mum does come for a meal sometimes, but it's not very good. I think she feels I'm being disloyal – she's so angry with him she can't see his side of it, though she knows he is very sad. She says I've taken her place as the one who's the victim in the family, and Dad has to have a victim. It's true when he's drunk he can be very argumentative and I just don't answer, there's no point. At other times, though, he does try to please. He is very lonely really and dependent on me. I feel guilty if I go out too much and leave him. People say it's better when parents part if they don't get on, but they don't realize the load it puts on the children.'

* * *

Paula's situation illustrates what happens when a mother has had enough of being a victim. What must have taken enormous courage appears as irresponsible to the family. Here is a mother who has betrayed the obligations appropriate to women, and has been aided and abetted by her counsellor (a fairly uncommon move: many counsellors do not empower women, but rehabilitate them to fit in with family life instead). The old guilt trip is no longer working, though it sounds as if Paula's mother is having to struggle to keep it under control.

Children know only too well the duties of a mother, and they are in an ideal position to commit emotional blackmail. If they choose to stay with their father, offering him support, they may try to justify their choice by blackening their mother's character. Paula feels responsible. She wants her mother back in the old role of smoothing things out, making things work for everyone else, and is perhaps shocked by her mother's abrogation of responsibility.

Blaming mothers is a time-honoured occupation, easier to do than blaming the average less responsive father. He, as Paula recognizes, is really the child, needing her care as the surrogate mother. She has indeed taken over the role, and it fails to occur to her that her father is playing on this. When passive wives have finally had enough they put husbands in a position of having to grow up, unless they find a substitute.

Paula is right, her mother is the stronger partner. Now her father needs to find his own strength instead of hiding behind the weakness of women. And she needs to relinquish the little-mother role, and allow her mother the freedom to do so too.

* * *

The theories and opinions of psychotherapists lead us to believe that children deprived of their mothers are immensely damaged. Many surely are, but more than anything else, the experiences recounted here suggest one very important thing: all cases are different and they need not conform to the prognoses of psychotherapy.

Mothers who leave may be loved by their children or disliked; they may be regarded as deficient in their attempts at being a parent or justified in their desertion. Their love might never be in doubt, though the children might feel they can choose to reject it. And while some fathers provide a stable home, others are totally inadequate. Perhaps the biggest gap, even with Mandy's 'good' father, is the talking, or lack of it. The conspiracy of silence, from parents, teachers (surely Mandy's were informed?) creates an extra burden for the children. However, teachers, and schools, also provide a stable, constant environment.

It is the quality of forgiveness that is so surprising among the first three people interviewed in this chapter. These people are not emotionally crippled, though indeed they may be scarred. And who isn't? Life itself is a scarring experience. While no one would wish a deserting mother on a family, the situation does not always have to be the psyche-damaging thing that it is made out to be. In some instances, it may promote understanding and tolerance of human deficiencies.

The standard view on children who love and forgive is to say that they are compensating for their own guilt, that somehow they feel their mother left because they were unlovable, and, as if propitiating the gods, they have to offer their own love to disprove it. Another view is that children often love the absent parent because they become fantasy figures – as happens with adopted children. These things are sometimes true, and they can have disastrous consequences. A leading psychotherapist in child guidance said, in response to the interviews above, 'Children who are very proud of a mother who has gone off and left them get depressed in adolescence because somehow they feel they weren't worth bringing up. They weren't wanted. They're no good. They're socially no good in relation to their peers. It all goes back to being not worth bringing up by their mothers.'

No doubt, many of the children who feel this or act it out end up on the therapist's couch or on a social worker's case list. But if such rigid theorizing exists, some may fulfil the script set out for them, propitiating another set of gods. And among those who never feel the need for psychotherapists are people who do have self-esteem and who genuinely reach a blessed state of love and forgiveness. To analyse and theorize in a totally negative way about such generosity is to devalue and degrade it.

Chapter 6

SACRIFICE IS A FEMINIST ISSUE

Most mothers who wouldn't dream of leaving their children will understand immediately the elements of obligation and sacrifice that the women in the previous chapters rebelled against, both as wives and mothers. This chapter explores the reasons why mothering is so akin to martyrdom, and why the idea of sacrifice is so alien to many women today.

The private experience of mothering may be enormously joyful and rewarding, but what every mother knows is that it is also extremely stressful. Never mind the beautiful mother and baby advertisements, the Madonna image, the reality is often demanding and unrewarding, not only on the domestic front but in public too.

At the most basic level in everyday life, the low status of motherhood reveals itself: the lack of public facilities for breast-feeding or nappy-changing, or for small children in restaurants; supermarket checkouts and public transport that make coping with a push-chair a nightmare; inaccessible toilets; department stores with children's equipment on the top floor: all these add to the stresses of being a mother.

If you can't beat it, you can always laugh instead. The following 'Images of Motherhood' arising from workshops run by the National Childbird Trust, and reported in their journal *New Generation* with accompanying cartoons, suggest a rueful sisterhood, sharing in adversity. 'Motherhood is scraping meals, prepared with love, off the floor and throwing them away' . . . 'Motherhood is being all things to all the family all the time – impossible' . . . 'Motherhood is having half a dozen jobs on the go and forgetting where you are in each one' . . . 'Motherhood is always thinking "they do grow up, don't they?" (But please not quite yet)' . . . Just as the traditional defensive male joke concerns being 'trapped' into marriage, so the equivalent female one is about being submerged by family life. In both cases, there is the underlying idea of being seduced by a loving liability, somewhat against one's better judgement.

This is not an ideal way of entering a lifelong commitment. Today, fewer and fewer men are asked to take on the sole burden of breadwinner, but women have to fight for the dubious privilege of being part breadwinner and main nurturer. The liberalization of women has merely increased their sense of stress as mothers. The 1984 General Household Survey showed that married women over the age of twenty-five are more likely to drink than their unmarried counterparts. On the other hand, married men drink less than the single, separated or bereaved. A survey by the Women's National Commission in 1988 discovered that seven times more married women than unmarried men are depressed. Around 83% of part-time working wives do most of the cleaning; 95% do most of the washing and ironing; 79% cook the evening meal and 64% do the shopping, according to a report from the Family Policy Studies Centre. The figures may apply to part-timers, ie women most likely to fit in work with looking after children, but full-timers hardly do better.

Adding to the martyring effect, a 1987 British Social Attitudes survey found that 76% of the 3,000 adults questioned believed that mothers with children under five should not work outside the home, even part time. The same opinion was held by 19% in relation to mothers of teenagers. An American national survey of women's feelings about mothering shows that it's not only men or stay-at-home wives who have this view: nine out of ten working women said that, ideally, it was best for a mother to be at home with her children, though most also felt the advantages in financial and emotional terms of having a job outside the home.

Such attitudes produce an inevitable conclusion: 'The general belief seems to be that in order to be a good mother, a woman should prostrate her life before her children, curtail her own cultural interests and make her own appearance second-best to those of her children . . . The birth process is also a burial process for the mother as an individual.' This was stated by a woman writing a personal column in the *Guardian*, someone who had no intention of leaving her children, but who felt moved to put down on paper her justification for depriving them of a clarinet and football gear in favour of buying herself a new tennis racket. 'I believe that mothers should give at least as much consideration to themselves as they give to their children', she wrote, concluding that such an attitude would be good for their selfish little souls, as long as it was accompanied by 'love, understanding, companionship, education'.

The trouble is that these four undoubted assets are very difficult to detach from the psychoanalytically approved idea of the good mother, the one who stays at home full time with her young children to provide the secure base so esteemed by, for instance, John Bowlby. She almost has to be seen as sacrificing to prove her credentials, and it is necessary to ask why. Why, for instance, do we hold motherhood in such high esteem on the one hand, but leave women to struggle alone on the other?

Bowlby is disliked for putting forward the idea of the necessity of practically full-time mothering. But even he is not suggesting that women cope alone. What he actually says in his book, *A Secure Base*, is that the mother usually bears the brunt of parenting during the early months or years, and she needs all the help she can get. He is not, it is true, talking about looking after the baby, but in helping with the household and providing the kind of support often found in less advanced societies. 'In addition to practical help, a congenial female companion is likely to provide the new mother with emotional support or, in my terminology, to provide for the kind of secure base we all need in conditions of stress and without which it is difficult to relax.'

Unfortunately, Bowlby has not campaigned vigorously for such a service, which may be why this part of his argument is not widely heard. But it is also because it is seen as *secondary* to the natural task of the mother. An American writer, Anne Wilson Schaff, suggests that women have a sense of 'the original sin of being born female', so that self-care appears to detract from care for others. They even carry within them an implicit idea that if women are concerned about women, they are not concerned about men. Presumably this applies even more to being concerned about children.

Susie Orbach and Louise Eichenbaum, founders of the Women's Therapy Centre, have come to similar conclusions. They say that women are over-preoccupied with the reactions of others and tend to experience anger as uncomfortable and dangerous because it is an assertion of self-needs over what they regard as the natural primacy of others. They judge themselves as lacking if they don't meet this standard, and come to identify the satisfaction of their needs through meeting the needs of others. Nowhere is this more apparent than in the roles of wives and mothers.

All this begins in childhood, when girls are encouraged to play cooperatively and to show consideration by mothers who have been brought up to value similar cooperation in themselves and want to pass on the tradition. Indeed, when mothers feel the need of care, they turn to their daughters to provide it – most certainly in later life, but even when children are young a mother might ask her daughter to make her a cup of tea, when she comes home exhausted from work or shopping, more readily than she might ask a son. Thus girls are brought up to be ever aware of the needs of others and to lose a sense of self-need. In other words, they actually lose the knack of recognizing what they want for themselves, and identify their wants to dovetail or coincide with the wants of others. If they do recognize their own distinct and separate needs, they experience guilt and conflict even when they put them into action. Here is the perfect foundation for the making of generations of masochists and martyrs.

These are the ideas that have come out of feminist theory, and they are inviting change. Women today are in transition, trying to free themselves of being 'perfect' in the sense of the values described above. They would be helped if they lived in a society that paid more than lip service to the status of motherhood and did not have to endure their nearest and dearest trivializing their doubts in the hope that things will quieten down. We do not listen to the real needs of mothers or offer them choices. Our counsellors and therapists and social workers, doing what they can but often subscribing to male values (ie the majority view), patch women up and send them home. Women are fighting alone, repudiating the notion of sacrifice and throwing out the baby with the bathwater.

One of the most important messages implicit in feminism is: thou shalt not be a victim. This does not mean repudiating motherhood or marriage, but for some women that is the interpretation. If they enlist feminism to disguise or justify what others might see as neurosis or immaturity, some of the neurosis and immaturity can be traced to the traditional expectations of women and the conflict that contemporary choices offer.

There is, throughout society, and not only within the bounds of feminism, a fear of obligation and exploitation, those natural enemies of self-fulfilment. Women are aware that they have been exploited as wives and mothers and some are making choices that avoid the predicament: they may remain single, or decide not to have children, or, in unconventional situations, have children in a lesbian relationship or bring them up without a male partner but in a supporting female network.

The majority of women do have children with a steady male partner, but they are watchful. As they become more detached from mothering, so they can tolerate it less, and they fear more the possibility of being a victim to sacrifice, since doing so stands in the way of a woman fulfilling her potential.

Sacrifice may be fine in a society that truly esteems it and does not exploit it, as may happen within certain religions. For women in our society, what sacrifice usually does is generate guilt and passivity, both regarded as undesirable features in healthy adults. Sacrifice also usually implies a victim, and any woman who sees herself as one might sometimes offer up her child instead. One way to do this is to batter the child, another might be to leave the marriage and leave the child.

Of course, we do admire the Mother Teresas of our world, those who give up worldly comforts in order to comfort others. The difference is that they have a choice, and in that choice lies satisfaction. Mothers feel they are offered few choices, and are aware that they incur disapproval when they try to make one. True, they can choose not to have a child, but for most women this is not the alternative they seek.

Salvation and self-fulfilment are to be found in work, even if that means doing two jobs and feeling guilty about at least one of them (which presumably is why men continue to get away with the minimum within the home). But work too serves to emphasize the idea of the 'mother as sacrificial victim'. Women's careers are blighted by having children. Being a mother can cost a British woman up to half her lifetime's potential earnings and is the greatest obstacle to equal opportunity, according to Bronwen Cohen in her report for the European Commission's Childcare Network. The lack of nursery places, or adequate childcare arrangements or provision for parental or sick leave suggest that both mothers and children are undervalued and are left to their own devices, rather as if having a child is a feckless thing to do if a woman is contemplating any other future for herself outside the home.

Women are offered invidious choices. Either they have children when they are young, but risk finding it difficult to progress in work later, or, if they are at all ambitious, they put off having children till they are established, aware that they will still be disadvantaged compared to their childless sisters, and still burdened with combining home and work. Those who can be mothers and career women, with their nannies tagging along so that they can breastfeed between meetings in the boardroom, only emphasize the gap between those who have power and can pay and those who have to rely on a nerve-wracking, clock-watching regime with babyminders or nurseries or neighbours.

These are the elements that make women today ambivalent about motherhood. They have a new, smarter image to live up to, far removed from the rueful sisterhood. The 'new woman' is nobody's fool. She is part of our free-enterprise culture (in practice very costly and requiring a large income). She boasts about being a rotten mother or a sluttish housewife or a dreadful cook, just as men do in order to get out of the unglamorous jobs at home. She pays others (often unqualified women, in fact the neediest and most disadvantaged) to do these tasks. She makes a great many virtuous noises about breastfeeding, which has become the token stand-in for devoted mothering, a commitment that lasts rather longer.

The luxury child of this new woman is of course one that comes to order. 'We are in the middle of a control generation in which consumers want to take control of everything they can, including gender selection' declares the blurb on a kit to plan a girl or a boy, marketed in Britain and America. This acquisition is the recipient of 'quality time', a mysterious, concentrated attention span determined by parents and resembling nothing in natural life. It, the child, gets the best of everything, but only if the commodity is something that money can buy.

The above is of course a stereotype, but it fits precisely with the ideal father-as-breadwinner role. While men are tentatively edging towards nurturing, women are being drawn into the role of material-providing parent, which is considerably smarter than being an exploited victim. It is becoming increasingly difficult for women to allow themselves to enjoy mothering. There is pressure on the young professional woman from her peers to go back to work soon after the birth. She may fear listening to the sirens that lull her into giving way to a softer, more responsive side. Maternity feels like a trap. The majority of men have failed to recognize or have suppressed this softer side; so must women if they want to succeed in a man's world.

But our anti-nurturing society affects far more issues than that of childcare. The traditional work of women outside the home is undergoing change too. The nurses, primary-school teachers, social workers, counsellors, all the caring, low-status, underpaid professionals who are mainly female, are also climbing on the enterprise bandwagon and getting out. Around 40% of new teachers leave the profession within five years: at the end of 1988, a serious shortage of primary-school teachers was announced by the Government. More than 27,000 qualified nurses leave the NHS every year, and nursing gets low rating as a career possibility among teenage girls, according to a survey from the National Advisory Centre on Careers for Women. Unfilled social work posts in London amounted to 15.6% in 1988, and the turnover is 28% as many social workers become private consultants. There is a shortage of marriage guidance counsellors, as more and more drop out of voluntary work and turn to private, and lucrative, counselling.

The enterprise culture is essentially a *male* enterprise culture, valuing success, prestige, material reward. Why shouldn't the social worker or the nurse, or the mother aim at similar goals? She will not achieve them through the traditional work of women, which makes virtue itself the main reward, so she seeks male-esteemed work instead, where her services are better appreciated. It is only just and fair that mothers should have real choices, on a practical and psychological level, and women in traditional professions should be paid amounts commensurate with their true value to society.

However, there certainly are dangers of throwing out the baby with the bathwater. Greer and Rantzen are not quite right – we are not a society of child-haters, but we are a society of anti-nurturers, a society in which women feel their deepest sense of identity is at stake when they experience that 'burial process' of becoming a mother. As long as women feel trapped and men remain detached, we will continue to see the former emulating the latter, and doing so could cost us dearly.

Women have for long supplied an important element in society. They have provided 'creative altruism', something that social philosopher Richard Titmuss defined (in his book *The Gift Relationship*) as 'social gifts and actions carrying no individual right to a return gift or action'. Once the action is paid for or is imbued with a power structure, it is corrupted. The traditional relationship between husbands and wives has been one of 'gift dominance', containing elements of compulsion and coercion. The traditional relationship between servant and master, no matter how steadfast and loyal, is similarly exploitable. The role of the trade unions, and the role of feminism, has been to defend against such exploitation. The problem is that in doing so these movements have stifled a great deal of natural generosity. Where we are paid, and where we feel we have rights, we are ashamed to give. Of course there always will be women and men who are prepared to put personal and professional satisfaction before their 'rights', but we have seen a reduction in personal pride in work, in service, and now possibly in the rearing of our children. Could future generations grow up with few examples of creative altruism with which they can identify and which they can emulate?

It is to be hoped that this will not happen, but we should not rely on women's charity. Rather, so that they can find out for themselves where their satisfactions really lie, they should be given the support that allows them to be working mothers or stay-at-home mothers, without pressures to be one or the other, and with the confidence that they will not be exploited or sacrificed. If you don't feel you have a choice, you don't feel you have the freedom to give – which is certainly true of many of the mothers in this book. And if you are not giving freely, not only is your own happiness at stake, but so is that of your children.

Attitudes to women today have not caught up with the major changes that have occurred in women's lives in the twentieth century. The widespread acceptance of reliable contraception allowed women to control their fertility – which they did in no uncertain ways. Legal abortion gave them further options. Released from childbearing they could begin to explore their sexual needs, their creativity, their personal ambitions. Modern feminism led them to think beyond domesticity and to campaign for wider opportunities in education and work. We cannot return to Victorian values without Victorian servants and kindly Victorian spinster aunts and unreliable Victorian contraception, all of which kept many women busily occupied within the home, bearing and rearing children or running the expanding and complex household.

There have been genuine advances in opportunities for women, and perhaps more are on the way as the supply of school-leavers drops, and women once again are wooed back to work, as they were in wartime to replace the men. But in the late twentieth century, in private life, once women become mothers they are supposed to remain as they were before the liberating advances of science took place: they are the centre of the family, unseparably linked with their children, needed in the home as an antidote to an anarchic and selfish world. The barriers may have been broken down, but the chains are still there.

Sweeping changes in the workplace for men are rarely related to their role as fathers. Perhaps this is why there has seemed no reason to relate sweeping changes in work opportunities for women to their other role as mothers. But society lays down specific rules for the ways women are supposed to behave once they have children, and no attempt has been made to pull those two strands together. The conflict for a woman remains a private one for her own conscience, often her own pocket, in terms of childcare and her own ability to combine two important areas of her life. If there had been a long tradition of men choosing to be working parents with the same responsibilities and demands as women, their role would have been unthinkable without organized support in the form of childcare, tax relief, leave after childbirth. The business of bringing up children would have been shared by everyone who pays taxes, whether they themselves have children or not. The rising generation is the future for any society. Those who have and rear children should not take on the burden alone.

If women's lives were stripped of the guilt and the notion of sacrifice, then many basic needs would be removed – the need for women to be dependent in marriage, the need to choose children or a career, the need to postpone having children, the need to succumb to pressures to produce a child, the need for economic dependence after divorce. And, to return to the subject matter of this book, the need to leave children.

SECTION II

Consequences of Adoption

Chapter 7

THE WOMEN WHO GAVE THEIR BABIES AWAY

When Mary Woolliscroft founded the Natural Parents' Support Group, a self-help organization for mothers like her who had given up their babies for adoption, she suffered enormous malicious abuse. She made a BBC Open Space television programme in 1988, and that was when the trouble started. There were obscene telephone calls, complaints to the police and social services that she was battering her child (though she has no child living with her), veiled threats sent through the post, even an attempt to set fire to her home. Some people, or maybe somebody, felt extreme hostility to a woman who was offering help rather than condemnation to other women who had given away their children.

Mary's baby was fostered when he was eighteen months old. The baby had been born prematurely when Mary was twenty-five. Her marriage was stormy and her husband violent – he tried on one occasion to pull his son out of the incubator; later at home he threatened to batter the child. The couple separated and Mary, under severe stress, had what she describes as a minor breakdown. Under pressure from her social worker, she agreed to have her baby put into care and fostered. She was advised to let the baby go for adoption but did not wish to. Through the efforts of the social worker the child was eventually made a ward of court.

Mary was alone with no job, and she felt she could not win against the system. She resigned herself to losing her child and tried to look on him as having died. Seven years later, after she had remarried, she received a letter from the foster parents saying that due to an oversight the adoption papers had never been signed, and they now hoped that she would cooperate with them in putting this right. Suddenly Mary had the chance to regain her son.

After six months of wondering what to do, wondering whether she was being selfish, she signed, having satisfied herself that her son was in excellent hands. And so she experienced a second grieving for her son, with no help and no counselling. Realizing how desperately a support group was needed for women in her position she set up the organization for which she was subsequently vilified.

The Natural Parents' Support Group is one of several organizations established in recent years to help women who had children adopted or to guide people through the difficulties of reuniting with their natural parents. Through these organizations, women are beginning to tell stories from their past, in some cases revealing secrets which they feel they can face only now that the stigma of illegitimate birth is no longer so great. It was a stigma that plagued women for centuries, until the more relaxed atmosphere of recent times.

In some ways, things actually got worse before they got better. Before church marriages became the norm (a process which began around the thirteenth century and reached its peak by the nineteenth), betrothals and unofficial wedding ceremonies produced many illegitimate births with few eyebrows raised, as is the case with cohabiting couples today.

But a different set of rules applied to women without recognized partners. An unmarried woman who bore a child by a man married to someone else was liable to be whipped in public and confined to a house of correction for a year, her main offence being that she had brought financial burden to the neighbours of the parish where her child would have to be supported. More fortunate women would benefit from close family and communities ties, with an illegitimate child absorbed into the network or informally adopted.

By the nineteenth century the evangelical movement established a widespread desire for 'respectability' and conformity. Unmarried mothers in rural areas would have their newborn infants taken to the foundling hospitals in the cities to save themselves from shame and ostracism. Domestic servants were in danger of losing their jobs if they had children. When the New Poor Law Act in 1834 eliminated relief to be given by the parishes to destitute individuals – including unwed mothers as part of a move to discourage motherhood outside marriage – the workhouses filled up and the number of abandoned babies left outside the foundling hospitals increased. At one point, 5,000 babies a year were 'abandoned' – though the word is both inadequate and inaccurate to describe the deed. Like the one hundred babies a year left by their mothers in the UK today, usually for similar reasons, the foundling babies were deposited in a place where they would be discovered quickly. Now it is likely to be a public lavatory or a railway station, or of course a handbag. Oscar Wilde's invention may have seemed bizarre, but it actually made as much sense as Moses left in the bulrushes near to the place where the princess bathed.

Victorian philanthropic bodies, church-based organizations, and, by the twentieth century, charities like Barnardo's, took children into their care or provided mother and baby homes, some being more tolerant than others but all inevitably reinforcing the idea of the fallen woman. Even today, the anti-abortion societies provide discreet homes for young pregnant women who will give up their babies for adoption after they are born and then slip back into 'normal' life again.

Adoption was legally recognized in England and Wales in 1926. It came into its own after the Second World War when some returning soldiers were not pleased to find a cuckoo in their nest, and others chose not to return to make an honest woman of their erstwhile partners. And of course, there were the men who, tragically, could not return.

Virgins, virtuous wives and strict abortion laws being the order of the following two decades, the adoption rate was around 16,000 a year in Great Britain in the fifties, rising up to nearly 26,000 in the sixties, when nearly half involved babies under a year old. Now the figure is around 8,000 a year, and few of the children are newborn or relinquished only because they are born out of wedlock.

It was the 1975 Children's Act that put both fear and hope into some of those children and their natural mothers, by giving adopted children over the age of eighteen the right to access to documents to help them seek out their real parents. Mary Woolliscroft's television programme in 1988 elicited responses from women all over the country, some of them confessing to a clandestine birth twenty or thirty years ago, and a longing to see their offspring. The Post-Adoption Centre began running group sessions in 1987 and offers counselling to natural mothers. Norcap (National Association for the Counselling of Adoptees and Parents) was set up in 1982 and gives advice to people wanting to meet their natural parents.

What was it like for the women then and now? How do the children feel? What are the pressures on young women giving babies for adoption today? Here are some personal stories.

* * *

'I think we were punished twice. Once for getting pregnant, and then for giving the children away'
Geraldine is forty-two, married for twenty-one years, with a

daughter of twenty and son of sixteen. She is a serious, thoughtful woman, a mature student in social studies. Her oldest daughter, born before her marriage, would be twenty-two now.

'I was nineteen when I had her [*in 1965*]. It was someone I knew a bit and I met him at a party. I was training to be a nurse at the time. There was an ambiguous attitude in those days. Temptation, opportunity, yet restrictions like having to be in by ten o'clock. I was treated abominably by this bitchy ward sister and I was very miserable.

'It was in Liverpool. The idea of abortion wasn't possible. I was made to leave nursing immediately and I went home for a month and then to a mother and baby home. It was run by a church and was rather like a strange boarding-school. Very punitive but within it we had fun in a very immature way.

'My parents knew, but no one else. My mother told me later that my father would never have had me in the house again if I had kept the baby. You had to work till six weeks before the birth, and then you gave up and moved into the next door house which was a nursing home. So you lived with the midwives. Looking back, it was the most natural delivery of the three children. Nobody had to have forceps, though the facilities were there. The expectation was that we would have normal deliveries, and we all did.

'I stayed there with the baby for six weeks. They insisted on that. When I gave her up, I went into one room and the new parents came to the other room. There was a communicating door, and the social worker would come in and take your baby and you could hear them receiving the baby. I heard them say to their son who was two and was also adopted, "look, isn't she lovely". I thought they sounded like parents who would be supportive.

'I've spent twenty-two years thinking about how did I feel when I gave up my baby. It was like a script that had already been written for me. My parents wrote it and I colluded with it. Therefore part of the script was that I felt very good about it. It was the right thing to do and I would come home and get on with my life.'

Geraldine returned to nursing and a few months later met her present husband. They were married fourteen months after the birth and she knew that more than anything else she wanted another child.

'My husband had no moral judgement on me at all and I probably did think at the time that I could have my daughter back now. But we had our own daughter very quickly. You can't hide the fact that you've had a child from the doctors, so I said this was my second, and everybody assumed that was his child as well. He was at the birth and they said was it like this with your first child and he didn't let me down, though it was his first child and the most wonderful day of his life.'

It was at this point that Geraldine experienced her first bout of depression. It was partly post-natal depression, exacerbated by the fact that her mother was developing a serious drug dependency. The cause was said to be Geraldine's first pregnancy since her mother started taking sleeping pills at that time. When the third child was born, Geraldine herself was put on drugs to counteract severe depression, and her mother was recognized as a drug addict. There followed for Geraldine several years of periodic depression which reached a peak when her mother died in 1985. Geraldine does not attribute her depression solely to her first pregnancy and its aftermath, but feels she has followed a classic family pattern, since her sisters and mother had made suicide attempts. However, she felt she had blocked off her feelings about the adoption, and it was a psychotherapist who made her look at them again many years later.

'He said how many children have you got? and I said two. Then I said well three actually, but the first one doesn't count because I gave it away. He made me realize that I had been made to have the baby adopted. Eventually she stopped being an "it" and became a "she". He used her name and I found it easier and easier to refer to her by name. I told my daughter about this sister of hers and she was very positive. I told my son but he was completely unmoved. My daughter, she's a bit iffy about seeing her sister. She says she often looks at young women at university and thinks when she sees someone about twenty-two that it could be her.

'I did leave a letter with the adoption society when she was eighteen. If she has got it and hasn't contacted me in four years, what can I read into that? I think I would find it very odd if I met my daughter and found she had a very different name to the one I gave her and it was one I did not like. Or I might find that politically we are poles apart. Her home was in a frightfully expensive area where I should think they never return anyone but the rankest Tory MP, and my family are politically left-wing.

'I thought one day when I was ironing, that she is at an age when she can make choices, and it is her choice not to find me, and I stood there howling my eyes out. I wrote a poem, just for myself, and the main theme was that I was always going to give the baby away, and yet suddenly I could remember the physical feelings of almost sensuality when I held this child, the smell of her and the feeling of warmth. At the time I had distanced myself. You feed the baby, put it in the cot, whereas this bit of me was responding on another level. I had conceived as a hard mother, given birth on a hard bed, in a hard environment, and in a very hard way I gave her away, and she was the only soft thing.

'I remember feeling very angry with those who were not giving their babies away. I thought at the time that my anger was because they had broken the rules, but I recognize now that a lot of my anger was because they got a lot more care than we did, though we were keeping to the rules. They caused a lot of extra work because they changed their minds, but they were perceived to be natural women, so the workers saw them as being good, natural mothers because in the end they couldn't do the dreadful deed. Whereas those of us who were still going ahead were not natural. That's where a lot of my anger came from. And I thought, whose feelings are we feeling – our own or other people's? All those years ago, when adoption was the thing to do because children were supposed to have two parents . . . we were doing the right thing, yet I think we got punished twice. Once through being naughty and getting pregnant, and then for giving the children away.'

* * *

'I feel I am rejecting my daughter now, and it is a luxury considering all the years when I was denied seeing her'

Maureen is fifty and works in public relations. She is Irish, a Catholic, an exuberant, well-built woman now living alone in a flat surrounded by family photographs, bowls of flowers, chintzy armchairs. She is very successful in her career, and was previously in nursing. Her only child, Sally, was adopted as a baby and came back into her life six years ago. Sally is now twenty-six.

'I came to England in 1954 having trained as a nurse in Ireland. In 1961 I had this transient affair and found myself pregnant. All I could think of was the shame for my family so the big thing was to disappear fast. I worked as an agency nurse till about three days before the baby was born. I had no intention originally of giving the baby up but I met a doctor, Geoff, who used to take me out from time to time and he said I shouldn't keep her.

'I had the baby in hospital. My youngest brother gave me a little money and my sister came over from Ireland. She told my father she wanted to stay some time in London. No mention of illegitimacy, that and insanity are the killer conditions. I had a long labour, a horrible experience, but she was a beautiful baby. Geoff phoned to say he knew someone who wanted to adopt – you could do it privately in those days. I was torn to smithereens, playing with this baby, my sweet daughter, but when I brought her home I looked at her and thought the most generous thing I can ever do for you is to give you to a family.

104

'I phoned Geoff and he came to lunch. He handed me some flowers, and I thought this is in exchange for the baby. A most peculiar feeling. He went off with my baby in the back of the car. She was ten days old.'

Maureen visited her family in Ireland and then got a staff job in a London hospital. By chance she heard someone mention Geoff's name. 'She was saying that his sister had just adopted a kid. I didn't say anything. I didn't see Geoff again for ten years. He had never told me it was his sister. I felt cheated in some way.'

Around two years later, Maureen met Clive, the man she was to live with for eighteen happy years. He was already married and Maureen felt it was pointless for him to get a divorce. It was he who encouraged her to look for her daughter.

'He said he couldn't bear the agony I went through every July when it was her birthday. So we arranged to meet, Geoff, Clive, and me, and Clive left us alone for a bit, but I never said a word about Sally, my daughter. Clive said afterwards, you poor love, you couldn't say a word, could you? I had always said to myself that I would never seek her unless she sought me, so I let it go.'

Maureen nursed Clive through a terminal illness. He died in 1980, and on the second anniversary of his death Geoff rang to say that Sally wanted to meet her mother. Maureen is a woman who believes in signs and portents. The following day she found herself knocking at the door of the woman who had given her daughter a loving home for twenty years.

'It didn't dawn on me till I was standing there that I was holding a bunch of flowers. It was as if I was handing them back in exchange for my daughter, the flowers I had received when I gave up my baby. She was charming, sensitive. Every time I moved she kept saying it's like seeing Jessica here. Jessica is the name they gave Sally. She wasn't there. She moved out at sixteen. In fact, I don't think she is the same as me at all.

'**I spoke to her on the telephone. I said hello. I didn't know what to say. I didn't feel anything**. I had been assured that she would be brought up as a Catholic, and she came on a Sunday so we went to church together and had lunch, and it was all totally unreal. She is three inches taller than me, and I'm tall. She looks more like my mother than me, very beautiful.'

Maureen herself is a very good-looking woman, and photographs on her walls show an exceptionally beautiful daughter. This daughter, now called Jessica, decided to stay overnight on that first meeting, and what followed was an intense and painful experience.

'She wanted us to eat in, to be at home. Then she said I want to sleep with you tonight and wake up with you in the morning and have my rebirth. She saw it as a rebirth in her head. So I sat down, and she didn't go to bed till 4.30 in the morning, and I said Jessica, I'm not going through with a charade about you being reborn, but that was what she had been building up to when she was waiting to see me. I couldn't give her that. I've often had regrets that I should have, but I felt I was in some sort of charade. It wasn't right for me. I woke her in the morning and got her into my bed. I said, come in, you can have some tea, and she came like a little girl and cuddled in my arms and went off to sleep again. I felt she had been hysterical and she wanted to merge with me.'

For Maureen, it was too much, too soon. Perhaps feeling the resistance, her daughter could only ask for more and more.

'She was here with me morning, noon and night, staying for a couple of days at a time. Her adoptive mother came once but I couldn't bear it – the volume of her pain and her feeling rejected. She still feels that to this day. Her husband has never made any mention of me, Jessica says. He seems to deny my existence.

'Jessica kept saying to me, you're the only person I've ever met who understands me. She says she feels as if she has no secrets with me, as if I can look into her head. I don't feel that at all.

'I had given her a letter I'd written when she was born and originally left in the bank. In it I set out the circumstances of her birth. I said how much I loved her and what I thought she'd be like. I said because she was Irish she'd be very sensual and there was never going to be enough in the world to fill the towering needs that she'd have, and therefore she'd have to use all sorts of opportunities to develop herself and her mind and feelings.

'Jessica lives with this man, someone not particularly effective to my mind. She has studied psychology at university. She is very idealistic, into everything that's pure, natural, ecological. She doesn't see any sense in any form of defence whatsover. But the biggest thing for me is the intense sense of disappointment about her that I have at times. A shocking thing to say perhaps. You dream. All those years you have this mythology in your head. I know that all our children, my nephews and nieces in Ireland, are "feelings" children. There is not a single one of them who isn't warm and "touch-ey". Jessica is not like that. She's into herself. It is definitely to do with her environment. I see that remoteness in her. And then she has the kind of London accent that I detest. A very grating sound, undisciplined speech. The words aren't completed in some way. I come from ordinary stock, farming background. But I always believed that we were us, you know, the greatest. I wanted her to be more melodious perhaps. That's the first time I've ever said that. And dear God, the fact that she stoops when she walks . . .'

Maureen's unspoken rejections, her feeling that her child is alien, not a part of her or matching up to her fantasy are met with strong verbal criticisms from her daughter in the true style of a dependent adolescent struggling to get free and yet wanting total understanding.

'She came over a few weeks ago and I could feel the tension in her, she was boiling up. She accused me of insulting her boyfriend and patronizing him. She is so over-sensitive about everything I do. She said the things I admire are facile. She referred to a day in a restaurant when I'd commented on the way a young man had pulled out a chair for his girlfriend. I'd said it was a charming gesture in today's world. She once said, I was prepared to find you in rollers, you know, or a hair net. [*Maureen dresses elegantly in designer clothes.*] She said that perhaps I was disappointed in her, that I expected her to be different. She criticized my clothes for being flamboyant and extravagant, and said I speak too loud in shops and she is embarrassed to be with me.'

And so, from Maureen, comes the deepest moment of disappointment. 'I feel I am rejecting her now, and it is a sort of luxury considering all the years when I was denied seeing her. It astonishes me that I am in a position in which I can pick up the telephone and speak to her any time, and I don't want to do it. I feel as if I am being made to pay. I've got an absolute consciousness of how much I feel for her, and I've got an almost equal or overriding one about keeping my distance. A bloody neurosis, isn't it?'

* * *

'I have never forgiven my grandparents for what happened, though both are dead now'

Norma is forty-one, a quiet, mild woman, mother of a daughter of nineteen and a son of sixteen. She is divorced and has been living with a second partner for five years. She became pregnant when she was fifteen and had her first child, a girl, at sixteen when she had just left school. This daughter is now twenty-five.

'I was living with my grandparents. This was because my mother had died when I was born. I had been with them since I was five weeks old. The father of the baby was my boyfriend and he was just nine months older than me. My father never knew about the baby. He had remarried and I wanted his respect. He had three more daughters, but my grandmother had said when she took me on that it would have to be permanent

107

and she would not give me up. I was sorry because I was brought up as an only child and they were in a big family.

'I got a job, and the father of the baby was living with his family, and his mother took in the baby for about eighteen months. Then she started to go out to work and the baby went to a childminder. I saw her twice a week.

'The family was unstable and my boyfriend did not get on with his mother. I had a lot of persuasion from my grandparents to have the baby adopted. His mother was upset but she did not take any steps. My grandmother said she loved the baby but she never gave me any money to help me support her, and never let me pay her less for my keep at home. I think she did not like my boyfriend and there was no incentive for her to help me keep the baby. So the baby went to a foster home when she was three and I went to see her a couple of times. The couple who wanted to adopt were living together because one of them couldn't get a divorce, and when the charity who were arranging it found out the baby was taken away and given to someone else. In those days that was a stigma too.'

By this time, Norma was involved with another man and about to marry. 'I wanted the baby with me, but when I told him I'd had a baby he nearly broke off with me and he wouldn't have anything to do with her.'

Norma has not seen her daughter since the adoption. Many years later she discovered that her mother was pregnant when she got married. 'It was with my dad. I was so angry with my grandmother. I thought my God, it happened to your daughter. Why couldn't you understand what I felt? She'd had a stroke when I found out and I couldn't confront her, and I was left with this terrible anger towards her, though we were very close. I have never forgiven my grandparents, though both are dead now.'

After sixteen years of marriage, Norma divorced. She told her younger children about their sister when her marriage was ending.

'My daughter's immediate reaction was, where is she now? My son did not say much. My daughter actually traced her last year. I knew the surname and my daughter went through the phone book.

'**I telephoned and she was very cool. She did not want to come and see us and wrote to say "I'm fine and happy and my adoptive parents have always been my parents."** She wrote, "Dear Mrs . . ." I wrote back and said don't ever think I didn't want you, and she wrote to the adoption charity complaining. I think she saw it all as quite a threat, though I would never have dreamed of pestering her.

'People were very kind at the charity, but I needed to talk to someone who would have given me time to find out how I felt, and to think of the pros and cons. I was carrying a lot of guilt, and I feel more settled inside somehow, just to know that she's all right. Obviously it is a rejection, the fact that she doesn't want to see me, but I can understand it. It could have caused problems. Supposing you don't get on? Is it better to have an ideal image of a baby than a daughter you don't really like?'

Whatever the answer is to that, Norma's guilt is still unresolved, a legacy from a rigid moral climate. Her grandmother had experienced shame twice in her life, and passed on that shame to her grandchild. Both Geraldine and Maureen speak of 'having to pay'. The dues appear to go on over several generations.

Chapter 8

. . . AND THE GIVE-AWAY CHILDREN

In recent years, a great deal has come to light on the subject of adoption. People who were adopted as children are beginning to speak out about their experiences. What they say suggests that it is not enough to tell a child that he or she is adopted. There is a strong need to know a great deal more. Here, two people tell of their search for their natural mothers, and a third, who was fostered throughout childhood but remained in contact with both his parents, provides a definition for the mother who nurtures and the mother who gives birth.

* * *

'What I felt was a sense of not quite belonging and not quite knowing what I looked like'

Stella is twenty-five years old. She was adopted as a baby. At twenty-one she sought, and found, her mother.

'I always knew I was adopted and so did my adopted sister. We were told as children, around three or four. I was told that I had not come out of my mummy's tummy, but from another lady's tummy, she couldn't look after me because she had so many children. And I thought of the Old Woman Who Lived in a Shoe. I had great compassion for this woman who was in this household washing, cleaning and ironing, and that's what I held on to. This poor woman was quite good for giving me away, to make sure I didn't live in such a chaotic household.

'But then gradually the thing became less positive and became more of an issue about what I was like because physically I didn't resemble my adoptive parents at all. I was blonde with big teeth and a big smile. They are both very dark-haired. People would even point it out and I would say I am adopted. Later I was told off. I was told I shouldn't have said it. I think we all lived with the belief that it hadn't really happened. You get into a mutual protectiveness. I didn't talk about it in order to protect them,

110

and they didn't talk about it to protect me. People say well, the children don't ask. They don't realize that the children don't like to ask.

'What I felt was a sense of not quite belonging and not quite knowing what I looked like. I could never work out whether this very big smile I have was part of me or not, whether I had a cheeky face or whether I didn't. There had been issues about my teeth. A dentist had said they protruded because I had sucked my thumb as a child. When I actually met my natural family they all had this big smile and big teeth and I realized that that was me, and that's where it came from. I wish I could have said, well, if you'd seen my family, you'd see that's not odd about me.'

Stella started her search for her mother when she left home, at twenty-one. She got her mother's address at the time of the birth from her birth certificate.

'It was a few miles away from where I had grown up. My first reaction was to have my photograph taken by a friend standing outside the house. I discovered it had been a lodging house and found names of people living there twenty-one years ago from the rates directory. Then I traced through all the telephone directories in England for the same names. I tracked down someone in Luton who remembered my mother. His mother-in-law had been the landlady. She had a photograph of my mother. She said my mother was Canadian.'

Stella went through every telephone book in Canada House looking for her mother's maiden name. She found 150 names, went home and started dialling.

'On the third phone call I found a cousin in Toronto. I found out later that there were only four names connected to the family – three cousins and an uncle. I wrote to my mother, not saying who I was because I did not know who would open the letter. I said I was the landlady and was now very old and was writing to people who had stayed with me. My mother had originally called me Julia, so I wrote that I, as the landlady, had seen Julia, a woman my mother had shared a room with, and she wanted to hear from her. Nobody could have known what I was really saying except my mother.

'For eighteen months there was no reply. Then I received a very trivial letter saying I have been married nineteen years, I've four children. The letter ended: "I was glad to hear from you but I was disappointed because I thought it was my daughter writing. I have been searching for her." She hadn't caught on to anything I'd written. When I wrote back and received a reply she said that her marriage had been breaking up at the time and she had avoided thinking because her life had been in chaos.

111

'I wrote back and quickly got a letter saying I can't believe it, this is wonderful. We spoke on the phone and then six weeks later I flew out to see her.

'That was incredible, indescribable. Very difficult to describe the actual, physical thing of touching your mother. We had never touched. She had given birth and I had been taken away from her straight away. She had never seen me, had no physical image of me whatsoever. We were both crying, and there was the physical energy of hugging my mother for the first time. What was odd was the similarity in very odd things, like laughter, and the smile. I think we both went through a process of wanting to identify with one another which lasted three or four years. We were fighting to find similarities. Now we have the confidence to say we are different here and there, which is good.'

'It was incredible to find the next child down, my sister four years younger than me, with the same bolshie personality. In adolescence she had been with my mother very similar to the way I had been with my adoptive mother. That helped me to reduce my feeling that I was wrong in some way. How I behaved was part of my personality. My adoptive mother is quiet and unassertive and couldn't really cope with an assertive female child.

'We thought what is this relationship going to be about? Was she my mother? What did "mother" mean? At the end of the day I was very clearly able to decide that my adoptive mother is my mother, and that my natural mother could never be my mother. I was actually quite relieved that she was in Canada because, well, one mother is enough, and that confirmed for me that my mum, who brought me up, is my mum, and that was it. She doesn't know. I think they would be devastated. Partly I'm protecting myself too. I do contemplate telling them, and I will know when it's the right time. Perhaps when I have a child. I think I would like to say, "You are my mum as far as I'm concerned. Don't be fearful that I'm going to reject you." I have not told my adopted sister. We are very different. I've never asked her if she has contacted her natural parents, and she has never asked me. We get on but we never talk about the adoption, it's a secret none of us talk about.'

*   *   *

'I didn't know I was adopted . . . For years I've felt totally different to my family, and now I know why'
Catherine is forty-two. She has been married twice and has four children. She found her mother only two years ago. She also left her older children, and that part of her story is told in Chapter 1.

'I only found out I was adopted when my adoptive father died. I dragged it out of my mother. It was just before my second marriage, I was twenty-six, and it was one reason why I married again. The ground had gone from under my feet. I had nobody. It wasn't just that they didn't tell me. My mother actually showed me the bed she said I was born in. The room I was born in. When I couldn't feed my oldest son she said don't worry darling, I couldn't feed you either. She made up a fantasy and she still doesn't know that I have found my real mother.

'When I was young and a bit wild, and writing poetry and sitting down in Trafalgar Square to ban the bomb, she'd say I don't know what you're doing. You're not a bit like the rest of us. And now I've found my mother and she writes poetry. It's all very simple. For years I've felt totally different to my parents, and now I know why.

'**Of course I still love my adoptive mother. The first thing I said when I knew was why didn't you tell me before, I don't love you less, I love you more**. But equally I went through a period of rejection, and things went through my head. I felt everything that had gone wrong in my first marriage went back to my parents as the model, but they weren't the right model for me.

'It was only a couple of years ago that it suddenly appeared to me that an awful lot of my problems were based on the fact that I don't know who I am. That sounds awfully silly when I was getting on for forty. Why did my mother give me away, was I that bad, that horrible? I knew that I had some brothers and sisters and I wanted to establish my roots.'

Catherine wrote to various adoption services and discovered eventually that her mother had had a wartime affair when her husband was away. Her mother had planned to leave the marriage for the father, but then he was badly injured in the war and the couple lost touch. When the husband returned home he did not want this illegitimate baby in his life.

'I found out from my research that he had died, so I knew I couldn't hurt him. I found an elder sister, a half-sister. My mother wants me to trace my father. The biggest thing I hated was that I found I had a younger sister, about eighteen months younger. I felt replaced, rejected. I was renamed Catherine by my adoptive parents and what do you know, I found this younger half-sister was also called Catherine.

'I see my mother a lot. She was really pleased I found her, even though I was forty. I think it would kill my adoptive mother if I told her. She is eighty-two. My real mother is in her early sixties. One is forty years older than me, the other twenty years older.

113

'About twenty years ago I had three epileptic fits. I went to my mother and said is there any epilepsy in the family, and she said no, not at all. When I found my real family, I discovered that my younger sister is an epileptic, so it was in the family, and so is my asthma and hay fever. Because my adoptive father was diabetic, the times I was tested for diabetes when I was pregnant! It was so stupid not to tell. A waste of everybody's time and money.'

* * *

'Visiting my mother every week was like visiting an aunt'

James is thirty-nine. He has been married for eighteen years and works in a bank. He has two young children aged three years and fifteen months. James was fostered at the age of eighteen months and lived with his foster family until he was twenty, though he remained in contact with both parents.

'My parents separated but I saw both of them regularly once a week for as long as I can remember. My father would come to my foster home and we'd stay there or we might go to see cricket or visit an elderly aunt. He took a great interest in my school work. I always felt he cared for me.

'My mother is a singular person, quite fiery and quick to rise. I stayed over with her most weekends. I don't remember how I got there when I was small, but I remember being with her. I'd go by bus when I was about eight. I remember being a bit taken aback when she took a coat to the cleaners and gave her maiden name. I thought at the time that it didn't sound right. On one of those occasions I met her future husband and I didn't ask anything about him. There is a flaw in my nature in that I accept things too easily. I think I didn't want to know certain things because I didn't want to hear anything that would put me against one of them.

'I was about nine when my mother remarried. I was happy where I was and did not expect to go back to live with her. She didn't ask me to, and she went on to have two more children. It was my father who had custody. He paid for the fostering and the schooling, and he was the one who chose my foster mother. She had been a day boarder at this private school and as an adult she went back to take the infants class there. She had looked after my own father and I think he had appreciated her softness and kindness compared to the strictness in his own family. And when the situation arose with me, that's where he sent me to live. I attended that same school and so did my foster parents' own son.

'They are to me my parents, though my mother and father hold very special places for me. My foster parents' son is eighteen months younger than me. We did everything together, like brothers. There was one bad time when I was in my early teens. I

114

had this strange thought that I could get my parents back together though my mother was remarried. I don't remember thinking that it was for me, but the all-important thing was that it was for them. That was the time when seeing them caused some inner turmoil. The other bad time was when I went through a period of resenting my foster parents, when I was eighteen or nineteen, though I can't think why now.

'I can't remember having any feelings of anger when I was young towards my mother. Visiting her every week was like visiting an aunt. You were on your best behaviour. Though she was very familiar, it was not the familiarity on a day to day basis that you get with parents you live with. You do hold something back.

'If I had something important to tell, like winning a prize or being in a play, I'd tell my father first, without doubt. And then my foster mother – I call her Aunt Mary. If I had any problems I'd go to my father first and then her. If I was in a school play, I'd want my father there but also my mother and Aunt Mary. It was natural if you were proud of something to take it to your mother. She was somebody I wanted to include in that circle.

'I'm part of her family, and I get on well with my half-brother and sister though I don't see much of them. But I am very much on the perimeter. I feel at the centre of my foster family. They went out of their way to create that atmosphere. My foster father is also a tremendous person and has treated me like a son. I've felt the weight of his hand more than I've felt the weight of my own father's.

'My father died three years ago and at the funeral we found out that he had remarried over twenty years ago. I had met his wife once and had been made to think that she was the wife of a friend. They had no children and she has told me she tried many times to get him to invite me over, but he said I was part of one life and she was his new life. Learning about that marriage did knock the stuffing out of me because I had always been concerned about him that he was by himself. But I could never say that I felt rejected by him during his life. He would always ring me and see me every week. With my mother, it's always me who's doing the contacting. If I didn't ring her it would take some while for her to get round to it. I get a bit upset at times that it's me who has to do all the chasing. I do wonder how long it would go on before she contacted me, but I'm not going to risk it.'

It is clear that right from the start, James made the overtures. In their different ways, both parents rejected him, and he seems to have been saved by the warmth and stability of his foster family. His own marriage is a happy one. Audrey, his wife, is loyal and

115

concerned. It was she who was enthusiastic about her husband being interviewed. She felt it would be helpful for him to talk. She is over forty, a late mother, and worked as a secretary until the children were born. It is interesting to note that Audrey and James were married for fifteen years before they had children. Why did they wait so long?

Audrey: I used to say to my sister when she asked, no, not yet. I come from a very stable, happy family and sometimes I think that James was just a little bit of jealous of it. He was brought up in a good home but I have sometimes had that feeling. I've said that to you.

James: I said I didn't think we ought to have children straight away but wait a couple of years.

Audrey: But then we enjoyed what we were doing. We lived in a beautiful flat and then a house in Kent. We were out all day and home late in the evening. I don't like not going to work. I worked till just before the baby was born.

James: The trouble is, you went from being someone with an identity to being an anonymous mother. When you're a mother you're just someone among a group of other mothers. Not your individual person.

Now here are a few revealing statements. What Audrey appears to be saying is that she feared James might be jealous of a baby, perhaps because he needed undivided attention to make up for his own divisions. This may have complemented her personal doubts about motherhood. What James seems to be saying is that mothers are non-people, or are treated as such – a popular contemporary notion. But how does this tie up with his own idea of who, or what, is a mother? His reply is as follows:

'I suppose my mother was, yes, just a figure, a figurehead with the title "mother", not someone who did the little motherly things like picking me up and dusting me down and being there for the trials and tribulations of life.'

Like the parents who couldn't and wouldn't get together again, the mother who gave birth and the mother who nurtured remain steadfastly separate, though mercifully not as rivals. That is a fact of life that all children who live apart from their natural mothers have to come to terms with. The mother who gives the everyday care is loved and valued for what she gives. This is true whether that everyday mother is the natural mother or whether she fosters or adopts or is a stepmother. The mother who gives birth is loved and valued for what she is.

Chapter 9

LEGACIES

In 1975, when the law was changed to allow people over eighteen access to birth records, there was some anxiety about the potential upheaval and disturbance for adoptive parents and children. The experiences recounted in the previous pages testify to the fact that the fears were well-grounded. And yet the system is working for the adopted children, for whom it was intended. It offers a chance for them not only to seek out their origins but also to heal wounds. Change is often painful in the short term, but it may clear the air. It is easy to understand why women like Catherine's adoptive mother fabricated stories about giving birth to her, and why Amanda, once told of her adoption, was promptly ordered to deny it in everyday life. There must be a fear in the heart of every adoptive parent that their child will reject them once the biological parent is found. In addition, the desire to conform compels people to lie in order to hide the irregularities, and in the end that serves to add to the sense of unease for all concerned.

But there are upheavals for the natural mothers too, as the case histories have shown. Phillida Sawbridge, of the Post-Adoption Centre, the charity that supports mothers who gave their children for adoption, points to some of their problems. 'Right from the start when the Centre was set up, we recognized that the mothers who gave up a child are a section of society who have nothing. The attitude has always been, now the adoption has gone through, you can get on with your life and try to forget about it. They might be told that they can come back if they have any problems or worries, but really the message has been: it's all over now, off you go. And of course, they bottled it all up, most of them.'

There is nothing in the law that prohibits a mother from seeking her child, but the right isn't spelled out either. Natural parents can leave information at the General Register Office, or with the original adoption agency or other organizations (see address list, p. 225). This leaves all the options to the adopted person.

The Post-Adoption Centre advises on where to leave a letter for the adopted person to find, and also offers natural mothers informal group counselling meetings with trained social workers. Phillida Sawbridge describes who turns up:

'People have come from all over the country, some who relinquished their child a few years ago, others in their fifties and sixties. Some of the mothers have met up with their children, and there are others who are still struggling about how they feel about the whole thing – their guilt, their anguish, their sadness. Most of them have never met a woman before who had acknowledged giving a child for adoption. They have never really been able to talk much to anybody. Some have told husbands, other haven't. Some aren't married. Most of them have said they couldn't really talk about it to their parents. It had become a closed subject.'

The Centre counsels young adults and adoptive parents too. 'We might get an adopted person ringing to say that they are not telling their adoptive parents because they don't want to hurt them, but they need help with their searching. We will write a discreet letter to the birth mother for them, and occasionally they reply saying I never told anybody. My husband doesn't know. Please don't get in touch again. That is devastating for the adopted person and we do prepare them for the possibility.'

Many natural parents and their children end up as companions in due course, though their expectations may have been greater. Phillida Sawbridge sees the build-up to the meeting between natural parent and child as enormous, but not necessarily something that makes for a lasting relationship. 'In some cases, the thing fades away. The adopted child feels he or she has solved the problem; found the roots, and there may not be that much in common. Others do want to make the person part of their lives and struggle with ways to do it. You haven't the shared background and yet there is a feeling of a tie.'

As one of the natural mothers in earlier pages demonstrated, the struggle may be equal on both sides. For the mother, there is the fantasy of finding a like-minded daughter who may in real life turn out to be a disappointment. Perhaps at one level there is a real need to reject in order to justify that original act of giving up the baby. And the rejection through dislike of physical characteristics – height, accent, looks – is especially significant. Shared physical characteristics provide the visible link, the badge of authenticity. The child who does not fit the picture physically and in personality is a stranger.

For an adopted child, there is the fantasy of finding the all-embracing, totally understanding mother, the one we all seek perhaps because we knew her once in the perfectly balanced

118

ecology of the womb. Maybe the temptation and opportunity to have another try at regaining this perfect state is irresistible though nerve-wracking for the unprepared parent, as it certainly was for Maureen – speaking in chapter 7.

It is also often irresistible for teenage children to give their adoptive parents a hard time. Linda Savell of NORCAP, the organization that advises people over eighteen on tracing their parents, comments that 'teenagers blame their adoptive family for their teenage problems, but half the time it isn't anything to do with it. Just a suitable hook to hang the problems onto.' These teenagers are also in an ideal situation for fantasizing that life would have been idyllic with their natural parents and can even go on half-believing this well into adulthood. Phillida Sawbridge sees the repercussions in some of the adoptive parents she counsels. 'They are not only suffering as parents of teenagers, they've also got the added sense of insecurity. They may think would the child have been better with someone else, have we failed? Sometimes they think: is it bad blood?'

This last question is not one that most counselling agencies will take on. Yet people who are adopted, like Catherine and Stella, appear to have little hesitation about thinking in terms of 'blood', and in the former's health history of epilepsy, it certainly tells. Today, we are happier talking about 'roots', partly because we still don't really know how much we inherit in terms of genetic characteristics and how much we acquire through our environment (and partly because we don't want to know for fear of racist inferences).

Some of the adopted children who seek help from NORCAP are long past childhood. A proportion are in late middle age and might have only just found out that they were adopted. Others have known about their adoption all their lives, but haven't got round to doing anything about it.

'A number discover on the death of their parents,' says Linda Savell. 'It's something you might discover in that little box of papers you might get given. But no one seeks out a birth parent till they are ready. An awful lot just get the certificates, learn the facts and that's as far as they want to go. Some will sit on the information for years before deciding to do something about it.'

Adoptive parents often feel very hurt when they find out their children are seeking their natural parents, but nevertheless the NORCAP advice is that the children should own up. 'It's not a question of asking approval, though some parents will give positive encouragement. But we do say they should be told, because the worst thing would be for them to find out from someone else. Most adoptive parents will go along with the idea in the way that any loving parents will go along with an idea their children might

119

want to follow – like taking a job abroad, or turning to a precarious profession.

'Girls tend to start before the men, often when they are thinking of getting married or when they are having their first baby. That's when they want to know what Mum went through – that seems to trigger the thing. Men seem to be well into their thirties and forties before they start. I presume they marry, get a mortgage, a couple of children, and it's always "I'm thinking about it but I'll do something tomorrow." Initially a lot of wives ring up on behalf of their husbands to get them started. It's just as important to them.'

Women and men are predictably different in their approach. 'The women will come in and they'll laugh and cry and get it out of their systems, and they'll ask questions. Men sometimes think it's soppy to ask questions. They are the worst because they make their minds up today to do it. They think they'll phone their mother up tomorrow and meet her the next day. That happens in so many cases. You try to pull them back and talk about the emotional side of it and what it's going to be like, but they don't want to know until contact is made and then they start thinking. They're not necessarily less successful. But it's very difficult for men to listen to what you're talking about, and especially when they come in and talk to us as total strangers. Afterwards they ring you up and say I realize now what you are trying to tell me.'

Since illegitimacy has become much less of a social disgrace, a new element has crept into the work. Says Linda, 'We run a register of everyone who joins, and this is something none of us expected, we are getting register matches – adopted people and also birth parents seeking their children. We can only put them together if the child comes to us and we know they both want to meet. One of the things an adoptee worries about is "will Mother want to know", so if the mother is registered with us, we are a couple of steps ahead. We know she wants to see her child.'

A natural mother may have problems telling her husband or her children about the reappearance of a child who was adopted. Linda Savell admits that the news could be too much for some husbands, and sometimes mother and child meet secretly and privately well away from home. 'But when a woman says she can't tell subsequent children and wonders what they would think of her, we try to explain that children are very different in their outlook today. They'd be curious if nothing else. The children say why didn't you tell us, and then curiosity takes over.'

While one can accept that this often happens, it is noticeable that in two of the personal stories recounted earlier (Norma's and Geraldine's), other daughters were curious but other sons remained noncommittal. Did they too feel it was 'soppy' to ask

questions? A Freudian explanation would be that they were con-
cealing oedipal jealousies. In any case, they were reacting in the
manner common to many males in potentially emotional situations
by revealing little.

Natural mothers are usually in for a shock when they meet the
child they gave away, according to Linda Savell. 'These mothers,
they are looking for their babies. It is logical because that's when
they last saw them and that's the picture they have in their minds.
Some ring up and say, I can't cope with this – a person aged twenty
or whatever. A number see photographs before they ever meet up,
and I understand this can be quite a shock too.'

And there's often a surprise for the children as well. Mothers
who had illegitimate babies in the past were often very young,
well under twenty. Adoptive parents are more likely to be in their
thirties. Catherine points out that her mother is twenty years older
than she is, while her adoptive mother is forty years older. Perhaps
it's not just the poetry-writing that makes her identify with her
natural mother, but also the smaller age gap.

One of the possibilities in today's more open society is that
an adopted child will want to inform a mother that he or she is
homosexual. Linda has come across one or two gay men who were
nervous about telling, but nevertheless felt they had to. 'In both
the cases I saw, they were accepted and not condemned. But that
was certainly uppermost in their minds. I don't think they saw any
connection with being homosexual and being left by their mothers,
by the way.'

On the other hand, it is perfectly possible for a natural mother to
reject a child because of sexual orientation, just as she might do so
because a child seems alien in style of speech or political beliefs.

In reality, the majority of adopted children are welcomed by
their natural mothers. A survey by NORCAP on adoptees who
had made contact showed that over 80% considered themselves
welcomed as family members, and seven out of eight felt their first
meeting with their family was positive.

Almost all adopted children want to find their mothers. Some
also go on to seek their fathers. This may be no easy task if
the father's name is not on the birth certificate. Today there is
probably as much paperwork on fathers as there is on mothers
when a child is adopted, but in the past it was a matter of luck if
name and occupation were given. A father might have been in the
Forces, a married man who might not even know that he'd left a
young woman pregnant. One might imagine the results of someone
turning up on the doorstep twenty-odd years later.

Asking a natural mother for details of the father can conjure up
further problems. She may find it very difficult to unlock memories

of a painful relationship from the past or does not care to remember an indiscreet episode, especially if the conventions of the time gave it the connotation of being sordid. Maureen looks back on 'a shameful, bloody liaison, degrading in the extreme'. She knows of the whereabouts of her daughter's father and says he has never expressed interest in seeing his child. Nevertheless, Jessica wants to meet him, and the beleaguered Maureen's response is, 'I'm not ready for that, not yet. But I might be prepared to let her know where he is.'

The significance of the mother is shown up very clearly by the almost universal need for an adopted child to seek out first the woman who has given birth to him or her. Here is confirmation of the need we have to know ourselves through knowing our mothers. This does not mean we care little about knowing our fathers. It is simply an order of priorities for which society has partially made allowances. As the paperwork expands on fathers, and the shame of illegitimacy and 'furtive' sexual encounters grows less, we can expect to find more adopted children seeking out the other half of their inheritance.

Men so far have been presented as shadowy figures, and even then mostly in a bad light. Of the women interviewed in Chapters 7 and 8, Norma's husband would have broken off the engagement if she had kept the baby she had conceived with her previous boyfriend. Catherine was given for adoption because her mother's husband would not have her. Geraldine's father threatened to banish her from the home if she did not give up her baby. Jessica's adopted father could not talk about the re-entry into her life of her natural mother. Whether through conditioning or some built-in pattern, or more likely both, many men often cope with matters that arouse anxiety by refusing to accept their part in the situation or by using their authority to block conversation.

Two men have emerged from these accounts sounding neither threatened nor anxious. Geraldine's husband and Maureen's partner displayed sympathy and tact. But it is also true that women themselves have in the past shown feelings of threat and anxiety. They did not shout out in defence of their persecuted sisters, but instead were muted, vicariously bearing the shame. Norma, who remembers her stepmother's hostility towards her when she became a mother at the age of sixteen – 'She said I reminded her of her sister, who had also had a baby before she got married' – now offers support to a half-sister, child of that stepmother. 'She is the youngest of my half-sisters, and she had a child and was allowed to keep it though she was not married. I told her about me and said if she wanted support I would give it because I had never had any myself.'

122

Today, there is no doubt of the support. Most unmarried mothers now feel they have a choice about keeping their children, just as they will have had a choice in most cases of opting for abortion. Illegitimacy has become socially acceptable, and the result today is that few newborn babies are available for adoption.

But there are other reactionary elements at work. A great many young single mothers are struggling in a system that offers little in the way of childcare facilities and is eroding child benefit. The Maternity Grant was abolished in 1987 and in a move reminiscent of the New Poor Law of 1834, supplementary benefit changes in 1988 meant that single mothers under eighteen no longer qualified for income support.

Nevertheless, there are pressures on young women today to keep their babies. 'Often what's thrown at you is that you give your child up because you want a good time,' says Mary Woolliscroft of the Natural Parents' Support Group. Rowena and Gaynor are two women who belong to the group. Rowena, twenty-two when she decided to give her baby up for adoption, was offered support by her mother and her boyfriend. 'My mum told me that if I wanted to change my mind she was sure I could keep my baby at home. I was given every choice. I could go and live in a flat – my boyfriend said he'd help me out there. I could stay at home and put myself on the housing list.'

Rowena did not choose any of these things. Instead, she had her baby adopted. Her mother, she says, was proud of her but other mothers failed to understand. 'They're the most difficult to talk to.'

The reality did not prove easy, and Rowena's moment of parting was 'absolutely terrible. I'd left her in the nursery for the night, and in the morning I walked down there and there were other mothers changing their babies. I wanted to pick her up and cuddle and kiss her and cry all over the place, but I couldn't. I just looked at her and walked away. It was awful, but I didn't cry until I got home.'

She met the adoptive parents and received a good impression of them. She does not know their address and they don't know hers. It was the way she wanted it, 'otherwise there'd be a great temptation'.

If the women speaking earlier in this section had had Rowena's choices, it is unlikely that they would have given up their babies. But Rowena arranged her priorities differently.

'I knew I couldn't bring her up on my own . . . She deserved better than to be with me. I'd have no money which would cause not just financial problems, but emotional problems and the stress that single mothers are under. I didn't feel I could handle it at all.'

Her outlook is echoed by that of Gaynor, divorced with one child, and about to have the baby that she is expecting adopted. 'I'd have to give up work, which would mean I'd have to rely on the state to keep me. I want a lot more for my child than that. If I did go back to work, the baby would be with a childminder, so I wouldn't see the baby anyway. I don't think that's any existence for a child . . . And someone who has been waiting four or five years on that list does desperately need children.'

There is no way of knowing how honest these sentiments are. They reflect a society with materialistic values far removed from the need for identity that can haunt an adopted child. How will Rowena's daughter read her mother's words should she ever see them, knowing that she could have been brought up in her natural family? Or Gaynor's baby-to-be? Gaynor wants 'a lot more' for her child and sees it in the material quality of life rather than in the roots from which come love and acceptance and a sense of identity. Of course, an adopted child can get these too, and in better measure than in cases where a natural parent batters or rejects or is oppressed by poverty. But the overriding materialistic values expressed here suggest that these young women are no more in touch with their own feelings than were the women of twenty years ago, who colluded with parents and others who told them what was best for them and their child.

Perhaps Rowena and Gaynor genuinely feel that their potential poverty and emotional difficulties might trigger depression or a tendency to abuse their children. They may be right. The living wouldn't be easy. But given their situations, are their values really in the right place or are they too faint-hearted and self-centred, perceiving themselves as potential victims and throwing away the chances denied to people like Geraldine or Norma? It is easy to see how those women were victims of their culture. Are Rowena and Gaynor victims too, or will the women who have kept their babies because of the current climate see themselves as the real victims in twenty years' time?

It could be said that we are all victims of a culture that wants to banish pain and stress, sees happiness in terms of possessions and offers women a choice but does not offer them adequate back-up.

There is one more question to ask on this impossible issue. What about those absent fathers who may be married or in another relationship and are unable or unwilling to contribute to their child's welfare financially or psychologically? The lack of an adequate father figure is said to be the cause of many behaviour problems in children, particularly in sons. Is it fair to impose a fatherless upbringing on a child, especially in deprived financial circumstances? Rowena and Gaynor may be right in their decision, if not in their reasoning. The sole constant in this shift in values and conventions is that the women continue to pay.

Scientific advances make the dilemmas and difficulties of un-married mothers seem comparatively simple. There is, for in-stance, the question of surrogacy. The Surrogacy Arrangement Act of 1985 banned commercial arrangements. This has not stopped women from giving birth and then handing over the baby to the natural father and his partner, secretly and no doubt with money quietly changing hands. Will these children be told the truth of their origins? There are moves to give a mother legal rights over her child which will make it virtually impossible for a couple who commission a surrogacy arrangement to adopt if the natural mother changes her mind.

New and imaginative ways are developing to cope with the dilemma of who keeps the child. In a recent celebrated case, an American surrogate natural mother, Mary Beth Whitehead, won unsupervised access to her child in 1988 after she had changed her mind about handing the baby over. The judge summed up by saying that he found 'no credible evidence or expert opinion that Melissa will suffer any psychological or emotional harm by continued and expanded visitation with her mother', according to newspaper re-ports. He also appealed to the adults concerned to end hostilities – something highly necessary and requiring counselling, given the fraught situation.

The sharing solution is becoming an acceptable custody arrange-ment after divorce. In America, this can often mean that children are allowed to live part of the year with one parent and part with the other. The idea of sharing is beginning to creep into adoption access too. The House of Lords ruled in 1988 that the courts can make it a condition of an adoption order that a member of the adopted child's natural family should continue to have access to the child. The ruling was made with a case concerning a thirteen-year-old girl who was taken into care and spent most of the first seven years of her life in children's homes. She was then fostered and remained in close contact with one of her brothers who preferred to stay in a children's home. The contact ceased after a few years as a result of discouragement by the social worker. The girl and the foster parents applied for adoption, against the wishes of the natural mother who feared that this would weaken even further the sister-brother relationship. The Lords agreed that the adoption should go ahead and access by the brother should be allowed, though they were at pains to suggest that the matter should be the exception rather than the rule.

Others would like to see it as the rule rather than the exception. Ariel Bruce, a trained social worker who runs a private tracing

125

agency, is a supporter of the idea of open adoption, even though it would put agencies like hers out of business. She says 'It must be the model for the future, with adoption societies looking for people who can share.' As an idea, it is not all that revolutionary. Informal adoptions in the past, and in underdeveloped countries in the present, have given children access to natural parents while they have lived with relatives or others in their community. Mothers in tribal societies have traditionally made many variable arrangements, from handing over a child to the grandmother in order to remain active in agricultural work to sharing in breastfeeding and general child-rearing with a pool of other women and their offspring. Even in Britain, it has been possible for informal contact to be maintained through private fostering arrangements, as happened with James, who told of his double family life in the previous chapter.

Open adoption is only another version of such arrangements. Schemes in America such as Friends in Adoption at Pawlet, Vermont, bring together couples who want to adopt and women who want to have their babies adopted, without involving official agencies. Natural parents and prospective adoptive parents are encouraged to choose each other and build up a relationship before the baby is born. This not only provides a sense of security in the natural mother about her baby's future home, it enables the child to have a sense of ease about its identity, whether contact with the natural mother is constant or not.

Private arrangements of this kind are not legal in Britain or even in many states in America, but the idea of open adoption is just one move in the direction of a more open attitude to families generally. Divorce, step-parenting, single motherhood, surrogacy, AID (artificial insemination by donor) – especially in lesbian mothers – are part of modern society. These circumstances and elements determine the structure of modern families as well as the standard once-married mum and dad and the kids, and they cry out for a new set of conventions. It may not be appropriate for all natural parents to remain in touch after adoption or other family changes, but the rules need to be sufficiently relaxed and flexible to meet different circumstances.

Just as couples after divorce and remarriage still remain parents and need to find ways to gain trust in each other, so adoptive parents need to reach out to natural ones and provide for parents who give their babies away some link, some assurance, and even some pride in their offspring if at all possible.

SECTION III

Post-natal Illness

Chapter 10

CYCLES OF DEPRIVATION

'**I** remember my shock at the state of your children and flat. Tracy opened the door to me. She was three years old, wearing only a vest, and filthy with matted hair. You hadn't taught her not to open the door to strangers, but I only thought about that later. Tracy took my hand and led me into the kitchen where Brett was drinking from an ashtray. "It's pee," Tracy told me with an anxious smile. I snatched the ashtray from Brett and the urine spilt on the floor. I gazed at Brett in horror. Just two years old, he was naked and shivering and there were marks on his face. "Ciggie burns," Tracy confided in me knowledgeably. "Mummy didn't mean it." '

The above words are taken from an article written by social worker Vicki Golding. They were addressed to a woman of nineteen, a single mother with two children. She was in a state of desperation when Vicki Golding found her, and was relieved to have her children taken into care on a voluntary basis. She herself had been abused as a child and had also been taken into care. Despite promises that she wanted her children back and would visit regularly, clean up the flat and get a job, she visited only four times in six months, and subsequently agreed for her children to be adopted, though she ran from the court in great distress when the proceedings took place. Later she went on to have a third child to whom she proved to be a loving and caring mother.

The story is a familiar one to social workers. The classic ingredients are there: a personal history of abuse and deprivation, extreme youth coupled with single parenthood, no income and inevitable poverty.

Another classic ingredient that affects the way a mother will care for her child is inadequate housing. Around 25% of babies born to mothers in bed and breakfast accommodation are of low birth weight, compared to the national average of 7%. The children are more susceptible to diarrhoea, chest infections and accidents. Both mothers and children are at risk of being under-nourished and are vulnerable to stress. Some of them will turn into abusers and abused.

But it would be misleading to imply that mothers who neglect and reject their children are solely among the underprivileged. Similar responses to motherhood have been found in all social groups, according to the National Society for the Prevention of Cruelty to Children. Wealthier families can employ nannies or send their children to boarding-schools as a way of disguising their rejection of a child. It is the poorer who show the visible signs of cruelty and abuse to the outside world and whose children may go into care.

The following account is from a woman who bears the scars of suffering from her own past and who found being a mother more than she could manage.

* * *

'He cried and cried . . . in the end I went over to his cot and I just tapped his leg, and he stopped. I thought, oh my Jesus, what have I done?'

Marlene is twenty-eight. Her son is three. She lives in a council maisonette which is shabby but quite comfortable. She is on social security. On the walls are photographs of film stars of the thirties and forties – Humphrey Bogart, Lauren Bacall. There are no photos of her namesake (which is not the one printed here but another of similar vintage). There are snapshots of her son, and children's picture books, and a Mother's Day card. Marlene is anxious to show to others, and to convince herself, that she is a good and loving mother, though her son had just been taken permanently from her.

'He had been a ward of court for nearly three years be-cause about a month after I had him I had a breakdown. What happened was, his father had him for the day and when he was brought back he wouldn't stop crying. Put it like this, he had a dad, or he had and he hadn't. He never supported me or lived with me for any time. I wasn't working. I'm not now. I used to do odd jobs, cleaning and things like that.

'Anyway, I changed him, I fed him, I could do nothing. He was nearly a month old. In the end I went over to the cot and I just tapped his leg, and he stopped. I thought, oh my Jesus what have I done, I've hit him. Next morning I phoned the social worker and she came over immediately and said right, we'll take the child to the doctor.'

Marlene did not wish to explain why she already had a social worker assigned to her, but later she revealed, somewhat ambiguously, that she had been sexually abused as a child.

'The doctor said I think we have to ask if there are any hospitals around here that have a mother and baby unit because you really do need some help. The doctor knew that I never hit the child, I didn't even touch him. There was no bruise on him – it was just that he wouldn't stop crying and I just tapped him and he shut up.

'They found one, and we packed his stuff. At the time, I didn't want to know him, my son. They had a nurse to look after him because I couldn't do it on my own. I was too frightened in case I hit him again. I wrecked the room. I smashed a window. I laid into him, he was like a punch bag.

'I couldn't tell anyone what I was feeling, the abuse I went through. Sexually, with my father and an uncle. I never told anybody. I kept it all to myself at school and I thought I can't keep this inside me any more. I let it all out to the nurse. Ha ha . . . They gave me something to calm me down and when I woke up they told me what I said and I couldn't believe it.

'I was under a psychiatrist, such a nice man. He said you've bottled that up for twenty-five years, and I can really understand why this happened with your son.

'I started to take care of Jonathan after that and with someone around I was all right. They gave me a social worker and she was a right bitch. She kept on saying you did hurt the child, there was a mark on his face, who did it if not you? I never marked him, he done it himself. Babies scratch their eyes when they're babies. She wouldn't believe me.'

Marlene was taken to a mother and baby home, where the warden appears to have been tactless and unhelpful too.

'She said oh you've just come out of a mental hospital, and I said no, not a mental hospital, a psychiatric hospital. I'm not mad. I had a breakdown. Jonathan wouldn't settle, and I was up with the nurse all night one night and in the morning I said I can't cope, I don't know if I am good enough to be his mum. So I always had it at the back of my mind . . .'

A meeting with the warden and social worker resulted in the decision that Jonathan should be taken into care. 'The social worker came with two men, two big men from her office, and they snatched Jonathan from the garden. I was feeding him, his father was sitting next to me. They came in the garden and snatched him and raced off. Then the warden came out and said you've got your just deserts now. Pack your stuff and piss off.'

This is Marlene's account, and it may or may not be true. There are many stories of social workers who take children

131

without warning, perhaps in order to avoid a scene that they fear they cannot control, though such an experience is likely to unhinge even the most balanced person. Marlene's next move was to a Salvation Army hostel which she found 'terrible, though the people were nice'. For several days she did not know where her son had been taken. The child's father proved unsupportive, 'swearing and shouting' at her. Finally, she visited her son in his foster home and found him thriving at three months. She was depressed and was visited by a health visitor.

'I don't know why I came out with it, but I said I wanted to kill my son. It was all part of being depressed. When I went to see him there was a policeman in the room and the social worker said we are going to stop your access.'

Following a solicitor's advice, Marlene went to the magistrates court where the verdict was that she needed help and the baby should remain in care. She was taken in by Arbours, the 'alternative' crisis treatment centre which does not use drugs and offers intensive psychotherapy with a great deal of personal freedom, though only for a limited time.

'I was there for seven months and I got therapy and talked about all the things I couldn't talk about before. Jonathan was made a ward of court and they decided I could go to see him because I was doing so well, provided I had my counsellor from Arbours with me.

'**I saw Jonathan three times a week by the end, and had a new social worker who was really nice**. Then I had to leave Arbours and they got me a place at a Richmond Fellowship house [*a halfway organization that offers supervision and rehabilitation before patients return to normal life*]. They said I could have Jonathan with me once I was settled in, and my new social worker collected him from the foster home. It was strange having him. He was nine months now. I managed all right. I had a lot of people around me who taught me things and encouraged me.'

After a few months, there was a review of her case and Marlene was offered her present maisonette. She moved in two years ago.

'Of course I was petrified. I'd been sort of institutionalized in a way. Jonathan was over a year old. I went to a psychiatric hospital for a bit on a daily basis, but it reminded me of the institutionalizing and I didn't want that. So regimented. If they say sneeze, you sneeze. My social worker found a day nursery just up the road which is run by social services. I don't like it. They arranged that I would have to go to the nursery as well every day to settle Jonathan in and so they could watch us together. They took him when he was nineteen months old.

'I wasn't getting any counselling at this time though the man from the Richmond Fellowship came down to see me. I could see my social worker whenever I liked. And then there was a bombshell dropped on me. My social worker was leaving. I couldn't stop crying. She said it was a real promotion and she had to go. I had one last meeting with her and she said she'd miss me and Jonathan more than I'd know. We were *really* close. She was a really nice woman.'

When telling this, Marlene's voice rose like that of a small girl's. She was near to tears, near to hysteria and despair. 'Mother' (in the guise of social worker) was giving up her child, somehow devaluing all of Marlene's efforts to hold on to hers.

'I had nobody. My parents didn't speak to me then. I get on with them a bit better now. Then I met my new social worker, the bane of my life. I don't have anything to do with her. If I saw her I'd kill her. I told her that.

'The minute I met her I hated her. She had done everything by the book. She said the nursery was getting a bit concerned because I was meant to be going there three days a week and I had cut it down to one day a week. None of the other mothers went. The social worker said they would take me to court if I didn't go, so I said OK, one day a week.

'When I was there I'd sit with Jonathan, play with him, and he didn't want me to play with him. I used to do all the sewing for them. I used to help clear up and everything. They never said anything about that in court. They said I just sat there on my arse and didn't bother to play with Jonathan. But he didn't want me to play with him. He didn't want me around.'

Again, Marlene's voice rose to near hysteria when telling this, a small girl protesting her innocence, fighting the terrible knowledge that her son was rejecting her as she was rejecting him, and as she had been rejected. She was fighting too, the failure of communication between herself and those who held her fate in their hands. There was concern about the child's development and Marlene was told he needed to undergo psychological tests. There were threats of a court summons if she did not cooperate.

'I said OK, I didn't want the hassle. He saw some woman – a right old miserable bag she is – she took a look at my son at the nursery and she said it's his mother. She's not giving him enough stimulation. Then we saw a man at the clinic and he had the gall to say that I wasn't a very stable influence on my son and he thought that Jonathan was in a lot of distress. Yet he could see that me and Jonathan loved each other and that he wouldn't be parted from me.'

Jonathan was found to have various difficulties. His speech was poor, and Marlene felt this was a severe judgement on her. She had to take him to a speech therapist every week who proved to be 'lovely, very encouraging'. The messages were confusing and contradictory, making it all too easy for Marlene to accept the judgements of those who praised and to reject those who didn't.

'But social services are never happy. They said I had to go back to the psychiatric hospital with Jonathan. There was a meeting with the nursery, and they were talking about me as if I wasn't there. I said will you talk to me, this is bad. I was crying, really upset, and then I heard them say see, you can't talk to the girl, she gets so emotional, she just can't listen to you and she gets really upset. And the woman from the hospital said Marlene is upset because she feels upset. I've seen improvement and I think she's doing well.

'**Then my social worker said but when she leaves here she will go downhill, and I said OK, if that's what you feel then you fucking take my son. You can have him**. Just take him. I can't do anything right. I'm not his mother. You're his mother. You tell me everything I do is wrong and if that's the way you feel then take the child.

'Jonathan was in another room playing, and I could not even look at the child, I felt so much hatred. I'd been trying so hard. I just told him to go away. I called him a bastard. I said go away I hate you. In the afternoon the hospital woman called me in the office and she was telling me to calm down and she said do you want me to phone up and say they can take him?

'I came home with Jonathan and do you know, that child must have sensed, he knew something was going to go wrong. He was very clingy. He wouldn't let me go. Next day he was at nursery and the social worker rang and said don't go and pick him up because he won't be coming home. We're taking him into care, and this time it's for good. They said it was for his own safety and he was emotionally disturbed and I couldn't blame anyone else but myself. I phoned my solicitor and she was really disgusted. She said these people took you for a ride. And they did.'

One must reserve judgement here about how the solicitor or any other of the 'experts' really behaved. What is given is Marlene's view and Marlene's experience. And yet there is much in the idea that she was indeed taken for a ride. The 'nice' man at the mother and baby unit, the supportive social worker, the Arbours and the Richmond Fellowship people were shoring up a sinking ship. While they could offer a secure base, they could also offer hope. They created certain expectations that could not be fulfilled in the long run, partly because they could offer no permanence. And then there were the 'experts' who seemed to reinforce Marlene's sense of guilt and failure.

Marlene, inevitably, feels that some were specifically against her. 'They wouldn't let me have therapy, they said I didn't need therapy. That was the social worker. She stopped it. I wanted personal therapy, not in a group. I was entitled to one to one.'

The court case was held up because Jonathan's father wanted access. Marlene herself was granted access and she saw her son at his foster home. 'I told him, this is the last time I will see you now. I just want you to know that I'll see you soon and I love you.'

And of course she does. The father was refused access. No social worker attended to his needs and one day he called round to see Marlene and beat her up, banging her head against the wall so that she was admitted to hospital with delayed concussion. 'He blamed me that Jonathan was going to be adopted. He said how could you give your baby away?'

The agony went on. 'In court, they were accusing me now of sexually abusing my son. And I said I never ever touched him. They were saying it because I kissed Jonathan on the backside when he was a baby. He had mentioned it to the foster mum. He had said I used to kiss Mummy's bum. I passed out when the judge made the decision and he came up to me afterwards and said I didn't want to do that one little bit. After the court case the fucking bitch, the social worker, walked out and didn't even come up to me. Now they're looking for adoptive parents. They won't let me find out from the nursery how he is any more. He's been told that he won't see Mummy any more. That was it really.'

Except for the anger that won't die and is rapidly turning into an obsession. 'They're real bastards at that nursery. Just because you have a bit of trouble – and I know I'm not all there really – I still looked after my son. But they can do what they like. When I used to collect him from the nursery he would often say he wanted to stay with them, with the Sister there. She made him cling to her . . . She made him want to stay with her rather than come with me. I feel so angry and bitter. It's just not fair. I don't trust anybody. If I trust somebody I get let down. I wrote to my nice social worker once but she never replied.'

Marlene is still under psychiatric care, though it's only one session in three weeks. She has been on and off drugs but doesn't know what and says they make her feel 'dopey'.

'I'm going to get a new social worker and I want to move out of this place because of its memories. The woman at the hospital told me that once I had grieved and know in my heart that I have done the right thing, I can start building a new life. But I'm finished with having children. I'm sure of that.'

Meanwhile, the Mothers' Day card remains on her shelf.

*   *   *

Around 69,000 children are in the care of local authorities in England alone. The majority are aged five or over, but 7,500 are under five. Some will grow up in residential homes. The majority are fostered and a proportion will eventually be adopted. A few will be reunited with their parents if they have been fostered temporarily because of a family crisis, such as parental illness, homelessness or some short-term problem that makes it difficult for a parent to cope.

The reasons for children being removed from their homes on a long-term or permanent basis are likely to be sexual abuse (almost always by men), or physical neglect or injury by either parent, or because a child is beyond control or is in what is deemed to be moral danger. A Place of Safety Order has to be obtained from a magistrate, and then a social worker has the right to remove a child from his or her home for up to twenty-eight days. A hearing follows which will determine whether a child is to be kept in care until a case is prepared or whether the child might return home. The number of children taken into care has increased by over a third since 1985.

Vicki Golding, quoted earlier, is a team leader with a London borough. Most of her social work experience has been with taking children into care and dealing with the mothers who feel unable to look after them. She said:

'Sometimes a mother doesn't bond with one child, but will bond with another. I had a case where a woman bonded with her first child, who is still with her, but not with the second, who was taken into care. He wasn't planned, she didn't want him. The first one was planned, though the couple were very young and the mother had been in care herself. When the second baby was a few days old there was a family row and she had dropped him on the floor. He was OK, but his mother said she didn't want him, she was frightened she would hurt him. But we have never been concerned about the older child. She had equated the younger with her husband, with whom she was on bad terms by the time the baby was born.'

There is a happy ending to this story. 'The child was fostered and his father remained in contact. When he eventually remarried, the child, now seven, was returned to him. His mother, who never visited, went on to remarry too and now has three more children whom she is bringing up successfully. It was the rejecting of her first husband that overflowed onto the second child.'

Bonding is thought to take place at a sensitive period immediately after childbirth, which is why it is current practice to give a new baby to its mother to hold as soon as it is born. Mothers who fail to bond have been observed to be less attentive to their child's cries and general needs as long as two years later. Failure to bond could be triggered by problems as above, or by a bad birth experience, or mental illness, or even a floppy, unresponsive baby. The painkilling drugs given in labour are known to affect infant alertness after the birth. Perhaps, too, the alien environment of a hospital, plus drugs, interfere in some subtle way with body smells. Newborn babies are said to respond to their mother's smell.

The significance of bonding and even its existence have become a subject of controversy in recent years. Sociologist Ann Oakley's study of sixty-six women having their first babies recorded 70% of them expressing lack of interest when first holding their babies. A paper by Robson and Kumar called *Delayed Onset of Maternal Affection After Childbirth* reported that 40% of 104 mothers had little interest in their babies for the first two or three days. By the end of the first week, only 4% still felt indifferent. By the third month, five mothers expressed detachment and three dislike. Of these eight, more than half had not been detached at birth. There was no association between the initially detached and those who had breastfeeding problems or who later developed post-natal depression. Perhaps there is too much emphasis on this bonding business – another aspect of the pressures on women to be good mothers and conform to some perfect pattern.

There are cases of rejection that baffle social workers and arouse horror in those who encounter them. Says Vicki Golding, 'The first case I ever had was an only child of middle-class parents. When I found him, he was five, and he was locked in his bedroom. His parents had expected him to love them and he hadn't somehow lived up to their expectations. They started punishing him. Because he wet himself, he was locked in his room. Because he was locked in his room, he wet himself more. He wouldn't eat, so they wouldn't feed him. And so it went on. They rang us and said if you don't take him away we will kill him. They said seeing him being taken away was like getting rid of a bad toothache.'

This is an extreme case which could well have led to headline-making murder. A couple who cannot between them operate as adequate parents constitute a huge danger to a child, especially if they collude in seeing him as the enemy who is the cause of all their problems. A decision has to be made by a social worker in such a case, and often the issue is far from straightforward.

It is possible that Marlene's son's life might have been in danger, and the decision to take her child from her was timely. But there was the lack of continuity and consistency in ideas and treatment between the psychiatrists and psychotherapists and social workers. The enthusiasm and encouragement of some were not taken up by others. The central policy of getting Marlene out into the community seems to have been unrealistic without permanent, close contact with a trusted mother figure, perhaps a warden in sheltered housing. Depressingly, the ultimate failure seems to be in our abilities to deal with severe mental illness. Like Humpty Dumpty with all the king's horses and all the king's men, Marlene has not really been put back together again.

For Marlene, the hardest part must have been to lose total contact with her child. There was no attempt by the social worker to pass on information about the child's likes and dislikes, his special needs and habits to the new carers. Like some of the women who suffered after giving their babies for adoption, Marlene might have gained some comfort from knowing a little about the people her son was living with, and even from hearing from time to time of his welfare. She did, after all, give birth to him, and tried for three hard years to be a loving mother.

In a book with the self-explanatory title *Long-Term Foster Care*, which looked at the progress of 145 fostered children, their foster parents and natural parents, the latter showed a need for news for many years, in some cases long after contact had ceased. The authors recommended that where possible foster and natural parents should meet before a placement occurs so that information can be exchanged.

The children too may want to know their roots, and social workers can provide the link, with memory scrapbooks, news of a parent, and perhaps some guidance as to how to explain themselves simply and directly to new friends and strangers who come into their lives. But more than anything else, the children need a home and long-term policy that gives them a stable life. If they are disturbed, they may need expert care in a therapeutic community. If they are put into a residential home, they should not be turfed out to fend for themselves at eighteen, as happens now, but should be given some systematic preparation and support for entry into adult life. And if they are fostered, they need permanency as soon as possible. In the book mentioned above, a one-year-old had experienced eleven moves since being taken into care, a primary-school child had had twenty-one moves. One in five of their own mothers had been in care. Constancy and continuity could perhaps prevent a third generation from entering that cycle of deprivation.

Chapter 11

WOMEN WHO LOVE AND HATE

Rich and poor, mothers can both love and hate their children, especially after childbirth. Post-natal depression can lead to a state of hopelessness that turns mothering into an unmanageable task. The more severe mental illness after childbirth, post-natal psychosis, can put a baby at risk of violence if a mother suffers delusions. These illnesses may be caused in part by disturbed nights and housebound days and the failure to live up to certain ideals of the mother-child relationship. They are also thought to be partly triggered by hormonal changes following the birth. In these situations women might voluntarily give up their children, especially if they are without a partner. Grandparents or other family members may rally round in some cases. Nannies and private health care may provide the necessary support. Today, for many women, work seems to be a major lifeline and a way back to health. Here, two women tell of their post-natal experiences and their fight for equilibrium.

* * *

'The hospital considered that I was dangerous to myself and possibly dangerous to other people . . .'

Jennifer is forty-five, divorced. She has a son of fifteen and a daughter of twelve, both of whom live with their father. She has, in the past, been diagnosed as schizophrenic but does not consider herself suffering from the condition now. She is a pretty, plump woman, nervous, sharp, on the edge; very proud of her newly decorated house, an Edwardian semi, furnished with antique pine and warm ethnic prints. She has little expectation of her children coming to live with her.

'I was twenty-seven when I married. I'd known Edward for about three years, I'd been training to be a teacher. I joined the family business when we married. His family were not too keen on me. They are part Asian and his brother had married an

Indian girl from a wealthy family. She helped to polarize them against me.

'I wanted children though I wasn't naturally an over-maternal person. There was a bit of post-natal depression with the first one. I got exhausted and had workmen in the house. I found it very difficult being in charge of a small baby. I didn't have any confidence. I went back to work two weeks after he was born. I suppose at an unconscious level I was trying to hold my life together.

'There was never any problem of money. My husband's firm was highly successful. I had an excellent nanny and after a while I shared the work with her. My son was fine if you gave him enough to do with his mind.'

Jennifer sees her problems beginning with post-natal depression after the birth of her second child, a daughter, and the arrival of her sister-in-law in the family.

'It is a very controlling family. I felt isolated. My husband was coming home later and later, and quoting his mother and sister-in-law. For the first six months after my daughter was born I was really out for the count. I was crazy about the baby, but I couldn't do anything for her. I'd have her in the room bouncing up and down with me, but someone else would have to come and change her nappy. I was seeing an analyst and I had a breakdown.'

Jennifer is a little vague about what happened during the first two years after her daughter was born. She talks of being 'exhausted and overwrought', of starting to do a university degree, of meeting other mothers and beginning to make her own life. She was in hospital for two months and when she was ready to go home she received a bombshell.

'My husband did not want me back. The children were aged two and five, and he had been told by the consultant "once your wife is as ill as this, she will be ill for the rest of her life, and it would be better for your children if they did not see her any more." They all agreed on that. The hospital considered that I was dangerous to myself and possibly dangerous to other people. Of course I was talking a lot of bullshit and I needed tranquillizers, but what you do not need is to be removed from everybody and everything that gives you support and be given mind-blowing drugs and be put with people who are much more disturbed than you are. I had wanted to leave the marriage, but not to be chucked out, and without my children. I went into a state of shock. Fortunately, I found a new friend who invited me to stay. I also went to a well-known alternative psychiatrist who took me off all drugs and said "stop behaving like a patient". He felt I was taking on emotions that belonged to other people in the family and was being made the victim of them. I stopped behaving like a powerless victim and found myself a flat.'

The psychiatrist wrote to Jennifer's solicitor stating that his client was sane and should see the children for their sake. Visits were arranged but Jennifer found them difficult and unsatisfactory, with the children clearly upset and torn between her and their new young nanny. Jennifer wanted to start divorce proceedings and was told that she had little hope of getting custody of the children. She moved into the flat and her husband agreed to pay the deposit on it.

'I had a plan. A friend advised me that the only way I would get my children was to snatch them because for my husband to go through the courts would take a long time and would give me a crack at being a successful parent. And by the time the case came up the children would be settled and the courts would hold that in my favour.

'I hadn't properly moved in when I made the snatch. The nanny had brought the children round and I was getting over-wrought because they were telling me she had locked them in the basement. They were crying and when she came to collect them, I couldn't take any more. She was hitting them in front of me, so I snatched my daughter from her and hit her three times in the face, not very hard. She tried to attack me and I said if you touch me I will throw you down the stairs. So she left. My husband turned up when I was out shopping and my cleaning woman would not let him in. The flat wasn't really ready, but I began to feel more relaxed over the months as it became apparent that my husband would not snatch the children back.'

For six months Jennifer was subject to surveillance so that the court could assess how she coped with the children. Her son was at school, her daughter at a morning nursery. She was stressed; she was told her son had learning problems and was possibly dyslexic. She changed his school and he settled quickly. When the court case came up she was awarded custody and care and control.

'**My husband paid me maintenance when he felt like it. I felt he had total control over me**. Originally he had access five nights a week, but he was unpunctual, erratic, and I kept a diary so I had evidence to change this. So it was reduced to two nights a week, and he didn't mind all that much as he was travelling a lot and being a bit of a playboy. I objected to him trying to get his girlfriends together with the children. I'd spent a long time getting these kids in order again and I didn't want them being kept up late and getting over-excited, so I stopped them going to him for a weekend or two.'

Jennifer began to renovate a luxury maisonette which was going to be her divorce settlement from her husband. During this time he stopped paying maintenance and school uniform bills, presumably as retaliation for reduced access. Jennifer accused him of 'playing games' but moved back again into the family home. After six months she was told by her solicitor that she would lose grounds for divorce if she stayed, so she moved out again into her not-yet-renovated maisonette, taking the children with her.

'Basically, I squatted there for eighteen months till I got a divorce. There was a relentless battle. I fell apart. I lost track of the outer world and I became paranoid. And of course I could not cope with the children. My son had permission from his father to disobey me. He is still disparaging and contemptuous. He would phone his father and say "Mummy is being difficult again" and his father would tell him he didn't have to do this or that if he didn't want. It might be about time to go to bed or eating vegetables. I'm not from his background where it is common to spoil children.

'I got to the stage where I was at such loggerheads with my son that I ended up threatening him with a knife. I didn't intend to do anything . . . he was eleven and acting out his father's total defiance.

'When I was seventeen, my mother did something similar to me. She made a very strong attack on me and actually stabbed me when I was getting boyfriends and she was very pretty and living a very hardworking life. I think maybe she was jealous of me. She had a difficult background. She was put into an orphanage by her mother – my grandmother – who was in service and found herself pregnant. Eventually they got together again and I myself have always found my grandmother very supportive, though I suppose I have never quite trusted my mother. It is a terrible thing to feel that you are making the same mistake as had happened to you.'

The episode led to Jennifer's husband taking both children to live with him. Jennifer was on tranquillizers, unable to sleep and very anxious. The divorce settlement was generous, which enabled Jennifer to sell the maisonette and buy her present house. It took her several years to recover from her second breakdown, and now, five years later, she is reasonably settled. She has resumed her part-time studies and has a 'steady man friend, a good friend'. She is under a psychoanalyst and feels much of her misfortune is due to having been in a National Health mental hospital after her daughter was born.

'Because they proclaimed that I was schizophrenic, I was considered not suitable for counselling or psychotherapy. I could have heavy drugs for the rest of my life. Most definitely I have been paranoid. It was not that I could feel other people's thoughts

142

in my head – more likely that other people could tell mine. I believed that there were plots that I was in. Not hallucinations, but paranoia based on fear blown out of all proportion. Fear that my ex-husband wanted to kill me. I wasn't that wrong actually, only his form of killing would be more psychological.

'I have talked with my analyst at length about my son. He is going to have to look for someone else to put his bad feelings on. He is not going to be able to use me as a dumping-ground any more. My daughter comes to see me on her own. I've kind of pushed my way back into her life by arranging to take her to lots of ballet, and that has become a nice thing to look forward to. She is a dear little thing and she's got her own sense of values which are fortunately independent of the rest of the household. I have talked about the past to her, and she says, "Look, I've only ever known you this way since I was born, so it does not seem so terrible to me." But I know sometimes she feels very sad. She is aware of the fact that I love her and that I loved her as a baby.

'**I think the hard part for me to bear is that she is more loyal to her father and his mistress than towards me.** She loves me, but she wants them to have a stable partnership together. When she arrives to see me she looks so pleased, I can hardly believe it. I expect her to look, I don't know, apprehensive or worn out from the journey, but she arrives full of beans. Our relationship is unusually good considering the circumstances.

'I don't think I have been a bad mother, though I would certainly say that incidents that happened because I was mentally ill would have been very bad for the children. I should have realized early on that I was going to need a lot more support to take on a full mothering role. Under the circumstances, which included a great lack of confidence, I actually feel that I did as good a job as I could.'

* * *

'**I ran away twice . . . but I found that I took the depression with me**'

Isobel is forty-three, a lean, energetic, stylish woman. Her flat is like her: spare, modern, elegant. In the second bedroom there are bunk beds strewn with toys and books, but it's a week since her twin sons, aged nine, visited. Isobel is American-born of an English mother and American father. She came to England in the sixties, married an Englishman and worked as a writer/researcher with a technical magazine before her sons were born.

'I'm a planning person, and my plan was to get pregnant after I became a member of the firm's health scheme so I could get back to work after the children were born. I was thirty-three. But there was a Pill scare and it happened six months earlier than the plan. My husband, Nick, wasn't doing the pregnancy with me as I had wanted him to in my fantasies. I wanted an involved, loving husband. We'd been married ten years and had had a good time together, and I had thought I knew him. But that was when I began to find out that I didn't know him.

'At seventeen weeks I found out I was going to have twins. It laid me flat. Nick hadn't come with me for the scan. I was devastated, he was thrilled. He was a man and it made him feel potent that he had produced two children in one go.'

The news made Isobel feel that they had to move, and the house they found, 'the dream house', needed total conversion which they decided to do themselves. Isobel was admitted to hospital at seven months, worried that the building costs were soaring and doubting her husband's ability to keep everything under control. The boys were born two weeks early and were fine. But again they were not according to plan.

'My first instinct when they were born was oh no, not two boys. I wanted at least one girl. I come from a family of girls and I know about girls. The house was barely ready, so I stayed in hospital for two weeks and I found myself getting more and more eye-poppingly what-do-I-do-now touch. I hadn't got a support group, my family were in the States. There was the house where I barely knew the neighbours. And Nick was fucking hopeless, no help at all. I had often heard him say, but I didn't know what he meant, that he didn't like tiny children or babies. I felt I had to do everything. I was breastfeeding every two hours and all the responsibility was mine. My husband wanted to be mothered and he couldn't mother me.

'I was waking very early in the morning, and by five weeks it was very obvious that I was depressed. It came to a point when I was staying in bed all day. Nick got that worried he had the doctor call round and I went on to the first of my tranquillizers and anti-depressants. I couldn't drive and if you've been active and free to do things, it's just horrifying. I had this double buggy, and the experience of wheeling that and balancing shopping in a crowded supermarket is something I will never go through again. And then the crying. My mother came over twice and she helped me to get the children onto bottle-feeding when they were three months old because I was getting so exhausted.

'**When the boys were four months I found a nanny and tried to go back to work. They'd given me my job back and I thought I could just go right back into it and be my old self**. But I reckoned without the fact that my responsibilities were quadrupled. And I was too ill. It is hormones as well as society's attitude. I really don't think it was something deeply psychological in my case. I have a very good relationship with my own family. I have three sisters and one of them is going through a schizophrenic breakdown, and that's the kind of mental illness which is more to do with your genetic make-up.'

Isobel started to see a post-natal depression counsellor attached to her local hospital. 'She was trying to paper over the cracks and keep me together. After six weeks I went to her and said I've got to give the job up, I can't cope, and I broke down. She said do you want to go into hospital, and I said yes please. Nick's parents came to help out and I was in hospital for two weeks. But it became obvious that he was not coping. He was broken over the fact that I was not the strong capable woman that he had married and he was totally at sea. I had to sign myself out. I thought right, I'll put myself together, I'll cope.

'But within a couple of weeks it became too much for me again. I was in the kitchen and the children were in bouncy reclining chairs, one on this kitchen table and I was trying to feed them, the other on the chair on the floor. I don't know what happened, or how I got that way, but I was so fraught, and they were both crying, and I thought what would happen if I pushed the chair over – and I did, just the one on the floor, not the table. And of course he spilled out and cried more. At that very point the phone rang and it was my mother in the States, and I told her what I'd done. And within two days I was in the States with both children. She paid the fare. She asked if Nick would accompany me but he wouldn't so a girlfriend came on the flight and turned round and came back again.

'I was there for five months. My father is a doctor and he took me to a woman psychiatrist. She felt my anti-depressant was a too low dose and that's why it wasn't doing me any good, so she whacked it up. That was the first time I began to have manic symptoms. I became over-active and I was getting very tired and not sleeping. My mother was in her element though, because she adores tiny babies, and they were settled. Things seemed under control and I said I wanted to go back home. The boys were six months old, Nick was writing me tender letters, though I was glad he was not with me.'

Isobel returned to England, and to her counsellor. She began to notice certain mood cycles: two weeks of depression, then a sudden switch to high activity, exhausting but euphoric. Then she lost her job.

'**I was engineered out of it. My husband colluded with the office to say she's not coping, you'd better ask her to resign rather than go back on sick pay again**. That to me was one of the most heinous things. What they had already done to a man who had multiple sclerosis was to give him an easier job to keep him going. They should have offered me a less responsible job to keep me ticking over and to keep sense of self. I would still have found it tough but it would have been a lifeline to normality.'

One can never know whether this really would have been the lifeline at the time, but certainly the idea of her husband colluding only reinforced her sense of disappointment about him and may have increased feelings of helplessness and being trapped.

'Nick's elderly parents came down to help out, and I was getting somewhat paranoid about them being there. I ran away twice. Once I managed to get to Greece on my own for two weeks, but I found I took the depression with me. The second time it was home to America. The children were eighteen months old and fine, not showing any signs of disturbance.'

Isobel returned after six months. There were attempts at family counselling, and talk of a divorce. Finally, Isobel was offered a place with her children in a new mother and baby unit. She accepted but found that she did not want her children with her. They were returned home and into the care of a childminder who took them to a day nursery.

'I was in the unit for five months, getting stable on lithium [*a drug used for manic-depressive symptoms*]. And in that time I faced my catch-22 which was "I'm not going to get better until I leave Nick" though they were saying you can't make that decision until you get better – and I was saying I won't get better till I leave him. And the other part of it was, but I can't do it with the children. So my first step was to say I'm not coming back to you Nick, and the second was to say I am going to live on my own and I don't want to take the children, because I am not strong enough to take them.'

So much of Isobel's rejection of motherhood is tied up with resentment at losing control over her own life and being dependent on a man who is perceived as ineffectual and unable to rise to emotional occasions.

'If he had been a different man, and if I'd had a different kind of ego strength and support group, what I should have done was to have chucked him out, gone back to the house, with the kids, with the council nursery and the council minder, and gotten myself better. But what happened was that I was given a council flat and I was seeing the children at the nursery one afternoon a week. Sometimes it was an absolute chore and a burden, but when I was with them, though I felt horribly depressed inside, it was great. I could see that I wasn't totally washed up as a potential mother.'

Isobel's lack of trust in her husband was heightened by the fact that he was beginning to drink after work and was arriving home late – hardly surprising, given his stresses, but not exactly appropriate for the children, given theirs. 'I felt the children were not getting proper attention or being fed properly. I had to have them back. The women at the nursery didn't stop me. She said OK go ahead, try. I picked them up one afternoon, and I didn't hear from Nick for a week. These two kids, I'm not exaggerating, they were fine. And that nursery was fantastic. It was their stable base of operations from nine in the morning till 5.30 in the evening, and they had a place and a life.

'They lived with me for three months. It was difficult, it was tiring. I felt less anxious about the children, but I felt depressed and trapped and had enormous anger towards Nick who refused to give me any money at all, and I was not working. Christmas came, with no money for presents, nothing, and I called Nick up and said you've got to get the children. I can't go on. I was lying in bed in the flat and the lady upstairs kept banging on the ceiling because of noise from the children. So he came and got them. The next day was totally different. I spent it with a girlfriend and it was time out, totally time out.

'And then the day after that, something extraordinary happened. There was a man I'd met in hospital, a fellow-patient, and he rang up that next day and invited me to visit Canada with him for a holiday while he was giving a lecture there. It was just what I needed. The plan was that I would come back after a break and Nick would give me the children back again. We'd sell the house and I would be able to buy a place with half the money and have the children.'

It was another plan that didn't and probably couldn't work out.

'**When I got back, there was this woman in Nick's life who had moved into the house in the two weeks I was away**. And Nick said we are keeping the children and we are selling the house but you're not going to get as much and the divorce is going through. I got so manic, seeing symbols and portents everywhere, that I began to fear for my mind. I got back into the hospital and they calmed me down. I had become an unstable taker of the lithium.'

Nick got custody and care and control when the divorce came through, and Isobel received a third share in the sale of the house – only £5,000. There was further depression, continued lithium and then rescue by Isobel's mother. Isobel stayed in America for three years, visiting the children three times a year in England, staying for two weeks at a time with friends. She regained her confidence as an 'OK mother', finding support from other single

147

mothers whom she saw as 'a unique breed, back in control of their lives'. Then came the idea of getting back to England permanently and finding a two-bedroomed flat where the children could stay when they visited. An unexpected windfall in the form of damages after a road accident enabled her to buy her present flat.

'It was here I could be a whole, independent, new woman, because that's what I was. I had learned and coped and survived. I am just about to come off drugs completely after a year's run-down. I've been doing some advertising-space selling. I want to edit, to write, to be in marketing. I take creative writing courses. I'd like to take a degree in typography. And my relationship with my sons goes from strength to strength. When they are with me, they say how long have we got, do we have to go? This may be true with any non-custodial parent but this is the way it is with us. There are friends of their own age we see when they come here and it is as much a normal weekend life as they would have were they living with me full time. I don't think they have said it out loud: we wish we were living with you. They know that I am their mother, and they call their stepmother by her name.

'I'd have to move to a bigger flat if they came to me perma-nently. I realize that. I think of this as an interim place. I don't have any of the old mood swings or feel that I can't cope with the children. I have no doubts about myself. Even my ex-husband has said of course I know that they will come and live with you eventually, though partly he is saying that he doesn't really want to cope with them all the time.

'My sons are entirely different, though they have had the same experiences. One is quiet, the other pugnacious. It's a comfort, one of the things I feel very fortunate about. If I'd had one child and gone through all I had, I think the guilt would be really very present and would be much harder to deal with. But seeing them, seeing how very different they are and the way they have dealt with a very tricky situation . . . They have no memory, thank God, of what I was like back then. But I tell them. I say that Mummy was ill, Mummy got very sad, and felt bad that she couldn't take care of them, that I lived away but that I came to see them.

'I don't think they have any turmoil memories of me, nothing they can't talk about. I do realize that if you don't ask children, they don't give words to their feelings, and are conditioned to give certain answers. They are also very accepting, if you are. If you are not showing anxiety or evasion or guilt they can accept. They have reported to me that their father says things like your mother's crazy. I've asked them: you don't think I'm crazy do you, and they say of course not. They can tell that it's his problem.

'I only had a small amount of psychotherapy. I put myself through my own. I did a hell of lot of reading. I pride myself on doing it for myself.

'Me and men? I haven't got one and I'm beginning to feel the lack. I don't want more children – over forty, that's too old. My fantasy is to find a man about my age who is also a non-custodial parent or part-time parent with girl children. I sometimes get lonely and a bit sex-starved, but the life I've got is the life I planned for, and the life that I wanted which is myself, my space, my learning, my children, my women friends, and the odd tangential man when I can find him.'

The plans are in order, in more senses than one. Isobel's post-natal depression appears to have burned itself out. She has found a new identity for herself, and sees herself as a liberated woman in charge of her life, able to share her sadness and loss with her children.

* * *

These two women, Isobel and Jennifer, appear to have suffered from a post-natal illness which they also, finally, seem to have mastered. Women like them, who are acknowledged to have been mentally disturbed, may be in a double bind in their own minds concerning their illness. If they admit to being ill, they feel less guilty about not making a success of mothering, but then they have to accept that they might be unsuitable (unnatural?) mothers who have damaged their children – which ultimately creates further guilt. They may have to blame and make enemies of husbands, psychotherapists, social workers, mothers-in-law, nannies, in order to reduce the sense of guilt. They may want to delude themselves into thinking that they can cope for no other reason than that they long for their children to be restored to them. And should they delude others and regain their children, they are even more damaged if they discover that the experiment doesn't work.

Their personal sense of disgrace is often compounded by intense public disapproval which only serves to exacerbate their problems. Both Isobel and Jennifer experienced a sense of persecution after giving birth, and both felt it was alleviated by going out to work. Working provides a diversion and a break from the demands of domesticity, but it also gives status and is an antidote to the heavy hand of authority from the medical profession, even from counselling, and from husbands and family. A job, to such women as these, could help restore a sense of autonomy.

Against this 'lifeline' there is the negative effect produced by a society that at a profound level disapproves of working mothers, especially those who openly express dislike of caring for young babies. The importance of work is discussed later. The following chapter contains an examination of post-natal illness, its possible causes and effects.

Chapter 12

ILLNESS AND INJURY

Emotional disturbance is common after childbirth, though usually it is of brief duration. The post-baby 'blues' – an expression used by medical researchers as well as the lay public – is said to affect about half of all new mothers and hits them from about the fourth day after the birth. There may be tearfulness, tension, anxiety, over-activity for no apparent reason. And then within a day or two it's all over as far as the medical profession is concerned. (In fact, adjustment to motherhood can be slow, wearing and worrisome, though there are usually increasing pleasures as a mother and child get to know and love each other.)

Post-natal depression is considered quite distinct from the blues. About 10–20% of women suffer from it, often developing symptoms within a fortnight after delivery, though it may not be recognized until weeks or months later. It is regarded as an acute psychiatric illness, possibly triggered at least partly by hormonal changes. Symptoms include feeling isolated, fearing loss of intellectual faculties, a sense of inadequacy, feeling misunderstood. There may be a constant search for assurance, exaggeration of small problems, constant fatigue, and of course an overwhelming sense of guilt.

Rest and the company of others who have been through it seem to be regarded as the most suitable 'cures', inaccessible as both are to most new mothers. The Association for Post-Natal Illness has a register of women who have suffered and recovered and who are willing to make contact and maintain support. A GP might suggest a short course of anti-depressants. Dr Katharina Dalton, who has made a study of the pre-menstrual syndrome and post-natal depression, is firmly convinced that the problem is hormonal and the solution lies in monthly progesterone suppositories as a general preventative and in a course of injections from the onset of labour for women who have a family history of the condition. An intramuscular injection of oestrogen and testosterone is another suggestion by

151

doctors who believe that it will ensure normal hormonal balance and act as a preventative.

Post-natal depression can last for weeks or months. It may actually go undiagnosed because doctors and health visitors and women themselves can fail to recognize the condition, seeing nervousness, incompetence, clumsiness and lethargy as qualities requiring a moral judgement rather than medical care. Health visitors make a routine home visit around the eleventh or twelfth day, which is not the 'peak' time for problems to show, and though there is a support structure provided by health visitors, mother and baby clinics and the sixth-week hospital out-patient check, surveys of mental health in the community suggest that 'the great majority of such problems remain unnoticed, or at least unremarked, by most health visitors and doctors'. The quote is from R. Kumar, senior lecturer at the Institute of Psychiatry, in the book *Motherhood and Mental Illness*.

There is a danger that social workers will consider a woman suffering from post-natal depression to be an unfit mother, especially if she has no husband or close family support. Mary Woolliscroft – see Chapter 7 – was a victim of such thinking, and she lost her baby permanently through pressure from her social worker, when the answer might have been short-term fostering.

It is impossible to know how damaged children of post-natally depressed mothers might be. Psychoanalysts have observed placatory behaviour in toddlers with disturbing and potentially violent mothers. Their modes of survival may include attaching themselves more strongly to their fathers or other close relative while at the same time they distance themselves from their mothers.

Children of mothers suffering from maternal depression respond with greater variation than is often assumed. A study of forty-nine young depressed mothers with two-year-old children showed that general intellectual levels and language comprehension of the children matched those in a control group of non-depressed mothers and children. Despite this, the depressed mothers made fewer verbal approaches and were less positive in their interactions with their children. Demands of high intensity were met, but lower-level requests tended to be ignored, and more confrontations occurred which ended either with the mother capitulating or ignoring her child. Depressed mothers were also more likely to have had a negative view of their own mothers when they were children, to have truanted from school and to have had their first child at a young age. Housing or environment were more likely to be poor, marital relations less than satisfactory.

About 10–12% of women suffering from post-natal depression (amounting to 1% of all mothers) do not respond to rest or counselling or a short course of anti-depressants. They go on to develop a full-scale post-natal psychosis, often a year after delivery, which can include frightening mood changes, hallucinations and an outright rejection of the baby, though in time most recover. Sufferers tend to be older mothers, possibly with premature or low-weight babies. They may be disappointed about the sex of their child and have a fear of life getting out of control, as Isobel's case demonstrates.

Abnormal ideas about the baby are the things that worry doctors and health visitors most. Consultant psychiatrist F. Margison of the West Didsbury Hospital, Manchester, made a study of 245 mothers suffering from post-natal illness (in *Motherhood and Mental Illness*), and noted a number of delusions and preoccupations, including exaggerated concerns about cot death and feeding, and delusional beliefs which were not open to reassurance, such as 'the baby is all blue, he's withering away to a bare skeleton', 'the baby has been poisoned by blowflies'. Other delusions revolved round special powers: the baby is the new Jesus Christ, or son of the Devil, or 'he can put thoughts into my head'. There were ideas that the child was a monster, ie 'a vampire bat', which led to rejection or hostility, sometimes an intense hatred and a stated desire to kill the child.

Women measured themselves against ideals of motherhood and found themselves guiltily lacking, making comments like 'I just don't seem to be able to feel love like a mother should.' They saw themselves as inadequate and unfit to be mothers.

The delusions distinguish them from mothers with post-natal depression, but in many ways they are not dissimilar, and not so far removed from any new mother. As Adrienne Rich says in her book *Of Woman Born*, 'What woman has not dreamed of "going over the edge", of simply letting go, relinquishing what is termed her sanity, so that she can be taken care of . . .?' Women can fear their own rage and despair and sheer ambivalence in the face of the enormous responsibilities of motherhood.

An American book, *First-Time Motherhood*, claims that the age of first-time mothers can affect behaviour and perceptions. New mothers in their twenties interviewed in the book felt less engulfed by motherhood than older first-time mothers. Demands on their time, and isolation, took older long-independent mothers by surprise. They felt the disruption of the newborn most keenly and were more likely than younger women to experience depression. They had greater fatigue, less of a support network, and felt that giving up employment for motherhood meant losing part of their identity. The older mothers who adjusted best and enjoyed motherhood most were those who kept their jobs.

Mothers who work part-time in the year following a baby's birth report less depression and anxiety and more satisfaction with their marriages than mothers who are full-time workers or full-time homemakers, according to research by psychologist Janet Shibley Hyde of the University of Wisconsin-Madison. Her findings also suggested that many women sought three to six months' maternity leave and there was a need for them to be guaranteed an option to choose part-time work during an infant's first year.

In another study of motherhood, Joan Raphael-Leff, American psychoanalyst and research psychologist, identified two different types of women at risk of post-natal depression. She calls one the Facilitator, the kind of woman who sees motherhood as a high point of her identity and who dedicates herself to the baby's well-being by adapting herself to the task and meeting all his or her needs.

The second type, the Regulator, embarks on pregnancy and maternity with a different attitude. She regards herself primarily as a person, and secondarily as a mother. Birth is part of a temporary retirement, a transient disturbance in her life. She aims to reinstate her pre-natal lifestyle as soon as possible.

Obstetric complications at the birth may trigger depression in either type. The Facilitator feels that natural childbirth enhances her baby's entry into life. Obstetric intervention is a source of anxiety and imbues a sense of failure. The Regulator assumes birth to be a surgical experience, with all modern analgesics to minimize danger and discomfort, but unexpected complications can also throw her. She may feel out of control and incompetent when well-laid expectations go wrong.

Once home, the Facilitator goes for total immersion and is upset by prosaic interruptions between herself and the baby. She will feel that separation – if the baby is hospitalized or in a special care unit – is an irredeemable loss which erodes her high standards concerning motherhood. Should she feel impatience or have any negative reactions towards the baby, there will be strong guilt feelings.

The Regulator is less likely to enjoy the closeness and the demands of a young baby. She may feel threatened by the helplessness, the messiness and greed. The seemingly full-time enslavement of the first few weeks can erode her self-esteem and threaten her sense of identity.

The horrors of enforced separation are principally what hurt Facilitators together perhaps with a fear of expressing any negative feelings. And the equal horrors of enforced togetherness unsettle Regulators. According to Raphael–Leff's research, 40% of Regulators and 36% of Facilitators experience depressive symptoms

154

which include sleep or appetite disturbance, tearfulness, diminished libido, especially in the first six weeks. There is another danger period later: after a year for Regulators, when the baby begins to walk and needs constant supervision, and after two years for Facilitators, when they feel they are no longer indispensable and all-providing.

Regulators sound remarkably like those older first-time mothers missing their personal freedom in the American study *First-Time Motherhood*. They also bear more than a passing resemblance to most fairly liberated young women today, some of whom may complicate the research by wanting minimal obstetric intervention (they will surely be conversant with modern arguments which are for natural processes and against things that interfere with them). Perhaps adequate provision for parental leave would tide them over just as well as drugs or even rest.

Of course, a job – or other facilities to reduce a mother's isolation and immobility – will not always prevent mental illness. No one can really pinpoint what tips the depressed mother into a full-scale depression or psychosis. Current uncertainties lead to inconsistency in treatment. Women and mental illness of any kind are a potent combination, inviting prejudices and assumptions about the nature of women, their expectations and conditioning. Post-natal mental illness is particularly at risk of varying opinions and attitudes which will determine the treatment offered. Anti-depressants, for instance, may be the last thing a hormonally-triggered illness needs. A side effect of some anti-depressants is manic-depressive symptoms. Manic-depressive symptoms are similar to those in post-natal psychosis.

Isobel reports having had strong mood swings, and feels that hers was a hormonal problem. After a course of anti-depressants failed to help she was eventually stabilized on lithium which is considered by many to be the most appropriate drug for post-natal psychosis and manic-depressive illness. ECT (electroconvulsive therapy) is also used for delusional depression and is considered superior to anti-depressants.

Jennifer seems to have resisted 'heavy drugs'. In the sixties and seventies, there was a strong reaction against anti-psychotic drugs and ECT. They were considered to be over-used by psychiatrists, particularly with women patients who did not conform to traditional ideas of femininity. No doubt in some centres they still are over-prescribed, but they have a central place in the treatment of post-natal mental illness which may have been denied to those who turned to the fashionable 'anti-psychiatrists' of the time.

Psychotherapy or counselling have their place too, even when hormonal disturbance is thought to be the trigger and drugs the

155

answer. If hormones affect behaviour, then the consequences of the behaviour must be taken into account. There is a strong case for bringing partners into the picture and looking carefully at the relationship. Women who want to go back to work, or merely maintain some independence, may experience conflict if their partners impose traditional ideas, no matter how subtly they do it. How often does a post-natal psychosis follow an unhappy marriage? Or to put it another way, how many women who reject their children are doing so as a way of rejecting their partners? Perhaps the direction and duration of both Isobel's and Jennifer's illnesses would have been different if some attempt had been made to involve their husbands.

Partners can bring various pressures to bear on the uncertainties of post-natal illness. Husbands, according to Frances Jones, a mental-health social worker, are very keen on the 'baby blues' label and they subtly encourage women to disguise more serious symptoms. 'Women learn to disguise symptoms in hospital anyway, because they want to demonstrate that they are good mothers and they feel guilty when they think they are not. They are motivated to appear sane because so much is at stake.'

They are also understandably reticient about all those devilish delusions and, says Frances, need to build up a real trust in doctors, nurses or social workers before they reveal their terrible secret. 'It takes skilled assessment by staff, and I don't think they always have it. Sometimes I've had women confess to me that they see it as their duty, a mission, to kill their baby since it was conceived by the devil. One woman felt it was all right when the baby was sleeping, but when its eyes were open they seemed to belong to the devil. These ideas may be kept secret unless you gain the woman's trust.'

In the mother and baby units where Frances has worked, there appears to be a great variation in treatment. 'It really seems to depend on the individual consultant. It could be drugs, psychotherapy, low-key counselling. Husbands almost never get any help. But they may be hurt, let down, and they may see the mother's rejection of the baby as part of a rejection of themselves. They might also genuinely be in danger, because some women show violence to their husbands.'

Women may show violence to themselves, their children or other close relatives when suffering from post-natal illness. A young woman of twenty-six was reported in a newspaper as having strangled her two children and taken an overdose after she was told that she had six months to prove herself a capable mother. She survived and was committed indefinitely to a secure hospital unit, having admitted manslaughter on grounds of diminished responsibility. The court heard that she was suffering from a chronic depressive illness.

A nineteen-year-old was given a life sentence but was freed after appeal judges accepted that she was temporarily unbalanced. She had given birth to a baby in secret and was said to be suffering from post-natal depression when she battered her mother to death with a hammer.

In Japan, where the Suicide Prevention Association reports about 300 cases a year of parent-child suicide, it is considered more merciful and honourable for a suicidal parent to kill a child than leave it behind. If a parent survives, he or she can face murder charges, but no charges are filed if a parent was considered mentally deranged at the time, a condition that is particularly applied to mothers.

Chronic depressive illness, post-natal depression, mental derangement . . . The labels are different in each case, though the condition may be the same. It is no wonder that treatment varies according to consultants in charge. If Jennifer had not been diagnosed as schizophrenic perhaps she would not have been considered incurable and unfit to mother, but might have received treatment to pull her through her crisis without the further conflicts and despair that dragged her down a second time.

Fear of the devil, or of being possessed – one of the common reasons for committing violence – runs through many of the case histories of women with a post-natal illness. In psychotherapy theory, this is most likely to be interpreted an an indirect means of expressing personal anger towards the child – an emotion which may be generated by anger towards the woman's own mother. The anger is so consuming that it has to be projected onto someone else, in this case a known figure of evil. For some women, a post-natal illness may be the only way they dare show their negative feelings about motherhood.

Other sources of the anger may fit less well with the professionals' view – they may themselves be part of the problem, for instance, and inspire feelings of impotence in their clients. If a woman feels helpless and trapped by motherhood, she may fear the weight of paternalism, and experience a sense of rage at being disbelieved or calmed down by male doctors and husbands or other authority figures. And there is the fear of male violence (it is after all, a male devil and not a female witch who is usually the evil figure).

Sexual perversion in women is often directed towards children and involves a compulsive desire to inflict pain, according to psychotherapist Estela Welldon. Motherhood is a suitable vehicle for perversion in women who hate themselves, hate their bodies and hurt their children as a way of wounding themselves.

Invoking the devil may be a more widespread and less abnormal fear than is supposed. Few who saw Roman Polanski's film *Rosemary's Baby* can forget the horror and the morbid fascination that the film inspired. Few at the moment of a child's birth will resist counting fingers and toes before they ask 'is it a girl or boy?' We are all susceptible to fear of the abnormal, especially in such volatile moments of existence as childbirth. In Spain, a medieval torture was to saw in half a woman who was suspected of being pregnant by the devil – hardly the poor victim's psychosis, more a case of mass hysteria and superstition. But a vulnerable new mother, faced with the urgency and greed of a small baby, may fear being taken over by its power, if only for one split second. Giving birth to a monster seems the ultimate defilement, the invasion of one's body by some alien creature, followed by the shame and guilt that one has brought this evil into the world. It is not difficult to understand something of the feelings a woman might experience once her mind has lingered for longer than that split second on the awful possibilities.

Will drug treatment without adequate counselling or psychotherapy take the logic of 'abnormal ideas' into account? Does counselling itself always acknowledge the external circumstances of women's lives, circumstances that can actually push some over the edge? Might the idealized view of motherhood and even of womanhood get in the way of understanding perverse sexual behaviour? Do high-tech obstetric techniques turn the process of childbirth into a battlefield and alienate women from their own bodies?

It is likely that hormonal reasons for post-natal illness can never be totally distinguished from other factors such as age or outlook or culturally absorbed ideas or family background, or the birth experience, and the best treatment must arise from taking all aspects into account.

The feminist view of post-natal illness, that it is culturally imposed, is only one part of a complex story. The traditional medical approach, that women are mentally unstable and need controlling drugs, is outdated and destructive. Assuming that a hormonal cause is less of a stigma than mental illness limits understanding and adequate treatment, as does the anti-psychiatry view that eschews all drugs. If professionals are uninterested in the state of the marital relationship, they ignore an important factor. The assurance of a job to go back to, a better understanding of the very real fear of being taken over that must assail any liberated woman, more active cooperation in parenting by fathers, adequate childcare facilities and housing and a more consistent approach to treatment by the medical profession might contribute to less mental illness among women after childbirth.

Chapter 13

WORK AND OTHER 'CURES'

One view concerning child-rearing is that children are the responsibility of parents, and it is they who should get the blame when things go wrong. Looked at more closely, this means that it is unnatural for mothers to want to pursue unmotherly interests like going out to work, a view that is out of touch with reality given that women increasingly see themselves as 'Regulators' in charge of their own lives, or have to earn money to support themselves. The American research on post-natal illness in the previous chapter suggests that women are less likely to experience depression if they have a job to go back to.

But finding adequate childcare can be a huge problem. Nursery hours rarely fit with a normal working day, so employment is often limited to part-time. State day nurseries provide for only about 1% of children under five. Holiday play schemes for children simply do not exist in many parts of the country. There are no provisions for sick leave for parents, or parental leave on the birth of a child, even today with the new interest in women returning to work. Whatever is said about parental responsibility, the bulk of it in practice is maternal responsibility, and it is women who have to make their provisions as best they can. New development of workplace nurseries, introduced by employers to attract women workers now that there is a shortage of school-leavers to fill low-paid jobs, are only part of the answer.

As a comparison, Denmark provides publicly funded childcare for over 40% of children under the age of three and over 80% of children aged between three and seven. Sweden offers a year's parental leave after the birth of a child (extending to eighteen months in 1991), followed by the right to work part-time until a child is eight. And parents are given 90 days a year leave to care for sick children or for other family reasons. In France, there are *halte-garderies* where children aged from a

159

few months to six years old receive group care, and home helps provide relief for exhausted mothers for several days if need be.

Peter Moss, research officer at the Thomas Coram Research Unit, sums up the effect on childbearing of our incoherent childcare services as follows: 'The present inadequacies in childcare, employment entitlements and in the division of family responsibilities between mothers and fathers have adverse effects on the welfare and health of substantial numbers of children and mothers, through exposing some children to under-resourced, inadequate and poorly regulated services; and placing unnecessary and excessive demands on many mothers, which increase stress both at home and in the workplace.'

When the stresses get too much, it is often the voluntary agencies and local projects that pick up the pieces. Schemes like Family Service Units provide social workers and volunteers to help families and sometimes run playgroups in inner cities. In recent years, small projects have been started by childcare officers and social workers to meet local needs in what might be called a new growth industry.

Wel-Care, a specialist social work agency, runs a small residential centre in Greenwich, London, to 're-educate' mothers who were abused when young. Birmingham's Holly Road Day Care Centre treats families having difficulties with their children, using staff chosen for their practical experience of parenthood rather than qualifications on paper. The Newpin programme – short for New Infant Parent Network – is largely a voluntary organization helping young mothers, first set up through health workers at Guy's Hospital ante-natal clinic in a part of London where child abuse is high. The Home-Start organisation operates in urban and semi-urban areas, assigning volunteers to a family in trouble for anything from six to twenty hours a week for on average a year or more. The schemes are run by independent voluntary organizations with links with social services or a health authority.

Mother and toddler groups at local clinics often aim to help mothers who are perceived as being 'at risk' – those in their very early twenties or younger, who have little access to a garden or local play area for their children, are short of money and have had little education. One study of such groups noted that what the mothers valued most was a break from watching the children and a chance to relax with other mothers.

Education for parenthood in schools focuses on the importance of play for small children, the supposed ignorance about ante-natal care facilities, and the need to inform teenagers, who in today's small families are often unfamiliar with babies, about aspects of infant care.

160

Research sponsored by the Health Education Council in 1986 suggests that the courses have got their priorities wrong. A study involving four schools, with 52 girls and 13 boys over a period of up to a year, revealed that the assumptions of ignorance and false expectations are at best exaggerated and often unwarranted. Before their course started, pupils were knowledgeable about child growth and development in the early stages. Ante-natal care, benefits and even some detail of clinical procedure were well-known. The advantages of breastfeeding and of giving a child love, care and stimulation were common knowledge. There was less awareness of childcare facilities, or lack of them, and almost nothing was known about women's employment rights in relation to maternity leave.

The girls in the study were under no illusion about the loss of social life, the day-to-day responsibility, the isolation and possible depression that can come with motherhood, and were thought to be fatalistic. They expected to get little help from fathers. Pregnancy and motherhood were regarded as a slight indulgence, something for which there might be a price to be paid. Many of the views were derived from personal reflection on what had been seen on television on news, current affairs, popular science programmes and soap operas.

Schoolgirl mothers are a group at risk of being overwhelmed by motherhood, and one scheme from Manchester's Booth Hall Children's Hospital provides home and classroom tuition in conventional academic subjects and in parentcraft. Pupils are mainly aged fifteen to sixteen, and the classroom centres have a crèche on the premises. Other cities have similar schemes – there is one in Liverpool, another in Bradford – but predictably there are too few to meet needs.

Mothering for those who are not at special risk can still be an overwhelming business, especially in the first months. The National Childbirth Trust has a network of post-natal support groups. Members of the Trust are contacted by their local group soon after the birth, which gives young women a break from isolation, a chance to meet neighbours which may not have been available when they were working, and of course the very necessary opportunity to share experiences. Gingerbread, the organization for single parents, and the Meet-a-Mum groups provide meeting opportunities for women with young children too.

There is a growing interest in improving parenting for those who feel they are not doing too well at it. The therapy-oriented organization Exploring Parenthood aims to 'bring together stressed parents and caring professionals in an atmosphere of mutual cooperation and respect'. Another organization, Parent Link, trains parents to set up support groups throughout the country, with the aim of helping to improve relationships between parents and children.

And what of the children who have suffered in their infancy and may still be suffering from parental neglect or abuse? NAYPIC (National Association for Young People in Care) is a small pressure group and information centre which wants to see more help given to people who have been in care and are no longer the responsibility of the State once they reach eighteen. NAYPIC is campaigning for better preparation for living alone, a wider choice of accommodation and more emotional and financial support.

The Child Psychotherapy Trust is campaigning for the training of child psychotherapists in areas where none exist. There are fewer than 200 trained specialists in the London area, and only a handful in the whole of the rest of the UK. The Trust would like to establish walk-in clinics for adolescents and weekly crisis sessions for mothers and babies. In child guidance centres where treatment is available, psychotherapists help children to come to terms with powerful feelings following such traumas as neglect, abuse and the breakdown of a relationship between parent and child.

What all of these schemes and services demonstrate is that the path of motherhood does not run smoothly for many women. Probably far more need help than currently receive it, given the patchy nature of the services. A report on a 1986 conference held by the Marcé Society, the psychiatrists' organization concerned with post-natal illness, included the fact that 'in Sweden over the past ten years there has been a distinct decline in post-natal depression'. No clear reason was given, but factors thought relevant were 'freely available abortions, paternity leave and good, flexible social/health support systems', ie factors that, on the whole, are lacking in the UK.

If schoolgirls in child development classes are resigned to the potential isolation and depression associated with motherhood, and regard the undertaking as an indulgence for which a price has to be paid, then there is something seriously wrong with the current demands made upon women to be mothers. If they want children, then they have to put up with the consequences, seems to be the message received. For some, like Isobel and Jennifer and others in this book, the burden is so great that it crushes them.

SECTION IV

The Price of Handicap

Chapter 14

TO CARE OR NOT TO CARE

In Doris Lessing's novel *The Fifth Child*, a mother finds herself isolated from her family after she gives birth to a strange, powerful, destructive infant and insists on bringing him up at home, though his presence and actions tear the family apart. The child is some kind of primitive throwback, not handicapped or even hyperactive in the conventional sense, but a genetic mistake, incapable of normal, loving responses. His presence, it is implied, is a threat to modern society. Yet his mother is driven to self-sacrifice on his behalf, at the same time sacrificing her marriage, her other children and her lovingly nurtured extended family. She does this because no one else will show compassion to the social outcast she has given birth to – neither her family, who see only senseless destruction in the child, nor the professionals who refuse to offer any constructive help for his unclassifiable abnormality. She also does it because she herself is a kind of throwback, a traditional family-building woman who has always stood apart from her smarter, self-seeking contemporaries.

The circumstances of Lessing's heroine are exceptional, but any mother of a handicapped child might find herself being persuaded by family or friends to relinquish her child to residential care on the grounds that she is being unfair to herself, if not to others. At the same time, she might receive pressure from professionals to keep her child at home. Both of these influences are very much part of contemporary trends. The first reflects a widespread resistance to the idea of the woman as victim; the second reflects current policies to integrate the disabled into the community – whether the community has suitable facilities or not.

Liberating ideas concerning women have a direct impact on mothers of handicapped children too. They may feel – and feel freer to express – love/hate emotions. They may experience great conflict over who could or should come first. They may choose to put their child into residential care, and evoke the disapproval not only of professionals, but also of other mothers who continue to look after their own handicapped children. They may live with a sense of guilt that is as searing as that of any woman who gives up her child, for whatever reason.

When a woman gives birth to a handicapped baby, she and her partner are likely to be stunned, but not necessarily rejecting. Feelings of love and protection are often uppermost, and there may be no question of 'giving up' the baby. But some parents are so shocked and ill-prepared for the news that a child is disabled at birth, that they have been known to leave it to the care of the hospital and blot the entire episode from their memories. Others fail to bond with the child though they do take care of it, at least initially. Often the mother will respond to her baby and the father will not. Sometimes it's the other way round.

In many ways those who are told of the problem straight away are more fortunate than those whose baby is not diagnosed as having some disability for many months or even years, even though they suspect the worst themselves. The medical profession has a poor record on really listening to what mothers say and accepting that sometimes the maternal instinct is in advance of medical detection. The imparting of bad news is often abrupt and lacking in sensitivity, reflecting a sense of unease and lack of training on the part of the professionals. Parents, often totally ignorant of the meaning of a diagnosis, may be given little information or support or access to a self-help group where they may gain knowledge and experience from others.

Keeping the handicapped at home is a cheaper solution than keeping them in institutions. There are also more humane reasons, though the humanity does not always extend to the carers who bear the brunt of looking after them. Help does exist within social services and through charities, and it has increased in recent years, since government policies have decreed that the disabled should live within the community, and hospitals are closing. But this help is exceedingly patchy and piecemeal. When support is lacking and information sparse or given with little sensitivity, a relationship between parents and a handicapped child is more likely to break down, or never develop in the first place.

Before the nineteenth century, it was normal in Western society to absorb the handicapped within the community. The village idiot, unkind a term as it is, illustrates both the normality of such a person and the somewhat low-key ostracism he or she was likely to experience. In a pre-industrial society there would be sufficient family members to share in giving basic support, and sometimes there would also be basic work that a handicapped person could perform. What was lacking was any serious attempt to educate or increase potential, though schools did exist for the deaf in England from the seventeenth century, and for the blind in the eighteenth.

With industrialization came greater ruthlessness in deciding who were and who were not valuable members of society, but at the same time newly-awakened philanthropic instincts brought into existence charities to aid the new misfits. Residential care grew, and fund-raising for the associated charities became an absorbing activity for well-meaning Victorian ladies. Unfortunately, institutional life for the recipients meant segregation, sometimes cruelty and neglect, often even less stimulation than they would have got at home.

Today, some residential care is still run on Victorian lines, but there are places which are excellent, with increasing emphasis on rehabilitation and self-help. Perhaps we are on the way to a genuinely pluralistic approach, though that can only occur if institutions are not closed and community facilities are available to all who need them.

The following interviews are with women who put their handicapped children into residential care, and with one woman who has her child at home. As will be seen, it makes little difference whether a child is physically or mentally handicapped, though some are both. The problems for mothers of children with any kind of disability are not that dissimilar. Even the degree of disability may be less important than other factors, such as the mothers' personal ability to tolerate certain difficulties, their economic situation, the support they can find or are offered, the state of their marriage. However, there is some evidence that mentally handicapped children actually present more problems than physically handicapped. Hyperactivity, speech and learning disabilities and emotional disturbances may put more strain on parents than, say, an inability to walk, or deafness or blindness.

* * *

'I felt so guilty. You do feel guilty if a child isn't perfect or has faults and you've put that child away.'

Jeannette was seventeen years old when she had her first baby, a son, Peter, later found to be mentally handicapped. Jeannette is now thirty-eight, a rounded, jolly-looking woman with an underlying air of frailty. Peter is twenty-one. She has three younger children, all normal. Five years ago she divorced and remarried soon after, and now lives happily with her second husband and her two youngest children. Peter has lived in residential care since the age of seven. Within the last year, Jeannette has

167

been having counselling in an effort to understand her feelings about Peter.

'He appeared normal when he was born, though looking back at old photos now he did look a little strange. It was a difficult delivery, but nobody said anything. I found out when he was about two. He hadn't reached the milestones other babies had. He didn't smile very much and he looked through you rather than at you. It was suggest by some people that he might be deaf, so we got that checked.

'He was fifteen months old and they said they'd take his tonsils and adenoids out. But there was no improvement. It became obvious there was something wrong, though I didn't assess it. He didn't sleep. He just wasn't like other children. We went to a psychologist at Great Ormond Street Hospital. He was two and a half, and by then I had an eighteen-month-old and I was expecting another. I remember we sat in this room and the psychologist said I'm sorry to tell you that your child is handicapped. He had brain damage and would be a bit slow, nothing more. They gave us a leaflet and said we'll make an appointment to see you in four years. And that was it. That was honestly it.

'We came out and it was as if my life switched off and has never really switched on again. I was thinking perhaps I ought to jump under a bus. My husband and I never really talked about it. I went and sat up in the bedroom and didn't want to speak to anybody.

'My GP said go out and buy yourself something nice and cheer yourself up. My health visitor, for whom I am eternally grateful, was very sympathetic. But it got worse and worse as Peter got older. He became difficult to cope with, doubly incontinent. He would be covered in shit from head to toe when you went in in the morning, and it would be on the walls, everywhere. At three, four, five, six, every day. We lived with my mum, but I had little support from outside. There was no help.

'He went to day school when he was four. He'd go off in a coach. In the holidays there was no relief till near the end of his living with me, when he went for short breaks. It was all really horrendous. I was in a wave of being, not really there. He couldn't speak, so he was frustrated. My little ones were very frightened of him. He would go for them and I think they suffered dreadfully. My husband adored him but we couldn't talk. I don't know why, guilty probably.

'I think I wanted him to go at the end because I was at the end of my tether. I was twenty-four. I had three other small children. I hadn't slept through the night for four years. I really wanted to kill him sometimes. I never hurt him but I may have neglected him a bit. I really wanted him to die, and I still fantasize that he dies and I fantasize that I'm at his funeral. I picture the relatives feeling sorrow and weeping.

'He went at seven, and it was a joint decision between the local specialist and me. I think I would have had more support at home nowadays, even though there would have been more pressure for me to keep him. Help with the incontinence, for instance.

'**So we just gave him away really. The day he went – how can you explain what that's like?** I remember packing his toys in a box. I was crying and my husband came and put his arms round me but I pushed him away. That was the last time we ever communicated about him emotionally I suppose. It was as if I put up a door that I never opened until now. What's so awful is that nobody took any notice. It was just like any other day. And I had had him for nearly seven years.

'We were advised in the early days not to see him very often. The matron was stiff and starchy and said leave it for six weeks to let him settle down. Visiting always has been very erratic. We went through periods of going every week on a Sunday, and we still go about every month and take him for a drive.

'I've never come to terms with having a handicapped child. I find it extremely difficult to be in public places with him. I'm very embarrassed. I'm very angry, with him, with myself, people, everybody. I don't know if he is happy or not. How can we know? He doesn't appear to enjoy life. He doesn't speak. He doesn't greet us with pleasure. He is physically very mobile and not usually incontinent now, but his quality of life is so poor. He kind of recognizes his dad. Mainly the people who visit are me and my second husband. I don't think he recognizes me. He bites his hands right through – they are scarred and bleeding. I get sick and revolted by him. When I visit, it's like I'm visiting a prison. I come out and the door is locked behind me.

'The guilt comes because you are relieved when they are gone. I felt a sense of failure as a mother because I couldn't cope. You don't want to tell people what you've done. You felt you had to make excuses as to why. But I was so cut off and very young. I think what am I saying now is that I want someone to recognize just what I did those seven years, someone to say, good work girl, you did your best. But I've got to believe that myself. The media tells you to be a proper mother, but no one looks after you.

'Two years ago, I felt I had to have a proper answer to what was wrong with him. We had been led to believe it was brain damage, but a specialist two years ago said this was not an adequate diagnosis. He said Peter was autistic, and in a way that made it easier because he had a label. I felt so guilty. You do feel guilty if a child isn't perfect or has faults and you've put that child away. That's something that's very hard to come to terms with.'

* * *

'As for the notion of self-sacrifice, well, it just wasn't me. I felt the pull to try, but I couldn't even sustain it when he was a tiny baby.'

Davina is fifty-six and a health professional. She is married and has two sons aged eighteen and sixteen. The older of the two, Philip, was born with Down's syndrome, and has grown up in a residential home. Davina is a powerful-looking woman with a strong personality. She has a high-status position within the NHS.

'We'd been married just over a year when my first son was born. I was thirty-seven and working full time as a health visitor. He was born just before amniocentesis was being used. [*A test for abnormalities performed on older mothers during pregnancy.*] The hazards of late pregnancies were known then and I had anxieties. When he was born they gave him to me in the labour ward, which struck me as a little odd. I didn't have my glasses on and I didn't see anything wrong. I remember checking that he had all his fingers and toes but I think my defence mechanism was so strong that I didn't entertain the idea of anything wrong. They told us about three days later.

'It was suggested by the obstetrician, whom I'd known from my nursing days, that I might leave him in the hospital and let them worry about it. I knew it wasn't a severe case and I couldn't do it.

'I married late but I didn't develop professionally in my early working life. I had tremendous expectations of marriage and motherhood. My life was going to be home-based. Before I got pregnant I was encouraged by my boss to go for promotion, but I said no because I was going to have babies.

'A year later, I had the baby and things had not turned out as I'd expected. Although I took him home because I could not face the empty-arm syndrome, I did not manage very well. I was desperately depressed, so disappointed. There was all that stuff about how you can do so much if you stimulate the child, and I stimulated till it was coming out of my ears. When he did smile, I burst into tears. I was terribly torn. My husband, well, he'd no idea what it was all about.'

Davina returned to full-time health visiting after her three months' maternity leave were up, just as she had planned. Her son was left with a local childminder, but she found the taking and fetching exhausting. A paediatrician friend arranged for Davina to have a break by taking the baby into hospital for a couple of weeks.

'When he came out, I was still depressed and stressed. My minder said she would have him on a full-time weekly fostering basis. We took him there on a Sunday night and I had him just for the weekend. I loved that. I had a baby. I could do my bit, and I could go to work. The minder's family was super, and it was an excellent arrangement.

'My husband had supported me extremely well at the time of the birth and for three or four weeks after. But he has never been happy or permanent working anywhere and he wants a great deal of attention and sympathy.

'When Philip was a bit over a year old, I was pregnant again. This time I was able to have a test and all was well. I was thinking about giving up work, not to have Philip with me, but to look after the new baby and do some work from home. We couldn't afford to go on paying for the fostering, and we approached social services to see if they would pay. Philip was two and a half by then. His development was slow, but he was a very happy child, very easy to manage.

'I was aware of criticisms within my family about all this. Though there was one aunt who had a child with Down's syndrome who wrote to me and said let him go. They do survive by the way, to a normal lifespan today, through better nutrition and encouraging mobility.'

Davina's application to social services was not accepted. She started to pull strings, and eventually her paediatrician friend came up with a temporary vacancy in a small home, really two suburban houses owned by a private charity. The local authority was prepared to pay for this, and Philip was duly installed. He is still in this home today.

'**The whole social work philosophy then and somewhat now is that the children should be in a nuclear family. Perhaps I am being defensive, but I do not see children like Philip growing into sufficiently independent adults to make a life on their own**. They are going to need some kind of protection and shelter, and that inevitably means living with other people. Philip has grown up with a family group that is going to stay together. His home is with them. If you like, they are his siblings. The staff change, but who are we to question the quality of the relations with the people there who don't change? There isn't anybody who is going to take care of them all their lives. As for the notion of self-sacrifice, well, it just wasn't me. I felt the pull to try, but I couldn't even sustain it when he was a tiny baby.'

The birth of Davina's second son was quick, easy and success-ful. She had taken a scholarship recommended by her tutor, and was able to return to teaching a couple of days a week soon after his birth. The baby went to a local minder on those days.

'I freelanced for four years, and was offered a full-time job when my younger son started nursery school. My husband had given up working in an office and was starting up a small nursery grow-ing plants. My job soon became very challenging and absorbing.

'My relationship now with my children? With Philip we've always had what is I suppose a fairly loose relationship. It has gradually got to the stage where he has more fun where he lives than he does when he comes to us. He probably comes about once a month, that's what I say if anybody asks us. But I think we delude ourselves and I would say it's probably about once in six weeks. He doesn't come on holiday, but does come two or three days around Christmas.

'He loves going out with us. We take him to my sister's. He is very sociable and loves doing all that. What has developed is the gradual acceptance that I am not the chief carer in his life. He went to school, and we used to go to their activities. So we're sort of back-up people. The first nursery nurse he had at the home still lives near, and she is his registered foster mother and has maintained a relationship with him. He goes to stay with her and her family. It is probably true that his contact there is stronger than it is with us. And with her children too, yes.

'My younger son has found it very hard. One Christmas, when he was at primary school, I had collected Philip and then went to collect him. The next term when I saw the teacher she said that was the first time she had ever heard about Philip. Whenever my younger son drew the family, he would draw Mummy and Daddy and Granny and never included Philip. But it was on the school record. I'd made no secret of it. The teacher said she had asked my son who Philip was, and he'd said, oh, he's a boy who comes to stay.

'I think he found it difficult to come to terms with it all. Philip is very uninhibited, and that was embarrassing. Philip is not at all physically handicapped, and he can look after himself, like wash and that kind of thing. He can lay the table and can do shopping, though you need to be with him. He can just write his name.

'We're at the stage when he is very jealous of his brother. That has gone on for quite a long time, and it makes my younger son angry and embarrassed. I am quite a strict parent with this one. He is not yet academic, but he is clever and can get away with the minimum. Yes, I suppose I am a little worried that he might be like his father and never stick to anything. I've learned to be direct and honest with him. When he comes home with stories about what all the other boys have got and how he'd like it too, I just say "tough – as far as I'm concerned I'm not parenting those boys, I'm parenting you, and these are my terms."

'Girls don't learn to make decisions that relate to the outside world. There's a book I've read about how to get to the top of the corporation if you're a woman, and it demonstrates that all the games that ordinary boys play are about the rules, how to score goals, who to trample on, how to make it up afterward. Girls have learned how to understand, how to be intuitive, how to respond to people, to the decisions that other people take, to show goodwill, not to show power. To take hold of your life is very frightening if you didn't spend your childhood doing that. I think being angry with my husband, and also at times being angry with male colleagues, was to do with that.'

* * *

'The future just terrifies me. Josh is five years old and he's difficult to cope with now. He's going to get heavier and bigger.'

Alison is thirty-three. She has a daughter aged six months, and also a son, Josh, now five. Josh is a spastic. He suffers from cerebral palsy, a brain abnormality that affects posture, speech and, in his case, intelligence. He cannot feed himself or sit up without support. He cannot walk or talk, and understands just a few words. He is in nappies but has control of bowel and bladder movements to some extent. He is taken daily to a special school where he can stay till he is sixteen or eighteen. Alison and her husband have Josh at home with them. Alison runs a holiday letting agency from her home.

'We started by taking Josh to doctors and saying hey, there's something not right with our baby. He was about four months old. He was not doing the things that other babies do, like with normal babies their legs just open so you can put the nappy on. But with Josh I couldn't do it. His legs were stiff. But nobody would believe me. It was "first baby isn't it, dear?" all that kind of stuff. Very patronizing. I kept saying I know what a baby should be doing. This baby isn't doing it.

'He was crying all the time, and the doctors passed it off as three-month colic, four-month colic, five-month colic, six-month colic. At seven months they started to believe me and said they'd do some tests. They diagnosed cerebral palsy, and it was very severe. They should have picked it up much earlier.

'During this time my husband and I went through a very bad period. He was convinced there was something wrong and he thought I wasn't getting anything done about it. I was convinced that there was something wrong, but was terrified. I didn't want it to be something wrong, I wanted it to get better, and it didn't. Being put off by the doctors didn't help.

'When the diagnosis was made, they didn't tell us anything about his potential, except that he might be able to hold a pencil one day. That was all. Did that mean he was going to be able to write? They didn't say. The dreaded word spastic came out, but they avoided telling us anything and didn't make it easy to ask questions. And this was in a big teaching hospital in London.

'The consultant lined up the students in the room and he lined up the parents, and he told us. I didn't even know what cerebral palsy was. But I knew the word spastic, and that knocked me out. Then the students all filed out. We had a good cry and a cuddle, and then they all filed back in. Oh it was dreadful, inhuman. They even measured our head circumferences in front of the students to show that our heads were normal and the child's wasn't. It was most degrading, appalling. But at the time I was so fraught I hardly noticed. This was in 1983, in a prestigious teaching hospital, not in the dark ages. My husband was in a rage for a year. He's still in a rage over it. The way they treated us had an effect on the marriage, I'm sure.

'**All we were offered was some genetic counselling if we wanted more children – the last thing we were thinking about at that moment** – and they sent me and Josh for physiotherapy twice a week to the local hospital. When I was there I said to them what would you do if you had a child with cerebral palsy, and they said I'd take my child to the Bobath centre.'

The Bobath centre is a small charity housed in north London, working with children suffering from cerebral palsy. It is supported through private donations and is a teaching centre for physiotherapists from all over the world.

'Going there was like a breath of fresh air. They said yes, your baby is handicapped. He's got A, B, C, D and E, and we're going to do this and that and we're going to stop him crying. Josh was ten months old by then so from seven months till then I'd had a bit of physiotherapy and a lot of heartache. When I was told the worst I could accept it, though it was brutal. It was necessary to be told. In the next two months they got him to sleep through the night. Before that I was up all night cradling this screaming, unhappy, obviously in pain child. And most of the day too. At that time if he lay down, he was like a banana backwards. He went into a spasm. And the doctors had said there was nothing wrong with him. Unbelievable.

174

'The Bobath taught me how to handle Josh, how to dress him, how to relieve his spasms, how to get him to bend in the middle, how to get him to put a hand to his mouth. He has got to be taught everything. You have to teach and repeat again and again and again, and eventually he does learn some of it. He is very happy. You'd never believe that that happy child was howling day and night.

'**Nobody has ever said looking after Josh is ruining my marriage, my life, or anything**. Nobody has offered me any alternative anyway. Twenty years ago your child was put into an institution and you'd visit once a week or whatever, and you were told that the best thing to do dear was to go and have another baby and forget that one. That's something that doesn't happen now. So you're not given that option. But even if I had been given it, I wouldn't have taken it. Maybe if I'd known the day after Josh was born . . . maybe . . . but by the time I'd learnt he was seven months old, and I'd put seven months' hard work into that. I loved him and there was no way that anybody was going to take him away from me.

'I was going to make sure that he'd do all these things that the doctor said he couldn't. Well of course I was wrong. But at the time I was absolutely fired – my marriage or anything else, well forget it. I was fired with getting this child working again. Of course I didn't realize then that he would never work again.

'To think it was a passing remark that led us to the Bobath. And we live a ten-minute drive from the place. I think basically you only get the help if you go and look for it. I've been offered the odd day centre where I can go with my child, but nowhere where I can actually dump my child for ten minutes, except one. There is a Parent to Parent scheme run by Camden council, where they find a family with similar social background but no handicap, and the other family takes your child for a few hours to give you a break. That was helpful for the first three years. The lady they found for me has become a great friend. I used to take Josh to her Wednesday afternoons and I'd go shopping or to the hairdressers or I used to have a bath, without a screaming child – the luxury of that – normally he'd be lying on the floor with twenty-five musical toys going round him and every now and then I'd get out, dripping wet, winding up musical toys, and then get back in the bath again.

'I started working from home a couple of months after Josh was born, at first for just a few hours when I had a nanny or a childminder. I'd been in the travel business before. It was very small then, I had a corner of the dining room. Now it's a full-time job and I have an office upstairs. I travel twice a year to Portugal, for business, and my husband then joins me for a family holiday.

'But very shortly it's not going to work. Josh is so difficult to travel with, and he's so heavy to get on and off aeroplanes and changing nappies. Can you imagine changing a five-year-old's nappies on a crowded aeroplane? He's nearly full height for his age, and he weighs 32 lb. Because he's spastic and because he's stiff he makes a mess, you can imagine. We last travelled with him nearly a year ago, when I was pregnant, and I don't know what we'll do this year. Unless I can find a nanny to take with me, I can't go. I could trust my husband, yes, but I don't think he'd be able to cope on his own. It was difficult enough for him when the baby was born. I had a week in hospital – what bliss, what a rest that was.

'I've had nannies, but they didn't stay. All my family live miles away. I'm thinking of getting an au pair. We haven't been out in the evening since the baby was born.

'She sleeps through the night now, but Josh wakes up two or three times every night. He shouts to me, and I go and I put his covers back on him and I say naughty boy, go back to sleep, it's the middle of the night, and he does. It's usually me who goes, because my husband's answer is to pick him up and bring him in bed with us, which is a disaster. Nobody gets any sleep.

'The baby is a delight, so easy. At six months old they're so wonderful. I feel cheated that Josh missed that. Not cheated for me but cheated for him because he missed that delight, that learning. He was in such pain at that time, such agony, in spasms. And we were handling him incorrectly because we didn't know.

'It's a helluva strain on marriage. For the first year of Josh's life I didn't get any sleep at all. So you can imagine what I was like in the sex department, the cooking-meals department, the washing-clothes department. Well, a husband can only stand so much of that. Also, he was missing out on the cuddles, the kisses, the attention. He had nothing. He didn't have a normal baby, a normal wife, or a normal marriage. And yet he coped, but only just. We had our moments. We had our marriage guidance. If a marriage wasn't as strong as ours, it would have broken up I'm sure.

'**I do understand women putting their child into care – if their marriage is on the rocks because of it, that's one reason**. Perhaps they've got other children, or they love their spouse and they've got to make a choice. It's a very hard decision to make. But I can't see how any mother can't love her child, having borne it. You can have a hundred husbands but your children are yours.

'If I didn't have my business, I'd go mad, completely and utterly mad. Even so, the future just terrifies me. Josh is five

176

years old and he's difficult to cope with now. He's going to get heavier and bigger. The thing that I've slowly realized – and my husband has been saying this since Josh was born more or less – is that he will have to be taken into care one day. That got my hackles up. There was no way anyone was taking my child away. I fought him, probably because I realized he was telling the truth and I didn't want to know. I didn't want to be told at that stage, or even now, that I couldn't cope with my own child.

'But I am beginning to realize that it is true. I'm quite strong, but fairly small, five four. Shortly I'm not going to be able to lift Josh. I'm not going to be able to carry him upstairs to bed.

'I have a friend with a four-year-old daughter with similar disabilities to Josh. Their son is one, and she is now heavily pregnant again. When her son was seven months old, she said that she'd "got rid of" her daughter all week in a respite home, that's a residential place and she is only home at weekends. I was absolutely astonished. I didn't think anybody could have the heart to get rid of their daughter during the week, just because they'd got a new baby. That's what it seemed like to me. She didn't need a residential home. She's little and light and she is more intelligent than Josh, and I couldn't believe it. It surprised me most how hard she was about it. Maybe hardness is necessary. I think I'm far too soft. My husband is hard though he doesn't want to be. But he has to be to keep me in check. I think I'd crack up if he wasn't as he is. He keeps my feet firmly on the ground.'

* * *

Attitudes to caring for the handicapped have changed greatly over the past twenty years. In the early 1960s, Davina was given the option of leaving her Down's syndrome child in hospital after he was born. As a health visitor, she was a professional 'insider', but even she would be unlikely to get such an offer today. In the 1980s, Alison, living in a progressive London borough, was offered minimal help or guidance from her prestigious teaching hospital, and was expected to cope as best she could virtually alone. The volunteer scheme and charity-run clinic came her way more through chance than design. The after-care and support that should back up a policy of keeping handicapped children at home does not exist.

The following chapter looks in a more general way at the cost of handicap to family life.

Chapter 15

ALL IN THE FAMILY

As the women in the previous chapter illustrate, public opinion has changed but public facilities don't meet the needs of women bringing up their handicapped children alone, especially those under school age.

Research reveals the high personal cost of families caring in the community. A government survey by Hilary Green, *Informal Carers*, found that half of all carers, including those looking after disabled children and the elderly, are at risk of psychiatric illness, and 58% are at risk of physical illness, possibly stress-induced. Many suffer from back injuries due to lifting the people in their care. Only one-third of carers looking after someone in their own homes get regular visits from health or social services or from voluntary groups. Facilities offered vary from one local authority to another, depending on their allocation of priorities.

When Jeannette says she would be helped with incontinence today, she speaks with more optimism than is warranted. Some local authorities provide incontinence pads – not necessarily the kind to suit the specific problem. Some have a laundry service. It is even possible to get a one-off payment for a washing machine. But the budget for such items is limited and discretionary.

Families suffer financial burdens through extra heating, laundry costs, special equipment or housing adaptation, as well as transport, especially for hospital visits. Many organizations concerned with the disabled find that people are getting a worse deal since the reorganization of benefits in 1988. Current flat-rate payments are less flexible or geared to individual requirements. Many who would qualify for special grants are unaware of their existence. Sometimes social workers are at fault for discouraging people from claiming, often because they themselves are not properly briefed, according to the Disabled Income Group, which advises the public and health professionals on such matters. The Department of Social Security does make loans available, but there are fears that repayments only add to the burdens of families with long-term commitments to caring and a limited income.

The problem of money and the problem of looking after a highly dependent or uncontrollable child must have an effect on a marriage. For some, the bond is strengthened. A survey of families with spina bifida children revealed that parents married for at least five years and with normal older children coped more successfully than others. When a marriage feels the strain, help is rarely forthcoming, and if anything, insensitive responses by doctors only add to the difficulties. Again there are parallels, this time with mothers suffering from post-natal psychosis, as mentioned earlier in this book.

Alison tells how doctors' dismissals of her fears caused friction between herself and her husband. The manner in which the couple were finally told of their child's condition was clumsy and humiliating. Alison's confidence as a mother had been undermined in the early months before the diagnosis was made, which surely interfered with her ability to share her fears with her husband. Something similar also happened to Jeannette, who still has not come to terms with her sense of failure as a mother.

Some women will look back on those early months as time wasted, time they could have been doing more for their child. Many disturbing emotions must follow the early days and months after the birth of a handicapped child, and there may be much anger against the professionals. Valerie Henson of the Children's Society, who works with young disabled people, speaks of one mother she knows: 'She had been convinced when she was carrying the child that there was something wrong, but no one believed her. Sixteen years on, she felt that the child, who was born with spina bifida and had been in a residential home since she was five, should not have been born. She said if anyone had listened to her, then something would have been done. The feelings are still causing pain, and I don't know how much visiting the child reinforces that pain. Contact is mainly one visit a year and the young person herself telephones once a week.'

As Valerie sees it, the mother somehow felt it was her fault that she had produced a handicapped child, and also her fault that she could not cope. 'And the turmoil has not been resolved sixteen years later.'

Parents are severely shocked when they learn that they have a handicapped child, whether they have already had suspicions or not. When they are told, there may be little opportunity for them to ask questions, but more likely they are too overwhelmed to absorb much information at that first traumatic interview. Too often, those who are available for questioning later – the GP or

179

social worker or health visitor – have little specialist knowledge about the disability. In any case, there is a tendency among the professionals to counsel 'down', ie to suggest a passive acceptance of the child's limitations, often because resources are lacking.

The self-help agencies tend to counsel 'up', sometimes offering unrealistic hopes in their prognoses. Alison was fortunate in finding a private clinic that was both realistic and practical in its help, but it is something she should have found at the hospital. Many young mothers today wish to help a handicapped child reach its full potential as a matter both of love and duty. If they are blocked in this, the sense of failure at having given birth to the child and the sense of hopelessness about the future can only be deepened. There is a truly therapeutic effect in being fired with a purpose and seeing some genuine results.

The main burden of caring for a handicapped child at home usually falls on the mother. Some fathers change their jobs or shorten their working hours, but many, as one father admitted, 'cut themselves off'. Even so, fathers are the chief source of any help the mother may receive. If there are other children in the family, especially daughters, they may be coerced into assisting. Research suggests that they aren't always too happy about it. The presence of a severely mentally handicapped child can interfere with their lives in many ways, curtailing such activities as entertaining friends, family outings, doing homework. Some mothers will be aware of this, others will block out the knowledge because their own needs are too great.

Sometimes the family closes in on itself, feeling misunderstood or even ostracized by the outside world. They may have good reason for this. A government-funded survey of people's attitudes towards mental handicap in the community showed that 25% were strongly opposed to the idea of integration and another 27% didn't like the prospect of community homes for mentally handicapped people anywhere near their own back yard. Reasons given were a concern for the safety of other children and a belief in the need for careful supervision. A more sympathetic 26%, consisting of sixteen- to twenty-four-year-olds, felt the family should take responsibility but lacked conviction about their own contribution in society. Only 22% said they felt comfortable at the prospect of mixing with handicapped people, and most of these were likely to have had contact already.

Jeannette points out the embarrassment of being in public places with a handicapped child, and it takes little imagination to understand what it must be like to avoid the gaze of strangers, or see them avoiding you. Valerie Henson of the Children's Society describes a recent walk in the park with two children in her care.

'They were both ten years old and severely mentally handicapped, and they were of different colour. I had a girlfriend walking with me, so we made a group of four. And the reactions we got from people in the park! We were able to laugh – not at the children, but at the way the general public reacted to us. At one point, I saw a woman watching. She spent a good twenty minutes looking at us. She sat on one bench, and then she went to another. She was fascinated by us.

'We had our hands full with the children, one was sitting and managing perfectly well with an ice cream. The other would have dropped hers if I had given it to her, so I was holding hers and every now and then she'd lunge forward and take a bit, then twiddle her thumbs or a twig and attempt to eat the twig. That was fine. But what does the general public think? My friend and I sat and talked about it and we said we could understand in all honesty why families actually stop taking their children out and keep them at home. They lock away their pain and sadness and humiliation, because they cannot cope with the way others will relate to them. We were able to in some way because the children were not biologically ours. I care about them. I love them. But they are not biologically mine, and maybe that is one aid for me in coping with them.'

Humour and some detachment are a great help. But Britain is not known for its accommodation of young children in public places, handicapped or not.

Retreating into the nuclear family is hardly a way of bringing the disabled into the community, and is not terribly good for the child, or for siblings, who may sense that their disabled brother or sister brings shame to the family. It can also turn mothers into martyrs, who refuse outside help because it is regarded as a slur on their ability to cope. A sense of failure will be all the greater if their dedication proves not to be enough and they finally choose residential care.

Women who do give up their children can suffer for many years. Whether they suffer more than other women in this book who give up children in different circumstances is hard to say. But they suffer differently, and to some extent can do so more publicly, being possibly less on the defensive about their decision since they do receive public sympathy. However, there is no thought given to any kind of counselling for such women or their partners, though they will be in contact with health professionals when they put a child into residential care. Jeannette is receiving counselling fifteen years later. She was seventeen when her autistic son was born, and had three more children in quick succession. It is hardly surprising that her action still haunts her, or that the first seven years seem devalued by her final decision. (Alison too speaks of 'seven months' hard work' that she had put into caring for her son, as if it would have been wasted had she given up her child then.)

Some social workers will put pressure on a mother to keep her child, especially if she had done so for several years. Why give up now? they may ask, thus putting a spanner in the works if the wife succumbs to their pressure but the husband resists. Valerie Henson thinks 'it is right and proper for families to admit that caring at home may not be appropriate any longer.' But how many social workers make it easy for families to confess such a thing?

Perhaps it was Davina's experience as a health professional or her career ambitions that made her tough enough to know what she wanted and to go for it, though her son is quite mildly disabled. She was also depressed and perhaps already disappointed in her marriage. And she was aided by a climate that accepted residential care.

What kind of support schemes operate to help mothers keep their children today? As with other kinds of aid, they can be good or bad, depending on the area. Alison mentioned a Parent to Parent scheme run by her local social services, whereby a family with normal children is 'matched' and the mother of this family takes the disabled child for a few hours a week. Such schemes are run by several local authorities, but they do depend on volunteers and don't offer great respite. Some local authorities have day centres where mothers can go with their children, though they have to stay too.

Where social services are lacking, a charity is sometimes able to fill the gap. Mencap offers a personal advisory service to parents, a support service to give carers time off and many other projects. The Children's Society runs a Parents and Children Together scheme in York, which links families with a substitute carer. Contact A Family puts families whose children have special needs in touch with one another, and also has a telephone service that passes on details of local and national self-help groups. The Crossroads scheme provides trained care attendants to help in the home. KIDS has a purpose-built holiday centre open throughout the year for children with mental and physical handicaps, and also teaches cued speech, a method of communicating with hearing-impaired children. This group uses volunteers to help at local centres during school holidays too.

As much as anything else, what these projects do is bring families together to share their experiences and exchange ideas and contacts. But there are no prizes for guessing that what most mothers want more than anything else is a break from being the carer on a regular, reliable basis. They want time to get away to shop, to go to the hairdresser, to have a bath, to have time alone. And also perhaps time to work. Schooling for the over-fives is provided. Weekday residential care is possible for some under school age. But nursery care is no better than it is for other sections of the community. There are a few statutory places for handicapped children at state nurseries, but nowhere enough to fill the demand. It is the same old story.

The next chapter looks at the alternative to home life, with accounts from disabled people living in institutions.

Chapter 16

INSTITUTIONAL LIFE

Nobody likes the idea of living in an institution. And yet institutions have their advantages. Here are two accounts from handicapped people who have experienced institutional life in very different ways.

* * *

'My mum would moan that I couldn't do anything for myself. But she never taught me about dressing myself'

Sonia is twenty-three. She was born with a condition that prevented her lower limbs from developing and she is confined to a wheelchair. Sonia was put into residential care at the age of eight.

'The condition was diagnosed when I was born. I was a third child, my brothers were aged eleven and ten, and my dad died before I was born. I definitely wasn't planned, and I'm not sure that he was my dad because she messed around.

'I wasn't happy at home because my mum was violent to me. I was in hospital quite a lot too. When I was seven she had broken my leg. My brother came to see me last year, and he told me that she would moan that I couldn't do anything for myself. She kept me in nappies for ages after other children weren't in nappies. There wasn't any money. We had an outside toilet and things like that. It was in Yorkshire.

'I didn't know at the time, but the social workers were watching us. They would come round, but my mum wouldn't let them in. They thought it was an accident when she broke my leg. But it wasn't.

'One day, about a year after the leg, I went to school and I had bruises on my face. They asked me, had I been a naughty girl, and I said yes, and then my family got it. But she had been getting away with it for years. I know that parents, when they have a disabled child, they feel it's their fault. Basically that's stupid, because it's not. I think she let out the guilt on me. Also it was a lot harder at that time, in 1966 when I was born, for women to admit that they were having problems, and please could somebody look after their baby for a while. But it's still no excuse for it to go on that long.

'When I was seven she married another man, and he didn't want me around basically. I remember thinking that when they got married, it would be the end of all the hitting. But he didn't stop her at all. He even allowed her to hit his own son, who was a year younger than me. He was weirder than she was.

'I was immediately put under section two, and that means they take you away from your mother. I was put in a school in Yorkshire, then I was taken away from there very soon after to a boarding-school in Sussex. I was there till I was eighteen.

'My mum used to come to the school to see me until I was about thirteen. My older brother used to come with her. The other one I didn't see from when I was seven till I was eighteen. He left home. She used to hit him sometimes. They didn't get on at all. She only wanted one child, and that was the oldest one.

'I wish I hadn't had to move so far away from Yorkshire. I was miles away, and I didn't know anybody. I wasn't very popular because I wouldn't do things I thought were stupid. Right from when I was eight. Generally, people would get cross because I wouldn't do things just because they told me to. Right through my life there have been a few people who agreed with me over that. These are the people I get on with. I became very independent looking after myself.

'I wouldn't let people pat me on the head. I'd have gone under. I was clinging on. I knew I had a mother I couldn't trust. But I still loved her. I did. I do. She's remained my mum. I can't remember the last time I saw her. I'd go for a week or so in the holidays. But I wouldn't stay with her. I did once, but after that I stayed somewhere else and she would come and see me, so we wouldn't start all over again.

'I read in my notes that he – her husband – asked her to choose between him and me. That's one reason why I don't write to her. Because when I was about twenty, I decided to get in touch and I wrote to her a few times, and I got this letter, written by both of them, and it said that in future if I didn't write to him and her then she wasn't going to write to me. I never wrote back. It made me upset. She'd chosen him over me twice.

'I think her parents died when she was ten, and I heard from someone, and I don't know whether it's true or not, that she was in a children's home herself. I think there is a pattern of children

185

who were hit, hitting their children. I haven't got any children, but I've got a cat that used to annoy me. There are times when I've lost control and I've hit her a lot. If it is a pattern, I suppose it can be broken. But at times I've thought, if I can't handle having a cat, then, you know, I may not have another one. I've still got her. She's really scared of me now. I definitely wouldn't have any children. I love my cat but there are times when she has just been so annoying. It's not her that's got to change, is it?

'I live in a house. It's like a hostel. It's got other disabled people there. Any decisions there are made by the staff. But I've got a flat in the house, and I can do my own cooking. I'm on the ground floor, and there's a lift to the first floor. I've got a job. I'm a secretary, twenty hours a week. I went to a residential college for six months to learn typing. Then I went back to the old place and stayed for three months, and then I came here.

'Was I glad to get away from my mother? Yes . . . I'm not sure. She is my mum after all. I don't know any of my cousins or anyone.

'I've got a few close friends. They are all able-bodied. I don't use the word handicapped. Disabled is better, but there should be another word. I'll be moving into my own place soon. It's a housing trust.

'Why did I want to talk to you? It's for revenge. I want to get back at her a bit.'

*   *   *

'At home, my parents thought for me and spoke for me'
Wendy was in her forties when the following interview took place. She was in a wheelchair and suffered from a spastic condition that affected upper and lower limbs. Wendy had been living in a very progressive local authority residential home for eighteen months.

'Living here is the best thing that ever happened to me. I lived at home with my parents for all of my life before that. I would never have been brought here if it had not been for the fact that my parents got too old to cope.

'Perhaps I ought to feel grateful to them, but I can't. All I can feel is that they wasted my life. I was given absolutely no independence. Never allowed to find ways of doing things for myself. They thought for me and spoke for me and did not let me have a life of my own.

'In this place we have facilitators. They are people who act as your arms and your legs. I have a bedsitter and I can entertain friends. I like to cook, especially Danish food, and I make up a shopping list. My facilitator gets the food and she cooks the dishes

186

I want from my recipe books. Everything I do here is my decision, and that's the most important thing for me.'

* * *

Both too little and too much protection can make a residential home a better place to be than living with parents. But age is the important distinction. A small child needs a great deal of protection, especially when that child is handicapped. Sonia would envy Wendy.

Sonia is at pains to show that her mother not only battered her, but also one of her brothers and a stepbrother. She is right in that it wasn't only her handicap that caused the rejection, but her handicap made her extra vulnerable. A remarriage can sometimes result in a stepfather refusing to support his wife's children from a previous marriage (and stepmothers, too, reject their husband's children, though more commonly when they are demanding teenagers). Again, a handicapped child is especially vulnerable.

Total rejection is very hard to take, and Valerie Henson of the Children's Society thinks that regular contact with the family, even if it is not very often, is better than nothing. 'Children in residential care see staff come and go, perhaps every two years. Though the staff may be caring and supportive, it is a blow for a child every time they go.' She has seen children sending their mothers birthday presents and never receiving a reply, and suggests that those who do get replies have greater emotional stability. Perhaps Sonia would not have had to take out her frustrations on her cat if her mother had not rejected her twice.

Regular, if infrequent, contact softens the blow. This is true of any woman living apart from her children. Those who featured in earlier pages in this book, and who remained in contact, showing love and constancy, will in the end surely prove that they did not reject, in spite of breaking the rules.

Wendy's experience of being smothered seems far removed from rejection, but nevertheless there may be an element there, and it is this that could be making her so angry. Handicapped babies are more acceptable than handicapped adults in some ways, and parents may unconsciously strive to prevent a child from growing up.

A normal child as it develops will snatch a spoon, put on its own shoe and make a claim for increasing independence. A disabled child who has to be stimulated into doing these things must rely on the will of its parents. Some will seek every means of releasing a child into personal freedom. Others will find it easier and more acceptable to carry on themselves, keeping the baby

187

and ignoring the maturing mind growing in the dependent body. It was Wendy's maturing mind that was rejected.

Poor residential care can also provide shoes and someone to tie the laces, but the best places aim to bring out the potential of the handicapped person. The facilitators in Wendy's home act as arms and legs, but only if and when the residents want them to.

The best kind of residential home for children and adolescents is one run on the lines of a small family. Davina's son has grown up in such an establishment with other handicapped children. He also has a foster family and his biological family with whom he remains in contact. Perhaps he feels rejected by Davina, or perhaps he shares with James, the boy in Chapter 8 who grew up with a foster mother and his natural mother, the feeling that he has an everyday mother and another mother, though he lives with neither.

Some handicapped children are fostered and live with their foster parents in a family home. A number are adopted, not necessarily by traditional nuclear families but by individuals who want to offer a child a home. Parents for Children, an independent adoption agency, counsels prospective parents and offers financial support to help people consider adopting a child who is mentally or physically handicapped. They are able to place children up to the age of fifteen or sixteen, often very successfully.

Why can surrogate parents tolerate what biological parents find intolerable? One answer may be that the children who are fostered or adopted tend to have fairly mild handicaps, but probably the overriding reason is that there are no dashed hopes and disappointments, no months and years of unresolved diagnoses and false reassurances, and no pressure from social workers. The decision is made by the prospective parents as a clear choice.

Once children reach eighteen, and are no longer eligible for many children's homes, they may be offered alternatives that range from a geriatric ward with no facilities for their age group to a hostel run by a charity or local authority, or sheltered housing, perhaps in a flat with other young people. The futures of these eighteen-year-olds depend on what is offered and sometimes on the interventions of their parents, who do not necessarily reject, but cannot always provide.

SECTION V

Beaten by the System

SECTION V

Beaten by the System

Chapter 17

LOSING THE DIVORCE BATTLE

Some women don't part from their children willingly. They lose them in battle. They might be driven out of the family home, feeling that their children's minds have been poisoned against them; or their teenage offspring may choose to stay in a domestic situation that their mother finds intolerable. Children after divorce often have two sets of homes to choose from, and they might elect to go to their father, feeling unwanted by a new stepfather, while their mother is torn between her new partner and her children.

Today the courts are basically in favour of mothers keeping their children, a result of legal reforms begun in the nineteenth century. As Caroline Norton's experience quoted earlier in this book shows, at that time the caring role of the mother was considered far less important than the legal right of the father. A judge is quoted in the book *The Father Figure* as saying in 1833: 'To neglect the natural jurisdiction of the father over the child until the age of twenty-one would be really to set aside the whole course and order of nature and . . . to disturb the very foundation of family life.'

But the times changed, and with them the so-called course and order of nature. Reforms over the next eighty years led to the conclusion that the welfare of the child should be given predominant consideration, with, in principle, neither parent's claim regarded as superior to the other. In practice, mothers and children were seen as naturally belonging together, and today more than 85% of children of divorce live mainly with their mothers.

But the times are changing again. The 'best interests' of the child still predominate, but views on what those best interests are have altered. As pointed out earlier, whether through male resistance towards the power displayed by some feminists, or male responsiveness to the invitation to share parenting made by other feminists, there has been a gradual build-up in the number

191

of men seeking custody. And they have been having greater success as judges change their attitudes. In Britain, there was a 10% increase in the number of fathers who won custody between 1980 and 1988. The trend is greater in parts of the United States. Among men in California seeking custody in 1968, only 35% were successful. In 1977, 68% were successful.

The advantages that men may carry – greater affluence, earlier remarriage – tend to go down especially well with judges (who are themselves predominantly male). If a father is a religious observer he may be more favoured, especially if his wife has been unfaithful. The preferred choice of the mother as the person most suited to provide a secure base, upheld within psychotherapy, is not always foremost in the minds of those in the legal profession.

On the other hand, psychiatry may be used to devalue a mother, too. Should she display extreme anxiety, insecurity, possessiveness or other emotions regarding her child – not unreasonable reactions when custody is contested – she could be labelled neurotic, uncooperative and ultimately unsuitable for mothering. Heartbreak newspaper stories of wealthy fathers snatching children from despairing, near-destitute mothers may end with a judge receiving a psychiatric report on the woman's mental instability, a report that often carries great weight. This may be right in many cases, but psychiatry contains fixed ideas about the way mothers ought to be, as displayed earlier in this book.

The Children Bill introduced in 1988 proposed to do away with the idea of custody. Parents will retain a shared responsibility even when divorced. There will be opportunities for arrangements whereby children might live part time with each parent. Children will be given greater freedom to make their own choices. But the courts will continue to deal with disputes, and how they will be handled remains to be seen. This chapter examines some of the ways cases have been dealt with up till now. What they reveal is a deeply unjust balance of power.

* * *

'He tried to turn the children against me. He said I did not love them. I was not a fit mother'

Beryl is a sweet-voiced, gentle, slightly bewildered woman, aged forty-one, mother of two boys aged seventeen and thirteen, and a girl of nine. She is a health visitor and lives in a neat, sparsely furnished one-bedroomed council flat on her own. Two years ago she was divorced, after having been married for eighteen years. Her husband was granted custody and the three children live with their father.

192

'For the first thirteen years our marriage had been a very happy one, and then for some unknown reason it started to break down. There was nobody else involved, but my husband's whole character seemed to change. He had been very ill with whooping cough, which is a bad thing for an adult to have. He was off work for three months, and the trouble seems to have stemmed from then.

'I'd say what's gone wrong? and he'd say it's you. And I'd say how? and he'd say if I need to tell you, you won't be changing yourself. He'd say you used to wear bright-coloured clothes and now you wear dull-coloured clothes, and I'd say that's to do with fashion. Or he'd say I'd spent a lot of time with a girlfriend, when perhaps I'd had a coffee with her during the week. He was very insecure.

'I could see him slipping away from me, and I asked my brother, who is a doctor, to see him. I couldn't get through to him that I loved him. My brother talked to him and suggested he saw a psychiatrist, and he said OK if I agreed too, and I did. Next day, he went to work and suddenly early in the afternoon, the front door crashed open and he stormed in and went absolutely berserk. He said, it just dawned on me what you and your family are trying to do, you're trying to make out I'm some kind of nutcase. You want me put away.

'And that was the end of it. I think it was the whooping cough. A vaccination can irritate the brain, so maybe the disease itself can too. He was very very ill. He was also held up by a shotgun a little later when he was doing some work in a bank, and he showed no fear at all. Well, that's not natural. His father died around that time too. And he built an extension and got quite paranoid about the measurements and the size of the foundations. He'd be up during the night recalculating and recalculating.

'I did love him very much, but in the end it got too much and I did agree to give him the divorce that he had been asking for, though as soon as I agreed he said that he didn't want one.

'I was working part time as school nurse so I could have time off for the school holidays. That was a bone of contention, that I was becoming more of a career person again, though definitely the family and the home came first. I would never have put my job first at that time.

'My husband said he would go for custody. That was a great shock to me. We were both advised by our solicitors to stay in the house because otherwise it would give the other person the advantage. Then it became a battle by him to try and get me out. He tried to turn the children against me. He said that I didn't love them. I was not a fit mother because I worked. I had read lots of books about how to behave with the children in this situation, and I lost out through that because I tried not to let them see me upset and tried to keep their lives as normal as possible. They knew things were going wrong and that's why Daddy and I didn't go out together, but we did hide the rows and I don't think they really realized the situation. They also got quite clever at switching themselves off.

'In the past, my husband had given the children very little time even at weekends, but when we were waiting for the divorce, he had to impress them and show what a great bloke he was. I was the one left at home on my own while they all went off to have a jolly good time.'

Beryl went to court to try to get her husband removed from the house, but her case was turned down on the basis that the house was large enough for them to have separate rooms. A downstairs living room was converted into a bedroom.

'He had made promises not to molest or touch me, but he refused to move out of the main bedroom, and I had been sharing with my daughter before. So I had to move downstairs, and I found myself cut off from everything. It's very easy looking back and seeing where you go wrong, but you are at your lowest physically and mentally . . . He was coming in at night and asking sexual favours, demanding his rights as a husband because we were still married. It was terrible. He was angry, hurt, sobbing. He'd be begging me to change my mind. He accused me of being a lesbian. He was jealous because I have lots of women friends. I could have gone back to court because he was coming into my room, but if I had done so it would have meant that he would go to prison.

'A court welfare officer came, and he seemed to find it difficult to talk to women. I found it difficult to talk to him. But with my husband, well they got on together, both talking about the fact that they had built an extension, chatting on, and I felt doomed. He came again and talked to the children. My oldest boy was confident, and being fifteen, wanted to be with his dad. The other boy didn't know, but he thought possibly his dad. My daughter told me afterwards she wanted to be with me, but she couldn't talk to this chap, so she hadn't said anything. She was only seven at the time.

'So that's how it was decided – one the welfare report said they should be with their father, and secondly in the summing up, the judge said there was no truth in the things my husband had been accusing me of, like being an uncaring mother, but that he felt the damage had been done and my character had been blackened with the children. If they were forced to be with me at this stage, they might harden their hearts towards me forever.

'**I was absolutely devastated. I had to leave the house that night.** I waited till the children had come home from school, I said goodbye and left the house. My daughter burst into tears and said I told you I wanted to come with you, and she looked so accusingly at me . . .

'At the beginning, they kept distant. I wrote them a letter each. I wanted to make it clear that though I wasn't allowed to come back to them, they could change their minds and come to me if they wanted to. My husband found the letters and I think he burned them. He was very cross, and he told the children that if I really loved them as much as I said I did, I would go back and live with them. That must have sounded pretty feasible to a child, don't you think?'

Beryl stayed with her brother for a few days, and then contacted her local health authority. She had already applied to go back full time to work as a health visitor, and she was given her present flat which was allocated for a health visitor. It is near to where her children live.

'I have to pay for the privilege of not having my children, £10 each a week. I ended up with 55% of the house, so when my younger son is eighteen or if there is any change in the number of people living in the property, I can get the house sold and claim my share. But I don't want the children disrupted at present.

'I think my husband will get remarried. He has had a string of girlfriends, and I don't think he will last out too long on his own. I live in hope that my daughter will come to me when she is older. She has hinted at it. For now, she is in a familiar environment. The three have become a supporting trio. She adores her older brother.

'But of course, when she gets to eleven or twelve I might not want her back. Is that a terrible thing to say? I think that as time goes on, the only way I can survive is to make a life for myself. I get more used to being independent. I can do what I like with my time, and being very work-oriented, I might have to weigh that against say a rebellious teenager. I don't know. Of course, she might not be a rebellious teenager. I want her now, that's the thing. I do feel desperately that I am missing out on so much.

'My children visit regularly. When my oldest son comes, he usually sits himself down and watches the telly and mutters a few words. Or if he wants to talk we have a long talk. It's just really like home, they all slot in. It was difficult at first, we had terrible times, in tears, awful, but as time goes on they feel more confident and I do too. They bring their friends here, and I love that. They can also see their father for what he is. I never ever run him down though he gives them so much hate of me. I don't want to add to it.

'They see now the way he over-reacts and explodes. They laugh and say do you remember when . . . and the laugh is always on me, I was always the one getting pushed out.

'My husband told the children, whatever you do, don't let your mum into the house. It's disgraceful. I laugh instead of getting angry. I don't shout. Yes I do have to fight back tears and fight back anger. The injustice of it all. If I start thinking too much about it, it gets too bad. I blank my mind off really. I went on holiday with the younger two a few months ago, and though it was so wonderful it was also so painful. Just to wake up in the morning and see my daughter asleep beside me was agony. I can't explain it. I couldn't believe it was going to end. I cried in the plane. I had to say goodbye to them on the pavement, and I didn't hear from them again for four weeks, because they were going on holiday with their father. It was a shame because half the fun of coming back from a holiday is sitting with people and telling them about it, and I couldn't bear to think back or even to look at the photographs. The two weeks have been blanked out.

'I know I have shelved all the thinking. I wanted to get rid of this terrible pain, and as soon as I start thinking, it's an overwhelming pain. There are times when I go off to work in the morning, and I see children going to school holding their mum's hand and I think oh I wish I was doing that.

'When I moved in here there was deep snow outside. I was cold and lonely, and I had no money. I had nightmares, and the strange thing was that the better I was coping in the day, the worse it was with the nightmares. But you can't just go through life thinking oh woe is me because you won't get anywhere. You've got to look at the advantages, and I have got advantages. Compared to the single mothers I talk to in my work, I'm the much envied parent, the parent whom the children go to for the good times, where you haven't got the everyday nagging and correcting, or the burdens. We have a very good time and off they go again.

'**I've got a boyfriend at the moment. I'm very fond of him, but I don't know about marriage at all any more. This period of being on my own has proved that I can do quite a lot on my own.** I do like company and going out, and I want someone around but I don't know that I want the hassle of living with them all the time. I always say to people who are perhaps afraid of going on their own, the thing is you have got peace of mind once you find out you can do it, and it's great. I was so lonely at home in that last year. Totally isolated.

'A sad thing happened the other week. My cat got run over. The children were here and were absolutely heartbroken. My son took it to the vet. I think they were so upset because they felt I now had nobody and would be on my own. And I did say oh dear everything I love seems to get taken away from me. I think I probably shouldn't have said that. When I took my kids back, their father didn't even come over to me. They followed him into the house hand in hand, and I could hear him say, what are you grizzling about?

'I don't understand what happened. We were an envied couple, so happy. He'd do anything for me. I can't believe it. He says why is it that nobody can understand what I mean? I said perhaps it's because you're not thinking along the same lines as everybody else. I think the way my children feel is that if they have got to let somebody down it has to be me because I am more understanding of them. They cannot upset him, and they want to keep things as calm as possible at home. Do you think one day they'll come and say to me "You did a jolly good job Mum"? Of course I want them to say to me "We love you and we want to come and live with you" and all those nice things.

'But it has worked out very well. I think my eldest would have gone to his father anyway, and that would have split the children. At the moment there doesn't seem to be anything wrong. There are no behaviour problems. The children have worked well at school. They are beautiful children. They have come out really really well.'

* * *

Mothers who choose to fight for their children, or who feel there is no choice but to leave on their own if the children wish to stay with their father, are in an exceedingly disadvantaged position. As Solomon knew, a loving mother will not allow her children to be split in two. Better that the other claimant has them. The qualities that allow someone to put the true interests of the children first make a person vulnerable. They make a mother vulnerable: not all judges are as wise as Solomon.

Mothers who under the current legal system (prior to the Children Act) lose custody or are forced to accept their child's loyalty to the father are still regarded by some as the guilty party – how selfish, how careless (neither careful nor caring), or even how spineless they are to lose out like that. Or perhaps there is the whisper of a suspicion that they manipulated or passively allowed the whole thing, and really wanted to leave their children.

197

A woman like Beryl had the dice loaded against her from the start. Rather than allow a 'scene' she was bullied into a corner. Because she kept her distress to herself, she was seen as the stronger parent, so that the children rallied to the father. Because she was the one who was driven into leaving the marriage, she was seen as the home-breaker. Because this is how she was represented in court, the judge was prejudiced against her. Because the case had been conducted in an adversarial 'male' style, she was confused and overwhelmed, though should she have shown toughness, this too could have told against her – nice women don't fight. Because the children were equally overwhelmed, they could not express their views. (Beryl's daughter did not understand the welfare officer, and perhaps was merely doing what her mother did, ie she tried to remain noncommittal in an effort not to betray either parent.)

When men are out for revenge, especially against 'uppity' wives who go out to work and show independence, women can be made to feel powerless, challenged against their will, and often unable to compete over adequate accommodation or childcare because of their more limited incomes. Because the withdrawal of sexual favours is seen as humiliating by some men, accusations about lesbianism and jealousy towards friends are used as ammunition to sow doubts in the minds of the children, the welfare officer, the judge.

At least Beryl tried to resist. Others might be tempted to give up at the idea of such a no-win situation – only to be considered even more reprehensible, though they would be simply displaying the lack of confidence and self-esteem wished upon them by circumstances as above. A woman who loses custody under the present system against her will, whether she fights or not, is likely to feel ashamed and inadequate. She has failed on all fronts and feels the disapproval or contempt of the judge, of health professionals, of relatives and strangers, of husband and sometimes children. Even the paying of maintenance, which can be perceived as a kind of validation of parenthood, can be felt as a punishment if it is imposed in a fashion suggesting the mother as miscreant. Women who leave and pay through choice are in some ways in a better position psychologically.

In future divorce cases, conciliation services and mediators are likely to be called in on disputes over children, and they should reduce the browbeating effect on women. But prejudices don't die that easily, and some men will continue to use their powers to persuade or bully women into giving up certain rights. Mothers like Beryl will continue to be vulnerable to moral judgements.

They might discover what many fathers learn about living away from their families, which is that living alone can be enjoyable and there may be a reluctance to relinquish freedom and independence should the chance of recovering their children occur. When Beryl said that the prospect of living with a teenage daughter was daunting, she was voicing an attitude that many women living apart from their children acquire. Some find this harder to admit than others, and most find it much harder to admit than most men do. They know that to admit their reluctance openly is to invite censure, even though they may also know that they have made a healthy adjustment to a painful situation.

Judgements are felt equally acutely when the children choose to stay with their father, or go to their father later. To a mother, this can seem like desertion, rejection, proof of inadequacy as a parent. If a family row results in a child leaving to live with the father, there may be guilt and the feeling that the child is being sacrificed, is being 'ruined' by its mother's selfish actions.

Mental illness, depression, irrational behaviour are still somehow not quite male territory, and that makes it easy for men to deny such things in themselves, and to concentrate on the faults and irritations they find in others. Beryl's husband may well be enraged by his wife's innocence and bewilderment and facility of blanking off emotion. He may feel the injured party, and influence his children to think this too, while his own inner disturbances are ignored.

The true story is often complex, involving many facets of character in both partners and their degree of dependency on each other. One very crude and generalized way of looking at the interaction works like this: when one partner behaves in an erratic fashion, the other tends to react by being extra 'reasonable'. The tradition is that women make emotional scenes and men remain in control. When the pattern is reversed men continue to assume they are in control, regardless of reality, and perceive women as deceiving, devious creatures who are deliberately making their real feelings inaccessible. This appears to them to be the reason for their own inflammatory reactions. It's a case of 'Mummy makes me feel bad, and I blame her for it.' Women, responding to this in their mothering/placating role, collude, humour, acquiesce, and can lose their children because of it.

They do it with husbands, and they do it with children too. Beryl could not share her distress with her children. They had to cry over a cat rather than over themselves. Men are often accused of not being able to cope with women's tears, but women find it equally difficult to accept their children's tears – not those of babyhood, but those of adolescent loss and heartbreak. Just as the woman who chooses to leave her children cannot explain, cannot always face seeing her children because of her sense of shame, so the woman who is ousted cannot always share her own unhappiness, her own sense of loss with them.

Chapter 18

LESBIAN MOTHERS

Whorenow future of their children is considered after divorce, lesbian mothers are more disadvantaged than others. Overall figures are hard to find, but a survey published by Rights of Women, a feminist legal collective, in 1984, found that 45% of lesbian mothers lost in cases where they wanted custody with care and control (ie day to day care plus either joint or sole custody). This is perhaps a smaller figure than one might expect – less than half – and it might be in the interests of lesbian pressure groups to publicize the fact that more than half of lesbian women are deemed fit to have major responsibility for their children.

However, there tends to be a rather defensive attitude among those active in groups, caused no doubt by deeply unhappy experiences that feel more comfortable when translated into anger. One campaigner said, 'The way the courts operate is that they are theoretically concerned with the best interests of the child, and they argue that these tend to lie in normal, heterosexual families. But if your husband has got pissed off and gone off with some other woman, the court would still prefer that to the child being with a lesbian mother.' True, but clearly not always true.

She also said, 'Unlike lesbian mothers, homosexual fathers are bad for children. Well, they are into paedophilia, aren't they? Men shouldn't be involved with childcare.'

This point of view does not win friends or influence people, especially those dedicated to the cause of joint custody. However, there is a genuine case for indignation and protest against injustice, prejudice and decisions that appear to be in anything but the best interests of the child.

In five cases among the group of thirty-six women who filled in the Rights of Women questionnaire, the court was prepared to move a child from its mother's home because of her sexual orientation, despite the fact that he or she was settled and happy.

One daughter had been living with her mother for six years, and a boy of four had been living with his mother for two years. The age range of children of mothers who lost custody was from eighteen months to eleven years. A child's wishes are rarely taken into account before the age of ten or eleven. Some women said that they had not contested, believing that the odds were too much against them.

There were claims that some husbands had no intention of bringing up the children themselves but had contested purely out of revenge. One father got care and control and joint custody, despite a history of violence and a previous injunction against him. Stipulations were made about the mothers, such as that there should be no contact with a lover. In one case there was a supervision order empowering the local authority to appoint a social worker, in order to ensure that the mother 'did not have sex in front of the children' with her lover.

Rights of Women feels that the system is deeply biased against lesbian mothers, and considers that prejudices are held by the probation officers or social workers who draw up the court welfare reports, as well as judges who may ignore evidence favourable to the mother. The group cites research which dispels certain myths surrounding lesbianism and its influence on children. Susan Golombok and others at the Institute of Psychiatry compared 37 children from lesbian households with 38 children from single heterosexual households, and found no significant difference between the two groups in terms of emotional development, peer group relationship, or psychosexual development. An American study of two groups of 20 children, by Kirkpatrick, Smith and Roy, came to the same conclusions.

There is a theory that children of lesbian mothers may be victimized at school or singled out in some unpleasant way. Work by Richard Green on the incidence of teasing of children in homosexual or transvestite families showed no prevalent teasing of lesbian mothers' children, though when teasing occurred they could cope with it adequately. Another American, Hoeffer, looking at sex-role traits, found no significant difference between lesbian and heterosexual mothers' children, and hypothesized that peer influence was greater on sex-role development. One needs to remember that homosexuals and lesbians emerge from heterosexual families.

The consensus from a body of research concerning overall emotional adjustment, sexual interests, sexual identity and relations with peers produced verdicts of 'no significant difference' between children of lesbians and children of heterosexual mothers. Commonsense would suggest that if a lesbian relationship is working happily, then it should be able to provide stability and a sense of normality to children, who after all do not participate in the sex life of the adults any more than they do in a heterosexual stable family.

None of this necessarily carries weight in the courts. Stereotypes abound, including the widely held belief that one woman must play the role of the man while the other plays that of the woman, a notion said to be not at all true for the majority of lesbian relationships. Even if it is true, any relevance to the quality of nurturing is obscure.

'Sex between women can be intense, passionate and loving, warm, caring and friendly, and also disappointing or destructive' writes Celia Kitzinger in a contribution to a book by her mother on women's sexuality. 'But lesbianism is *not*, for most women, centred around sex. Lesbianism is a way of experiencing reality, a way of being in the world.' Unfortunately, that reality often fails to come across.

* * *

'The judge declared my love for a woman to be "a cancerous one which must be severed forthwith" '
The following is an extract from a paper written by Judith Priestley published by the Lesbian Custody Project run by Rights of Women.

'If a mother is a lesbian, all the usual assumptions about the importance of mothers are overturned. Women like myself, whose caring and competence as mothers was never in question, find ourselves suddenly depicted as dangerous and unfit. Our children are interrogated and our personal lives are open to scrutiny.

'Lawyers acting for fathers know only too well that if lesbianism is even mentioned in court, their client's chances of gaining custody are significantly increased. It is claimed that lesbians corrupt children, tamper with their "normal" development and expose them to anti-lesbian taunts from their schoolfriends. The strength of feeling against lesbians is such that judges and magistrates tend to take these accusations for granted, despite evidence to the contrary.

'It is not surprising that many mothers keep their love of women a closely guarded secret despite the stress this causes. Others may even deny their lesbianism and live out the next years in fear of being exposed. Some mothers choose not to fight for custody, not because they don't love their children enough, but because they don't want their children or themselves to be exposed to the anxiety and distress involved. They do deals with fathers, hoping at least to retain good access to their children.

'In my own case it was a complete shock to find myself in the middle of such a dispute. At the time my predominant emotion was fear that I would lose my three, much loved, small children. Today, five years later, I also feel extremely angry about the way I was treated in the courts. I had no idea that British courts had the power to impose restrictions on my personal freedom that are reminiscent of the banning orders of more repressive regimes. The judge declared my love for a woman to be "a cancerous one which must be severed forthwith". To that effect he imposed court orders forbidding my lover and I to have any contact what-soever. We could not meet, exchange letters or phone calls. Think how you would feel in a similar situation. We had committed no crime. We had broken no laws. We simply loved each other.

'It was pointed out to the judge that this order would prevent me from doing my job because we worked in the same university department. His reply was, that was all very well, but what might happen in the tea breaks. He was unable to imagine that we might be drinking tea with our students because the only thing that registered with him was my sexuality.

'When I challenged the orders, he accused me of being more interested in my job and my lover than I was in my children. He won. I backed off and gave up my job.

'Apart from being grossly insulted and having dire financial and emotional consequences, such orders constitute a major infringement of civil liberties.

'What happens to lesbian mothers today could happen to other mothers tomorrow. It won't be long before other women in custody disputes, who want to work, or who are active in political parties, will be judged as not caring enough about their children. They will be accused of not putting their children first.

'Some might say what's wrong with joint custody, what's wrong with men having custody of children anyway. We don't want our lives restricted by the exclusive demands of mothering, yet we feel we have a greater right to bring up our children than men. Perhaps when there are real changes in popular notions of child-rearing; and when the system of paid work and rewards no longer reflects the view that women are expected to put the children first – then men may have an equal right to custody of children. But until such time, the emphasis placed on the mother-child relationship makes it worse for women to lose their children and worse for children to lose their mothers – as any child will tell you.'

The logic of the final points made above are undeniable. The one thing left out is the love and loyalty a child might well feel towards its father. Joint custody arrangements might be abused by men in some circumstances, but they also make it more difficult for a father to remove himself from the commitments of parenthood and they offer him a way to show his love and loyalty to his child.

Lesbian mothers who have suffered humiliation from the courts and have fought to keep their children, have particular reason to feel bitter. Unlike many women who choose to leave their children, they may be prepared to sacrifice their job, as Judith Priestley did, in order to keep them or get them back. What they are not prepared to do is sacrifice their sexual identity, though they know it may take their children from them. Since there is no evidence that living in a lesbian household harms a child, there is no reason to expect a mother to give up being a lesbian. In terms of sex abuse, there is more risk statistically attached to a child living with its mother and a stepfather. The courts should be prepared either to examine all partners for their suitability for parenthood, or none.

Chapter 19

RACIAL INDIFFERENCE

Minority groups within a mainstream culture, unless they are both wealthy and worldly, are easily used and abused, sometimes unknowingly, by their host society. Values are imposed insensitively, 'help' offered may be distinctly unhelpful, though the helper might fail to understand why it is less than rapturously received. Immigrants with their own cultural identity often develop a resistance towards the mainstream, and a sense of privacy which is quite easy to maintain since few people outside their circle take anything but a marginal interest in them. This marginal interest, often dismissive and lacking in insight, reinforces prejudices and allows myths to develop. Though there are signs of improvement, as for instance when community leaders and pressure groups act as a liaison, and social workers from an appropriate ethnic group are assigned to a case, a mother from a minority group is at special risk when she turns to professionals. Her approach to child-rearing may be challenged, her needs wrongly assessed. Like the other types of women looked at in this chapter, she may find her role as a mother threatened or be living without her children against her will.

* * *

'When I went back for my children, they were different . . . telling all sorts of lies about me'

Veronica is forty-three. She has a daughter of nine who lives with her, and a son and daughter, both in their teens, who were taken into care. She is a diffident, shy woman, who gives way at times to extreme intensity of emotion. She is clearly devoted to her youngest child, who appears sympathetic and affectionate. She has not had contact with her husband for several years. On the walls of her flat are religious pictures, photographs of the Pope.

'I came here from Nigeria in 1972. I was twenty-seven. My husband was here already studying. I worked to earn the money, and when I became pregnant he decided he should send the children to somebody to look after them. In fact I did not even know the day it happened. I went to work and the baby was gone when I came home. I didn't know where. He was five weeks old.

'I cannot forget the experience when I first saw him again. The tears, the agony. I saw my baby every three or four weeks. It wasn't easy to maintain contact because he was very far away in Derbyshire. I always paid. I didn't know anyone or what I could claim. His father wasn't interested and I was hurt to find that I married a man who did not want children and made me have my first baby terminated and then this one taken away. Then my second child was born the next year, and she was fostered in the same place. I tried to build up relations with this family so I could visit and bring the children back in the holidays.

'I was paying them nearly a hundred pounds a month and it was too much. This family was a white family and they were beginning to foster too many black children. Every time I go I see new faces, and I did not like that. There were four children in one room.

'I wrote to the director of social services and asked them to find me a daily minder who could look after my children. I wrote to so many places but I was turned down. You see, once it had happened, nobody wanted to do anything. In the end I said to myself, I can go and bring my children back any time. So I went to the family and told them they had always been kind and I would come back and visit them with the children, and I brought my children home.'

Veronica's husband left her when her two older children were aged two and three. She brought them back to her home when they were four and five. Her health visitor found her a child-minder and Veronica continued in her job in a local factory. Her husband reappeared briefly, she became pregnant, and he disappeared from her life permanently before her third child was born. The baby went to a day nursery and the older pair were at school. A stable pattern was established for about five years. During this time, Veronica's father died in Nigeria. Shortly after, her mother died, and she flew over for the funeral with her children. Then she and the children visited the foster family and she left them with the family for two weeks while she returned home to nurse a friend who was ill.

'When I went back for my children, they were different. The older two were telling all sorts of lies about me. They say I smack them. The family had told them they should go and report this to the police. What happened was this. My big son is very stubborn and would not do his school work. He goes to somebody's house and I don't know where he is. You know, the Africans, we are

207

disciplined, so I say you do your school work. But he disobey me. I say, if you do not obey me, the girl will not obey me. Even the little one said I'm not doing it, though she is a good girl. So I picked up a stick used to prop up a plant, and I cane my son. I was so angry, I went to the school and told the headmaster I have caned my son because he would not do his work. I said all I can do is see my children educated. He is going to work because he has no father. The principal called my son in and rebuked him.

'I told this to the foster family when I left my children with them, and they said look, his report is very good, and I said his report is useless. Not every mother can stand behind her children in this country. When I come back and I see my children are different, I ask this family, why are my children like this? My girl of ten was putting on make-up and nail varnish. I said what happens when she goes back to school? Why do you let my children watch television till two o'clock? This man was treating my son as a servant. He was given paint and told to paint the toilet. He got paint on his trousers. This man also told my youngest, you've been making your mother punish these two.

'**I said to the children when you leave here you never come back.** I had taken my children there as a matter of courtesy because the family said other African children had not come back or written.'

Veronica returned home with her children. But without her knowledge, the foster father had given her oldest child, then eleven, money. One day she returned from work to find he had disappeared.

'I was afraid. I called the police. They said give us the number of the foster family, we will contact them. I had no idea he was there. But they rang and he was, and I spoke to the man and said I've worked so hard, I've always paid you. Why do you want to ruin my home? I spoke to my son and he said he was not coming back. The man said you have not been treating these children well. I said yes I cane them, not to hurt them. Weren't you caned at school?'

Veronica approached her local social services department the following day, to find they were already informed. Her son appears to have been brought back to his mother and pleaded with her to let him live with the foster parents. He wanted to work on a farm. The situation worsened when one day on her return from work she found the two older children beating the youngest one. Eventually, both were taken into care by social services.

'According to the social services, I hated both of them and I loved my young one, so they hit her. You know, they hated this child. I'm a Christian, and I'm telling you, they hated this child.

They started to pick on her and they tell lies about her. They told a social worker that they don't know me as their mother. When people tell stories about innocent people you know they are not right, and they injure you so much, it hurts. I could return to my country and leave them forever, and it is them who would suffer because when they are sixteen people will say go away, we don't want you. It is sad for me because I wasted my life, my energy, and I lost my parents. I think that when their father left them, I should have left them as well. But they are my children and I want them back. Nobody wanted to listen to me when I asked the social services to investigate the foster family, because this man was a white man. Nobody wanted to listen.'

* * *

It is very difficult to disentangle Veronica's story completely. Did she reject her older children and batter them? Or did she merely treat them fairly if over-strictly, according to Western standards? There is no doubt that she herself has been battered emotionally. Fostering in some African cultures is acceptable, even an act of love, but when it is done partly against one's will, the result of sexist domination by a husband and with an inappropriate family, the effect can only be disastrous.

During the 1970s it was common practice to foster black children with white families, and perhaps because there were insufficient numbers of homes available, social services cast their net wide. In addition, a great deal of private fostering took place, and this continued in the 1980s. This can result in children from African cultures being placed far from their own parents, often in remote rural areas among people who live a totally different way of life. A report from the Save the Children Fund in 1988 revealed that at least 2,300 West African children were placed with families in Britain through magazine advertisements on an informal basis, often in inadequate conditions such as overcrowding or living with unsuitable foster parents – in one case someone who had been convicted of sexual offences.

Private fostering could bypass local authorities or the various voluntary bodies that handle fostering with increasing skill and expertise. Changes in the law at the time of writing should mean that such practices will be abolished and local authorities will be informed of all fostering arrangements. Without strong powers of intervention from local authorities, children of ethnic minorities have undoubtedly been in danger of being fostered by people who wished to make a profit out of them or were insensitive to their culture, their psychological needs and those of their natural families too.

It is not clear whether Veronica's children were fostered through a local authority or through some private arrangement, but the cultural and geographical distance created between them and their mother was disastrous. Veronica, a stranger in a foreign country, was expected to work to support her student husband, then had an abortion and lost her two children to a foster home. Added to this was the disappointment with her marriage and the loss of her parents, and the feeling that she was not listened to. It would not be surprising if her experiences resulted in an over-the-top reaction. She must have had an immense need to impose some kind of control over her life. Sadly, that control might have extended to battering her own children.

What is glaringly obvious is the lack of support. It was bad enough that the fostering placement caused a huge cultural gap between Veronica and her two older children. But no effort appears to have been made to bridge the gap between the permissive standards accepted in modern British society and the stricter Victorian values of Veronica's background. Did no one tell Veronica that it was not the norm to cane in British schools, or that getting paint on trousers is acceptable, and doing a bit of decorating is regarded as fun? Where were the upholders of the religious faith to which Veronica belonged? Surely they could have helped her understand.

Ideas about fostering have changed radically in recent years and remain the subject of much debate. Many local authorities in major cities operate a 'same culture' policy regarding fostering and adoption precisely to avoid the kinds of problems encountered by Veronica and her children.

Vickie Shaw is a fostering project leader with a London local authority, and is of Afro-Caribbean background. She holds strong and uncompromising views on fostering. 'I see a situation where black children are placed in white families as sheer racism in that the white society feels it knows what is best for the child, and it knows better than black society. Fostering has been widespread here because there was no extended family in this country, but a majority of black children are in care, I believe, because the white social worker understands black society only as deficient and doesn't understand black child-rearing practices.'

Vickie herself was parted from her parents when she was eight. 'They came here from the West Indies to work, and I stayed with my grandparents till they sent for me and my brother and sisters. Grandparents in black society are important people. They are highly respected and loved. They offer to help automatically. We see it as our responsibility to care for them till the end of their days. That's part of our culture that a white worker might not understand. Our children learn that it is important for them to take care of themselves and to take care of other people.

'A white family taking a black child can't give what they haven't got. The child might find most of the crises taken care of, but to be proud of their culture is hard for them. If a child doesn't get a positive black image when growing up, they will have a low esteem of black people and of themselves. A family would need to understand what a child might feel when it comes home from school and says a teacher or another child has picked on them. If the child says it is because he was black, how should that be handled? A parent has to understand what might be discrimination and what is simply part of normal experience. It is an extra dimension to deal with.

'If a child asks am I different? because children at school have commented on his or her colour, a mother might reply in God's eyes all are the same. This may be a comfort but it bypasses the question. The answer should be yes, you are different, and there should be a pride in the difference. Children coming home from school and trying to scrub their skin white, or being told by a well-meaning foster mother that if they drink more milk their skin will get white, or feeling different from other black children because their white parent does not know how to plait a child's hair, which is something all black parents know because the hair is very tangled in the morning if they don't, all this causes identity problems.'

Same-culture fostering can mean a child has to wait for an appropriate place, and there have been criticisms on the basis that few black families have come forward. Vickie thinks the wait is worthwhile. 'I'd say the same for a Chinese or even a Scottish child. But we are recruiting and finding the families now. In the past black families were not sought. They were not seen as good enough by white society.'

This view can only be acceptable when it is not taken to extremes. When a black child has the option of waiting in a children's home or going to a white foster family, the latter must surely be the more humane answer. And once the situation appears successful, it must be best for the child to stay there. A child's future is too important to be determined by racial resentments and rigid principles.

That said, it is undeniably important that white society recognizes and respects the culture and style of other groups.

Long-term fostering has been known to be used as an easy option by social workers for any families they regard as 'deviant'. As Veronica says, 'once it had happened, nobody wanted to do anything'. Social workers have also been criticized for having a tendency to devalue the natural family once a child is removed, concentrating on parental weaknesses and not their strengths when writing up reports. From a child's point of view, there is a subtle devaluing of roots which can have disastrous effects later, and this holds true for fostering and adoption with any colour or creed.

In the section of this book on adoption, there are examples of white adopted young people searching for their roots and experiencing a kind of homecoming when they discovered some recognized family characteristic like an expansive smile, or, more tenuously, through a liking for poetry. The compatibility of their adopted families, culturally similar though it was, did not truly fill the need for this special recognition. Children of different colour will be even further removed from their roots if they live in families that cannot teach them their identifying links with colour or custom or language.

However, it is not always true that cross-culture fostering is a failure. It can be highly successful, especially if the parents themselves mix easily with various ethnic groups and the social circle is racially tolerant and varied. There can be no hard and fast rules on this delicate issue, only the kind of open-mindedness that breaks down all kinds of racial prejudice and resentment.

Chapter 20

WOMEN IN PRISON

When a mother goes to prison, she is highly likely to be parted from her children. According to a report on women in prison from the London Strategic Policy Unit, there are forty prison places in England and Wales for pregnant women, and thirty-four places for mothers with babies. But the issue is not whether there should be more places, but whether more mothers could be given an alternative to a prison sentence.

The numbers of women in prison rose from approximately 988 in 1970 to under 1,350 in 1985. It is not an enormous number, but proportionately many more women than men serve prison sentences for relatively minor offences. These offences are mainly non-payment of fines, theft involving stolen goods worth less than £100, non-payment of a meal or not having a television licence. Theft and handling of stolen goods constitute 75% of crimes. Foodstuffs and children's and women's clothing are the main items handled, reflecting poverty among women, especially those who are single parents. As well as those convicted, proportionately more women than men are remanded in prison pending medical reports. They can be in prison for weeks or months, though in the end they do not necessarily receive a custodial sentence.

* * *

'When I came out of prison I told my social worker I wanted my children back, and she said it wasn't as easy as that'

Irma is twenty-nine. She has a son of six and a daughter of ten, each from different fathers. Her background is one of loss, rebellion and violence. Her mother died when she was seven. Her father was a strict disciplinarian. Having served a prison sentence for criminal damage and arson, she now lives with her children in a council house and is on a training scheme to help her set up a small business. She is a dark, thickset woman, direct of manner, probably intensely loyal and ready to fight for those she defends.

'I got into trouble when I was a kid. Approved school, borstal. My father made it hard for us. He wouldn't let me and my sister mix with the other children in the street. I found out later that he'd been in trouble a long time ago for shooting a taxi driver and for drugs. He said we were different and the other children would take the mickey and say I couldn't go out at night and had to stay in after school. My two brothers ran off when they were eleven and twelve. But he wasn't so strict with them, I think it was because we were girls. He thought we'd get into trouble. He looked after us, but really it was my older sister who did everything.

'I haven't seen the father of my older child for a long time. We only lived together for a few months, and then he left. It never worked out with the second one either, though I do still see him and it's not as if he doesn't care about the little boy. I've done odd jobs from time to time, but nothing permanent.

'I was living in bed and breakfast accommodation with my kids. I had no support for them. My only money was from the DHSS. I felt I couldn't cope because the little boy was hyperactive and he was getting on top of me. So I decided he should go and live with his dad and the little girl went to her godmother. This was two years ago.

'I was drinking and taking drugs because I was so depressed. But I wanted to sort myself out, so I went into a psychiatric hospital. I was allocated a social worker, and I just couldn't get on with her. She'd be sitting there with her nose in the air when my little boy was running around wild, like I couldn't control him and was a rotten mother. Once when she brought my little boy to see me in hospital, I told her, piss off, I can't get on with you, but she said it took time to change your social worker, though I did later.

'Anyway, I discharged myself from the hospital, and I was taken back into bed and breakfast, even though I was on my own. I had nothing much to do, I was angry, you know, and frustrated. My kids weren't with me. I decided to go to a little supermarket round the corner and I bought myself some cigarettes. And – it was an impulse really – I picked up this can of deodorant and I sprayed it – you know how you can do that in chemists. Anyway I didn't like the smell and I put it back. When I went to buy the cigarettes I give him £5 and he charged me one pound and something over. So I said excuse me, I want more change. And he said you tried the spray, and I said you can do it in chemists, and he said this isn't a chemist, and he refused to give me my proper change. So I just smashed one of the shelves, right? He called the police and they were very nice and said leave it at that and they didn't take me in. So I waited for them to move off again and I just walked round to the shop and wrecked the whole lot. I went mad.

'The police came again and it was the same lot and they said we're gonna have to nick you. So I was put in the back of the police car, and I put my foot straight through the window. When they got me in the cell, they didn't know I had a box of matches on me. They searched me, but she never went too far and it was in an inside pocket. So when I was in the cell I felt so mad, I took all my clothes off and put them in a pile and the mattress and blankets, and set the lot alight. So next morning the charge was changed to criminal damage and arson.

'I was already under a probation officer. I'd had a record since I was twelve really. But they got me a duty solicitor for the court in the morning, and I didn't have any clothes so I went in front of the judge with only a blanket on. He said I will remand the case for another three weeks for a social enquiry report. A friend came and she had some money, so as I had unconditional bail, we went out and I bought a track suit in a shop across the road.

'Then after the three weeks I went back in front of the same judge and he said I am going to remand you in custody while waiting for the report, because he hadn't got it yet. I was put in Holloway prison in the wing for disturbed women for three months, but the report still didn't turn up. It was all a terrible waste of time.'

Irma was visited by her social worker while in Holloway, but relations did not approve. Irma rejected her social worker's reports – no doubt this contributed to the delay, though she does not say so. And eventually she was allocated a new social worker whom she found helpful and understanding.

'Finally, my barrister talked about my mental condition in court, and the judge recommended I went to a psychiatric hospital. I was put on a 28 day section to remain at the hospital for further medical reports. In the hospital I was followed everywhere, watched all the time. I thought, if I get a chance I am going to run. I just got cheesed off. If I went to have a shower there was somebody sitting outside waiting. And some of the other patients were mad, really mad.'

Irma got out the following day when there was a changeover of staff.

'**I just ran from the hospital. Went to friends, got pissed. Next day I was trying to make arrangements to see the kids.** I went to my social worker's office, the new one. She had already had a phone call from the hospital saying I had run from there. She said I should go back myself otherwise I'd be nicked again. She phoned them and arranged it. The doctor explained to me that I

215

needed to be watched for forty-eight hours and then I'd see my doctor with a report. I expected just to see my doctor and a psychiatrist but when I opened the door to this room I saw fourteen or fifteen people sat all round and that put me right off. I looked in and shut the door and went right out again. If they'd explained beforehand that there was going to be a lot of people there I might have been prepared. All those people frightened me. They explained that these people were training.'

After a few more days, Irma was allowed out of hospital during the daytime. She was on major tranquillizers and was going out and drinking heavily with friends. She was also getting drugs from them.

'The nurses did try to help, but I said I tell you what, I'd rather go back to Holloway. So I went back to court the next day and he dropped the section. I could have run off then, but I didn't want more trouble, so I went back into Holloway for about another month.

'When I came out I found out that the dad of my little boy was not looking after him properly and was leaving him with all sorts of different women and he was really upset. The little girl was different, she was being spoiled. I told my social worker I wanted the children back. I didn't realize I'd have to fight to get them. We ended up in Somerset House and the dad was there, but the godmother never turned up. The dad said he had no objection to me having my son back, but he had just started school where he lives and he should stay there. But I shouted out I'm not having that. I was in this three-bedroomed council house now, with a local school five minutes away. I said the travelling backwards and forwards every day, which was a good half an hour on the bus, would be very stressful for me. And the judge understood and agreed with me. The little girl was also going to that school, but as her godmother wasn't there there was no objection.

'But they didn't bring the children back right away. I was getting maybe one day a week with the social worker with them for a couple of hours. That's the procedure, it wasn't that they thought I wasn't fit to be a mother. It was upsetting because my little boy was crying and saying he didn't want to go back to Daddy, and I said I'll get you back soon.

'Then they came to spend weekends. The social worker explained that I hadn't had them for so long that I might crack up if I had them back all at once. I agree with that. I wasn't sure I could have them back so quick. I'd been used to being on my own. I explained to my social worker what I felt and she said don't jump in, I understand because you haven't had them for over a year. She said when you're ready you do it. But when the court hearing came my little girl kept saying when are we coming back, and I thought I've got to do it, so I said I'll have them then. So I got them back, and touch wood now they are happy at school and have got a lot of friends. It's six months now. The father never comes to see the boy, and the godmother is hardly ever in touch.

'I'm doing a course with CAST (Creative and Support Trust) and helping on a video they're making about women prisoners. It's voluntary but I'm getting social security, and CAST have helped me get a grant so I can go on a business course. I want to set up a small business making things with leather. I need money for materials. I heard about CAST when I went to see the solicitor and spotted one of their leaflets on the wall. I'm getting on my feet now.

'I still do get depressed now and again, and I'm still under a psychiatrist at the hospital. I'm still on tranquillizers because I do get in a panic now and then. My little boy is still a handful. My girl says I let him get away with things she can't get away with, and I suppose it is because he is the younger. But I'm managing. It's terrible to think I nearly lost my children.'

* * *

Irma was luckier than some. Her sympathetic and insightful second social worker gave her the opportunity to express her doubts about having the children. Perhaps for the first time in her life she was able to see solutions that did not have to be violent or an abuse of privileges. Hers may well be the beginning of a real success story.

According to research from a report called Breaking the Silence, published by the London Strategic Policy Unit, many women in prison live in constant fear of what may be happening to their children and to their homes. Single parents are especially vulnerable, so much so that some have been known to avoid disclosing the fact that they have children in case they are taken into care. The majority of children stay with relatives, usually the maternal grandmother, which is not necessarily an easy solution. There can be economic hardship, overcrowding problems, difficulties if the relative works full time. Child benefit allowances can take months to be transferred. Family resentments may blow up, or children and the grandmother or other relative might get very attached and resist separation when the mother is released.

When children are taken into care, they might be involved in long-term fostering (with possible consequences as discussed earlier in this book). Social workers may see a woman prisoner as an unfit mother, though the offence may have little connection

217

with her ability to mother, and evidence of her care and devotion may be ample.

Mothers, along with the rest of the female prison population, are allowed one visit lasting one and a half hours every two weeks if convicted, and a daily visit of fifteen minutes if unconvicted. Sometimes the children's carers are reluctant or unable to bring the children. The alternative is one supervised half-hour telephone call a month. In Sweden, Denmark, Australia and one or two American states, regular use of telephones is allowed.

Home Office guidelines stipulate that no children over the age of nine months should live in a close prison unit, and none over eighteen months should be in an open prison. If a woman's sentence continues beyond that time, then mother and child have to be parted. There is only one open prison for mothers and babies, Askham Grange in Yorkshire. While there have been some campaigns to provide units for mothers with children up to the age of three or four, there is much concern about the incarcerating of these women. James Anderson, governor of Styall, one of the closed prisons with a unit for pregnant women and mothers, is quoted in the London Strategic Policy Unit report as follows:

'I am interested to know what response there would be to pressing for a change in legislation to enable all mothers with newborn babies to be immediately paroled . . . It seems to me that a mother giving birth to a baby should always be given the opportunity to make a fresh start and that a caring and compassionate society should, if anything, err on the side of leniency.'

Anderson made his statement in 1984. In 1988 he still had had no official response.

There remain other, more manageable ways of reducing the numbers of women in prison. Imposing a fine is a pointless solution for many mothers in the grip of poverty, which in itself may have been the motivation for their offence. When they cannot pay, they are sent to prison. Some magistrates, knowing this, impose a suspended sentence instead, but this too can inadvertently send a woman to prison, when, for instance, the offence is non-payment of a television licence. If the woman does not have the money to pay, then the sentence may come into force.

Women do not get community service orders as an alternative to prison or fine. In 1982 1% got such an order, as against 9% of men. One reason is that the types of jobs allocated are deemed more suitable for men, such as painting and decorating, though this must be more assumption than fact in many cases. Another is that probation officers feel that community service is difficult for mothers with small children and babies, which it often is, given the paucity of childcare facilities. One suggestion has been to provide community service options with women's projects and other agencies where children might be accepted. How about helping in a local authority children's nursery or day centre?

Irma, though under psychiatric care, might have been better off doing some kind of community service under tactful supervision. The remand sentence seems to have served no useful purpose and in no way helped her get on her feet again. Disturbed prisoners may well be instrumental in delaying reports, especially when they dislike and distrust their social workers. But there should be quicker ways round this and more flexible procedures for changes of social workers.

Clearly the best thing that has happened to Irma was finding out about CAST, which was set up in 1982 by a group of women ex-prisoners and helps women to find their way through claiming benefits, organizing housing, reconciling relationships with families and generally putting their lives together. Her story suggests that there is appropriate help out there, from social services, from voluntary agencies, and from sensible and compassionate judges.

Conclusion

BACK TO US AND THEM

If it is truly desirable that men and women should have equal opportunities in life, then it might be only fair to suggest that the leniency men enjoy when they live apart from their children should also be enjoyed by women. When a marriage breaks up, few men consider the idea of being the main custodial parent, whether they leave to live alone or to be with a new partner. Even the father of a handicapped child is less involved with the decision about that child going into an institution than its mother is. Rarely does a father consider whether he might be the better parent for the child, except when circumstances such as post-natal illness force him to do so, or when the children are old enough to be companions and he can influence their choice (sometimes through a mixture of concern for their well-being, fear of being alone and, regrettably, sheer malice). Even more rarely do a couple consider together whether the father might be the better parent for the child, not only in material terms but for reasons of stability and emotional links.

In opposition to the idea of fathers and mothers being equal, whether absent or otherwise, is the high value placed on the mother/child relationship. The majority of women, having invested the months of pregnancy and years of loving care in a child's development, have no hesitation in accepting this value. But some find that they cannot do so. They may be women who themselves were denied contact with their mothers when they were children, and who have somehow failed to gain the learning experience or the concept of reward or any confidence in the nurturing role. They may be overwhelmed with the task of mothering, or so out of love with the father that they have to reject the children too. They may see no way of making a life for themselves while having to support their children alone, or they may feel that they have to make a choice between their lover and their child and are not empowered to claim both.

The economic system which discriminates against women in terms of pay, childcare facilities and job opportunities, does not make it easy for a woman to match her husband as a provider or allow her sufficient independence to assert her needs to her lover. And then of course there are the women who repudiate the discriminations and are prepared to walk away from the family home in search of self-development and personal freedom, on the basis that if men can do it, so can they.

How much understanding and tolerance should we give to these women, in their varied and different circumstances? There is the view that we need to make a judgement, if only to liberate the offender. Punishment is said to have a cleansing effect. A woman who is given the opportunity to admit to the guilt she struggles to avoid, in facing it may experience a release. And there is no doubt that more than anything else, a woman who leaves a child needs to forgive herself.

But it is impossible to say that it is always wrong for a woman to leave her child. We know that cannot be true for mothers suffering from post-natal illness, or those who are in prison, or those who are forced to put a handicapped child into an institution. Moreover, in our post-permissive society, it is impossible to ignore the fact that some women appear to be ungifted for motherhood. We may call them handicapped, because they themselves lacked a proper bonding with their mothers, or immature because they appear to be unable to take on the responsibilities of motherhood, or so desperately self-involved that they fail to understand the hurt they are causing when they choose freedom above motherhood. To condemn them is irrelevant. It is far more important that we recognize the unpalatable truth: that there are in our society mothers who cannot or will not mother. If they remind us of our own potential weaknesses and selfishness, they should not be blamed for it.

We do not allow women to be weak, to be immature, to break the rules of motherhood. We do not forgive them their trespasses as we have grown to do with men. A man can sublimate his childishness in pursuing a career while neglecting his family, being one of the boys, rushing from one broken marriage to the next. He is allowed to forget and is forgiven. A woman does not have this privilege. Her proper destiny is to be mature, to be good.

This book has shown that children want and need both their primal mother, the woman who gave them life, and their everyday mother, the person who nurtures and nourishes them. Ideally, the two are one and the same. But women are children as well as mothers, and some are locked into immaturity, or feel so trapped

221

for some reason that they cannot provide that ideal combination. They need help, not condemnation.

Rigid views regarding the 'maternal instinct' affect the way women are counselled. Negative feelings are damped down with tranquillizers. Counsellors appeal to the conciliatory instincts in women. There is a tendency to patch up a woman and send her home to get on with the job of keeping the family together, with husbands supporting that aim and rarely being given the opportunity to examine their own position. The idea that the best 'everyday' mother, the person with the most developed 'maternal instinct' does not have to be the mother, and does not even have to be a woman, is seldom seriously considered.

The woman who refuses to be patched up, or simply cannot be, is given a rough ride by psychotherapists, with their simplistic view that a mother who leaves her child cannot really love it. Other than the two self-help organizations, MATCH (Mothers Apart From Their Children) and Mary Woolliscroft's Natural Parents Support Group, no organizations exist to support her through the morass of ideas and opinions, and there is no body of knowledge to help her build a new relationship with her children. The judgements, the sometimes overstated fears about what might happen to the children, are often sterile, providing neither illumination nor guidance.

Where is the professional guidance to help with such problems as women feeling unworthy and being confused and/or disbelieved about their motives for living apart from their children? Who helps those who feel the weight of family disapproval or find difficulty in telling strangers of their situation? What is being done for those who fear being rejected by the children or endure their emotional blackmail, or perhaps having to admit that the father is the better parent?

The biggest punishment for these women is that they cannot live with themselves any more than they can live with their children. They cannot sort out their motives or face their inner truths. That is a terrible price to pay and provides a very poor basis for repairing a damaged relationship between a parent and a child. For in the end, that relationship remains, and some kind of trust and opportunity for expression of love must be regained.

It could be that the agony will reduce as gender roles are blurred, and more men become family-minded while more women seek autonomy. Then the load on mothers would lighten, and with it the guilt. This could in turn lead the way to making more women feel less committed to motherhood, and perhaps to more women leaving their children. But to keep women in their old subservient place for fear of their potential insurrection is unconscionable. In any case, insurrection is not the aim. For true equality, we should not seek to make women behave more like men, but to help men gain the learning experience, the concept of reward and the confidence to take on a more committed nurturing role. (Just as some women do not acquire these virtues through their mothers, most men do not do so through their fathers.) Then both will have equal choices, and both can if necessary decide between them who is the more appropriate full-time parent should the need arise.

We may be progressing towards this desirable state, albeit slowly. By the mid nineties, it is predicted that women will be taking up around 80% of new jobs to compensate for the shortfall in school-leavers – an estimated drop of 1.2 million. Private industry is beginning to provide nursery places for female employees' children. Perhaps ultimately, there will also be more public-funded nurseries and after-school facilities too. Women will then be able to find easier choices within motherhood, and ideally employers and government will begin to give greater status to fathers, and to offer facilities to *parents*, rather than mothers.

There is another demographic change which could profoundly affect the lives of fathers and mothers, and that is the increase in the number of men over women. Already, men aged between twenty and fifty outnumber women by over three-quarters of a million in the UK. There is a similar trend in the United States. Social scientists Marcia Guttentag and Paul Secord of the University of Houston predict that the change will mean a male population more eager for marriage, a protective morality that favours monogamy for women, and a return to traditional domesticity, with women marrying younger and having larger families. Their predictions are based on an examination of other societies in which women are scarce, but they seem in direct opposition to economic needs in the UK and the trends of women towards greater autonomy. Female independence, and an economy more dependent on female labour, will surely have developed too far to be halted by an urge among males to secure a traditional partner. Would it be too much to hope that any male sense of insecurity might be expressed in offering greater support to women rather than in imposing traditional-style domination?

The balance of power between men and women has an immense effect on children. The role and extent of mothering has been determined by a particular balance – of the nuclear family, the woman as homemaker, the father as breadwinner – which is breaking down in front of our eyes. Whilst that breakdown can be good

223

for women, and also for men, who have hitherto been deprived of a proper share in nurturing, it would be tragic if it meant that women chose to flee from motherhood while men, sometimes reluctantly, picked up the pieces. Our children offer us the greatest gift in the world. They allow us to experience altruistic love. We are enriched by them; we enrich those who do not have children themselves. They are everybody's future. And that means that everybody must take a share in caring for them: the State as public servant, parents ideally working together, the community contributing through local support. The burden that women experience once they become mothers is increasingly unacceptable. In a society that truly espouses equality of opportunity, mothers would be able to be free to choose and free to give their love.

Useful Contacts and Addresses

Single Parents
Mothers Apart From Their Children (MATCH), BM Problems, London, WC1N 3XX. Self-help groups for women living apart from their children.

Fathers Need Families, BM Families, London WC1N 3XX. Tel: 081 852 7123.

National Family Conciliation Council, 155 High Street, Dorking, Surrey RH4 1AD. Gives advice on custody, access, etc. to divorced parents experiencing conflict.

Gingerbread, 35 Wellington Street, London WC2E 7BN. Tel: 071 240 0953. Self-help support association for one-parent families.

Rights of Women, 52–54 Featherstone Street, London EC1Y 8RT. Tel: 071 251 6575/6/7. Helps lesbian mothers facing possible loss of custody.

Family support
The Parent Network, 44–46 Caversham Road, London NW5 2DS. Tel: 071 485 8535. Runs courses for parents wanting to share problems, improve relationships with children.

Home-Start Consultancy, 140 New Walk, Leicester LE1 7JL. Tel: 0533 554988. Volunteers offer support to families with children under five in their own homes.

National Childbirth Trust, Alexandra House, Oldham Terrace, London W3 6NH. Tel: 081 992 8637. As well as classes on preparation for birth, runs post-natal support groups, fathers' groups.

Meet-a-Mum Association, 5 Westbury Gardens, Luton LU2 7DW. Provides nationwide network of care to help mothers of young children, puts new mothers in touch with others nearby.

Psychotherapy, post-natal illness, etc
Association for Post-Natal Illness, c/o 7 Gowan Avenue, London SW6. Tel: 071 831 8996. Support group, leaflets, etc.

Women's Therapy Centre, 6 Manor Gardens, London N7 6LA. Tel: 071 263 6200. Therapy workshops for women.

Exploring Parenthood, 41 North Road, London N7 9DP. Tel: 071 607 9647. Runs telephone advice line for members. Also runs workshops on 'problems and pleasures of being a parent'.

Child Psychotherapy Trust, 27 Ulysses Road, London NW6 1ED. Tel: 071 435 1276. Supports projects concerning mental health of children, such as workshops, counselling services.

Mothers of Abused Children, 25 Wampool Street, Silloth, Cumbria CA5 4AA. Telephone helpline: 06973 31432. Wales: 0222 733929.

Working mothers
Workplace Nurseries Campaign, Room 205 South Bank House, Black Prince Road, London SE1 7SJ. Tel: 071 582 7199/7587. Works to abolish tax on workplace nurseries and to develop work-related child care.

Working Mothers Association, 77 Holloway Road, London, N7 8JZ. Tel: 071 700 5771. Campaigns to improve working parents' childcare needs.

Adoption Agencies
National Organisation for Counselling Adoptees and Their Parents (NORCAP), 3 New High Street, Headington, Oxford OX3 5AJ. Tel: 0865 750554. Support agency for adopted people, adoptive and natural parents.

Natural Parents' Support Group, c/o Mary Woolliscroft, 90 Harvey Place, Uttoxeter, Staffs. Support group for women who have given up children for adoption.

Post-Adoption Centre, Interchange Building, 15 Wilkin Street, London NW5 3NG. Tel: 071 284 0555. Support organization for adoptive parents, adopted people and natural parents.

British Agencies for Adoption and Fostering, 11 Southwark Street, London SE1 IRQ Tel: 071 407 8800. Can supply information on adoption, addresses of specialized agencies.

Children
National Child Care Campaign, Wesley House, 70 Great Queen Street, London WC2B 5AX. Tel: 071 405 5617/8. Publishes information, advice to parents on fighting cuts in childcare.

Family Rights Group, 6–9 Manor Gardens, London N7 6LA. Tel: 071 272 7308. Aims to improve the law relating to children in care, offers training, meetings, etc.

National Association of Young People in Care (NAYPIC), 20 Compton Terrace, London N1 2UN. Tel: 071 226 7102. Campaigns for improvement of conditions of young people in care.

Care for the handicapped
Mencap, Royal Society for Mentally Handicapped Children and Adults, 123 Golden Lane, London EC1Y ORT. Tel: 071 253 9433. Offers a wide range of services, including local self-help groups.

The Children's Society, Edward Rudolph House, Margery Street, London WC1. Tel: 071 837 4299. Runs various projects, residential homes, etc, for disabled children and young people.

Disabled Income Group, Millmead Business Centre, Millmead Road, London N17 9QU. Tel: 081 801 8013. Advises on benefits for the disabled.

Crossroads Care Attendant Scheme, 94 Cotton Road, Rugby, Warwickshire CV21 2PN. Tel: 0788 73653. Provides trained home care for families with a disabled child.

Contact a Family, 16 Strutton Ground, London SW1P 2HP. Telephone helpline: 071 222 2211. Puts families with disabled children in touch with each other. Provides contacts with other organizations.

The Bobath Centre, 5 Netherhall Gardens, London NW3 5RN. Tel: 071 435 3895. Provides treatment for children suffering from cerebral palsy.

KIDS, 13 Pond Street, London NW3. Tel: 071 431 0596. Runs holiday centres for disabled children.

Women ex-prisoners
Creative and Support Trust (CAST), 34a Stratford Villas, London NW1 9SG. Tel: 071 485 0367. Support for women who have been in prison or in a drug or alcohol or psychiatric unit.

Bibliography

Introduction
The Baader-Meinhof Group by Stefan Aust, Bodley Head, 1987.
'Fathers Without Wives' by Margaret O'Brien, unpublished PhD thesis, University of London, 1984.
'Mother Doesn't Live Here Any More' by Christine Moore in **New Woman** (American magazine), January 1988.
'Antenatal Identification of Women Liable to have Problems Managing their Babies' and 'The Importance of Childhood Experiences in Relation to Problems of Marriage and Family Building' by Dr Eva Frommer and Gillian O'Shea, **British Journal of Psychiatry**, August 1973.
Depression in Childhood: Developmental Perspectives edited by Michael Rutter, C. Izard and P. Read, chapter in this book by Tirril Harris, George Brown and Antonia Bifulco, Guilford Press, New York, 1986.
'Absentee Mothers' by Patricia Paskowitz, reported in 'Leaving as a Wife, Leaving as a Mother' by Karen E. Rosenblum, **Journal of Family Issues**, June 1986.

Section I
I Know Why the Caged Bird Sings by Maya Angelou, Virago, 1983.
'Mothers Living Apart from their Children' by Judith Fischer, **Family Relations**, July 1983.
'Custodial Dads and the Ex-Wives', Parents Without Partners survey by Geoffrey L. Greif, **Single Parent**, January/February 1984.
Recycling the Family by Frank Furstenburg and Graham Spanier, Sage, 1984.
'Mothers Without Custody and Child Support' by Geoffrey L. Greif, **Family Relations**, January 1986.

'A Victim of the Rights of Husbands' by Caroline Norton, in **Strong-Minded Women** edited by Jan Horowitz Murray, Penguin 1984.

Centuries of Childhood by Philippe Ariès, Penguin, 1973.

Yesterday's Babies by Diana Dick, Bodley Head, 1987.

The Myth of Motherhood by Elizabeth Badinter, Souvenir Press, 1981.

'Rural-Urban Child Fostering in Kenya' by Nici Nelson, unpublished paper, Goldsmith's College.

Maids and Madams by Jacklyn Cook, Ravan Press (Johannesburg), 1984.

'Mothers Without Custody – Reversing Society's Old Stereotypes' by Maggie Riechers, quotes Cora Lynn Goldsborough, **Single Parent**, October 1981.

'Mother Doesn't Live Here Any More', details above.

University of Exeter survey on relations with parents, 1987.

National Association of Social Workers reported in **NOW Times** (New York), April 1987.

Fathers by Lorna McKee, a **Citizen 2000** booklet, Channel 4, 1987.

'Are Men Who Hug Wimps?' report by Thomas Draper and Tom Gordon, **New Society**, 12.12.84.

'Lone Fathers' by Toity Deave, unpublished paper, 1987.

'Single Fathers Rearing Children' by Geoffrey L. Greif, **Journal of Marriage and the Family**, February 1985.

'Dads Raising Kids' by Geoffrey L. Greif, **Single Parent**, December 1982.

'Fathers without Wives' by Margaret O'Brien, unpublished thesis, 1984.

'After Mum Left', report on Anne Willis's work by Barbara Lamb, **Guardian,** 30.8.88.

Sex Discrimination in the School Curriculum in West Glamorgan Schools, report by Equal Opportunities Commission, October 1988.

Sex and Destiny by Germaine Greer, Secker and Warburg, 1984.

'Who Runs the Family?' by Ann Kent, **The Times**, 24.8.88.

'A Day in the Life', **Sunday Times**, 21.8.88.

'Images of Motherhood', **New Generation** (journal of the National Childbirth Trust), March 1987.

General Household Survey, HMSO, 1984.

Stress and Addiction Amongst Women, report by the Women's National Commission, 1988.

Inside the Family, report by the Family Policy Studies Centre, 1987.

The Motherhood Report by Louis Genevie and Eva Margolies, Macmillan (New York), 1987.

'Why I'm not a Martyr Familias' by Robin Green, **Guardian**, 2.2.87.

British Social Attitudes edited by Roger Jowell *et al* (Gower), 1987.

A Secure Base by John Bowlby, Routledge, 1988.

Women's Reality by Anne Wilson Schaff, Harper and Row, 1985.

What Do Women Want? by Louise Eichenbaum and Susie Orbach, Penguin, 1983.

Understanding Women by Louise Eichenbaum and Susie Orbach, Penguin, 1985.

Caring for Children by Bronwen Cohen, European Commission's Childcare Network, 1988.

Report by Kalyani Menon, National Advisory Centre on Careers for Women, 1988.

The Gift Relationship by Richard Titmuss, George Allen & Unwin, 1970.

Section II

Adopted Adults: their relationships with their families, NORCAP, 1987.

To Give Up a Child, leaflet on the National Parents' Support Groups, Open Space file, BBC2, March 1988.

Section III

'Mummy Didn't Mean It' by Vicki Golding, **Social Services Insight**, 8.5.87.

Prescription for Poor Health, report by The Maternity Alliance, 1988.

From Here to Maternity by Ann Oakley, Pelican, 1986.

'Delayed Onset of Maternal Affection After Childbirth' by K.M. Robson and R. Kumar, **British Journal of Psychiatry**, 1980.

Long-Term Foster Care by Jane Rowe and the British Agencies for Adoption and Fostering, Batsford/British Agencies for Adoption and Fostering.

Depression After Childbirth by Katharina Dalton, Oxford University Press, 1980.

Motherhood and Mental Illness edited by Brockington and Kumar, Academic Press, 1982.

'The Impact of Maternal Depression in Young Children' by A.D. Cox, **Journal of Child Psychology and Psychiatry**, June 1987.

'Neurotic Disorders in Child Bearing' and 'The Pathology of the Mother-Child Relationship', papers in **Motherhood and Mental Illness**, see above.

Of Woman Born by Adrienne Rich, Virago, 1977.

First-Time Motherhood by Ramona T. Mercer, Springer Publications, 1987.

'Birth of the Blues' by Joan Raphael-Leff, AIMS Bulletin, Winter 1982–83.

Mother, Madonna, Whore by Dr Estela Welldon, Free Association Books, 1988.

'Do Abused Children Become Abusive Parents?' by Joan Kaufman and Edward Zigler, **American Journal of Orthopsychiatry**, April 1987.

Childcare and Equality of Opportunity by Peter Moss, Consolidated Report of the European Commission, April 1988.

'Where Parents Get Time to Ensure Children Come First' by Peter Moss, **Guardian**, 5.7.89.

Knowing and Learning About Parenthood by Shirley Prendergast and Alan Prout, Health Education Council, 1986.

'Parenthood Education in Secondary Schools', **Health Visitor**, March 1988.

'Mother and Toddler Groups Among "At Risk" Families' by Shirley Palfreeman, **Health Visitor**, September 1982.

'Marcé Society Conference 1986', report in National Childbirth Trust journal **New Generation**, December 1986.

Section IV

The Fifth Child by Doris Lessing, Jonathan Cape, 1988.

Informal Carers by Hazel Green, OPCS, 1988.

The Child with Spina Bifida by D. Pilling, National Foundation for Educational Research, published by the National Children's Bureau, 1973.

Handicapped Children, Their Homes and Lifestyles by N. Butler *et al*, Department of Child Health, University of Bristol, 1978.

Mental Handicap in the Community edited by Alan Leighton, Woodhead-Faulkner, 1988.

Section V

The Father Figure by Lorna McKee and Margaret O'Brien, Tavistock, 1982.

Lesbian Mothers on Trial, Rights of Women, 1984.

Children in Lesbian and Single-Parent Households by S. Golombok, Ann Spencer and Michael Rutter, Institute of Psychiatry, 1983.

'Lesbian Mothers and their Children' by M. Kirkpatrick *et al*, American Journal of Orthopsychiatry, No 13, 1981.

'Sexual Identity of 37 Children Raised by Homosexual and Transvestite Parents' by Richard Green, **American Journal of Psychiatry**, June 1978.

'Children's Acquisition of Sex Role Behaviour in Lesbian-Mother Families' by B. Hoeffer, **American Journal of Orthopsychiatry**, No 3, 1981.

Woman's Experience of Sex by Sheila Kitzinger, Penguin, 1985.

Review of the African Family Advisory Service, internal report by the Save the Children Fund, December 1988.

Woman's Imprisonment – Breaking the Silence, report by the Women's Equality Group, London Strategic Policy Unit, 1985.

Conclusion

'Coming Soon: More Men than Women' by Jib Fowler, **New York Times**, 5.6.88, quotes work of Guttentag and Secord.

Index

abandoned babies, 100–1
abnormality, 165
  see also handicapped children
absence, parental, 49–50
absent fathers, 124–5
abuse *see* child abuse, sexual
  abuse
adolescent depression, 85–6
adolescents, disturbed, 36
adoption, 22, 97–126,
  of handicapped children, 188
advice, biased, 35, 222
Africa, practice of motherhood,
  34
AID (artificial insemination by
  donor), 126
Anderson, James, 218
Angelou, Maya, *I Know Why the
  Caged Bird Sings*, 26–7
anger, 81, 82, 83, 104, 135
Anna Freud Clinic, 35
anti-depressants, 155
anti-nurturing society, 5, 92, 93
apology for leaving, 83
Arbiter, Elizabeth, 49
Arbours, 132, 134
Ariès, Philippe, *Centuries of
  Childhood*, 31
Askham Grange Prison,
  Yorkshire, 218
Association for Post-Natal
  Illness, 151, 226
au pair girls, 33
authority, loss of, 40,
  41

'baby farmers', 32
Badinter, Elizabeth, *The Myth of
  Motherhood*, 32
benefits, state, 123, 178
'best interests' of child,
  in custody cases, 191–2
biblical example, 1–2
Black, Dora, 49
blame, children laying on
  themselves, 81
Bobath centre, 174, 228
bonding, 30, 136–7
Booth Hall Children's Hospital,
  Manchester, 161
Bowlby, John, 29, 30, 32, 33, 89
breastfeeding, 31–2, 92
British Social Attitudes Survey,
  1987, 88
Bruce, Ariel, 125–6

care, 165–77
  local authority, 136
'carer', 26, 42
CAST (Creative and Support
  Trust) 217, 219, 228
Chagall, Marc, 12
charities, 182
child
  'best interests' of, in custody
    cases, 191, 192
  choice in custody cases, 191,
    192, 194
child abuse, 37, 129, 130, 160
child benefit, 123

235

Oakley, Ann, 137
O'Brien, Maggie, 45–6
obstetric complications, at birth, 154, 155
open adoption, 126
opinions, society's, 28–41
Orbach, Susie, 89

parenthood, education for, 160–2
parenting, contribution to disturbed adolescents, 36
parent link, 161–2
Parent to Parent, 175, 182
Parents and Children Together, 182
Parents for Children, 188
Parents Without Partners, 28, 29
Place of Safety Order, 136
playgroups, 33
play schemes, 159
Polanski, Roman, *Rosemary's Baby*, 157–8
Post-Adoption Centre, 101, 117–18, 227
post-natal depression, 37, 127–62,
    cause and effect, 151–8
    damage to children, 152
    cures, 159–62
post-natal support groups, 161–2
poverty, effect on mothers, 129
Priestley, Judith, 203
prison
    alternative sentences to, 218
    women in, 213–19
psychoanalysis, 29–30
psychotherapy, 132, 142, 148, 155, 162, 192, 222
puritan ethics, 57, 61

'quality time', 41, 92

racial indifference, 206–12
Rantzen, Esther, 49, 93
Raphael-Leff, Joan, 154–5

'regulator' type of mother, 154–5, 159
rejection, 54, 62, 67–8, 69, 73, 199
    of children by mothers, 70, 106–7, 113, 118, 187
religion, influence of, 19
Rich, Adrienne, *Of Woman Born*, 153
Richards, Martin, 30
Richmond Fellowship, 132, 134
Rights of Women, 201, 202, 203, 225
Robson and Kumar, *Delayed Onset of Maternal Affection after Childbirth*, 137
Roman attitudes, 1
'roots', 119
Rousseau, Jean-Jacques, 31
Royal Family, 2, 5, 49, 50

sacrificial life, women's, 61–2, 83, 87–95, 165, 171
Save the Children Fund, 209
Savell, Linda, 119
Sawbridge, Phillida, 117–18
Schaff, Anne Wilson, 89
schoolgirl mothers, 162
schools, 85
search for natural parents, by adopted children, 110–22
Secord, Paul, 223
section two, 185
secure base for children, 16, 23, 25, 37, 89
self-fulfilment, women's, 4, 48, 83, 90, 91, 221
sexual abuse, 27, 37, 130, 135, 136, 205
sexual love, 12
sexual perversion, in women, 157–8
shared child-rearing, 34
shared control, adoption cases, 125–6
shared custody, 125
shared parenthood, 26, 47
Shaw, George Bernard, 11

239

Editor's Note: Read Luke 10:38-42 and John 12:1-11.

5

TWO WOMEN OF BETHANY

And Martha served (John 12:2).
Mary, which also sat at Jesus' feet (Luke 10:39).

These two sisters appear in three unforgettable scenes in the Gospels, and the artists who sketch them for us are Luke and John. Luke sketches them in the first and opening scene, and John in the two other scenes. The first scene shows the sisters at a supper with our Lord; the second shows them at a funeral; and the third at a banquet. But in every scene they appear with the same unmistakable characteristics. One is the busy efficient woman who cooks and serves; the other is the woman who sits at Jesus' feet, the woman who prays.

As you go out from Jerusalem, taking the road to Jericho, you come to Bethany—about three miles along the road, just where it begins to drop down toward Jericho. In this village lived Lazarus with his two sisters, Martha and Mary.

Martha seems to have been the head of the house, for Luke tells us that "a certain woman named Martha received him into her house" (Luke 10:38). Some have conjectured that she was the widow of Simon the Leper, for Matthew states that it was in Simon's house that the banquet celebrating the resurrection of Lazarus was held.

We do not know how the relationship between this family and Jesus was established. Perhaps Martha in her grief after the death

55

of her husband had gone to Jesus. Perhaps—and more likely—on one of His journeys Jesus stopped one day at their door in Bethany and asked for a drink of water. But however established, the friendship was beautiful and mutually profitable. Jesus once said that the foxes had holes and the birds of the air had nests, but the Son of Man had not where to lay His head. So far as ownership was concerned, that was true; but it is a satisfaction to recall that there were at least two homes where the Son of Man was always a welcomed and beloved guest. One was the home of Peter at Capernaum; the other was this home at Bethany.

Who can tell what that home meant to Jesus? There always awaited Him a warm welcome, great kindness, true sympathy, and deep understanding. All we know of the brother in the house, aside from his death and resurrection, is that Jesus loved him and wept over him when he was dead. It was a home where love reigned; and without love what is home?

Often on His journeys of mercy and teaching Jesus stopped at this Bethany home and was refreshed; and it was this home, Matthew tells us, that was His refuge and resting place in the week of His passion and death. I imagine that Bethany home was to Jesus what the home of the Shunammite woman with its prophet's chamber was to Elisha as he made his journeys up and down that land. I imagine it was to Jesus what the home of Sir Thomas Abney was for thirty-six years to Isaac Watts. I imagine that home of Bethany was to Jesus what the home of Mary Unwin was to William Cowper, the great poet and hymn writer. In her home Cowper lived for nineteen years; and in one of his noblest sonnets he commemorated the love and care of Mary Unwin:

> Mary! I want a lyre with other strings;
> Such aid from Heaven as some have feigned they drew!
> An eloquence scarce given to mortals, new,
> and undebased by praise of meaner things!
> That, ere through age or woe I shed my wings,
> I may record thy worth, with honor due,
> In verse as musical as thou art true,—
> Verse that immortalizes whom it sings!
> But thou hast little need: there is a book,
> By seraphs writ with beams of heavenly light,

On which the eyes of God not rarely look;
A chronicle of actions just and bright!
   There all thy deeds, my faithful Mary, shine,
   And since thou own'st that praise, I spare thee mine.

SCENE 1: A SUPPER

Let us look at these two sisters, first in the supper scene which is related by Luke. "Now it came to pass, as they went, that he entered into a certain village; and a certain woman named Martha received him into her house" (Luke 10:38). Jesus was traveling through the country with His disciples, perhaps coming up from Jericho; for He had just related the story of the Good Samaritan, who showed kindness to a man beaten and robbed on that road. No doubt, Jesus sent a messenger ahead to inform the friends at Bethany that they could expect Him for supper that night. His disciples, of course, were included among the visitors; and we can see Martha, when she received word of the approach of the considerable company, going energetically to work to prepare for the loved Guest and His friends.

One servant is dispatched to the market for food, and others are directed to get the guestchamber ready. In the midst of the bustle of preparation Jesus arrives. After the first Oriental kiss of welcome and the washing of the feet, Jesus sits down to rest in the cool shade of the courtyard, where the vines are clambering over the walls. There Mary joins Him, while Martha hurries off to direct the servants and prepare the repast. It was no slight task to prepare for so many, and Martha is somewhat anxious and heated as she helps the servants in the hot kitchen and prepares the table.

In the midst of her exertions she remembers Mary. "Where is Mary? Why doesn't she help me with the work?" Off she goes to search for her sister, and finds her in the cool courtyard sitting at the feet of Jesus, looking raptly and fondly into His face and drinking in His words of wisdom. For the moment Martha loses her temper, and exclaims to Jesus, "Lord, dost thou not care that my sister hath left me to serve alone? bid her therefore that she help me" (Luke 10:40). Jesus answers this rude intrusion and interruption in calm, patient words, saying to Martha, "Martha, Martha, thou art careful and troubled about many things: but one thing is needful: and Mary hath chosen that good part, which shall not be taken away from her" (Luke 10:41,42).

Jesus did not rebuke Martha for her zeal and industry. Somebody had to prepare the supper; and if Martha, too, had spent all her time sitting at the feet of Jesus, He and the disciples would have gone hungry that night. God bless all the thoughtful, busy, efficient housekeepers like Martha. A young man looking for a wife would do well to ascertain if the one he looks upon with favor has some of the qualities of Martha. Martha's housekeeping qualities will wear much longer than rouged beauty, enameled nails, and permanent waves. The divorce records would be cut down considerably if modern wives had a little more of Martha in them.

But it is clear from the words of Jesus to Martha that she was in danger of putting too great an emphasis on the practical, busy side of life, to the neglect of the devotional and contemplative side. The ideal woman would combine the practical and the devotional; but the devotional can be omitted only to the hurt of the soul.

There is too little quietness and meditation and prayer in the world today, and too little of it among our women, many of whom are stirring about in their various clubs and organizations, commendably busy and cumbered with care of the social welfare of the community, but somewhat to the neglect of worship and prayer. All the old-time Christian homes used to have in them works of devotion and meditation which were read and pondered. Today those books have almost all disappeared. Even the one great Book of devotion, the Bible, gets little attention in the ordinary home.

What about us? Are we cumbered with the cares of this world? Are we giving more thought to them than to the spiritual needs of our souls? We should heed the words of Jesus to Martha: "Thou art careful and troubled about many things: but one thing is needful: and Mary hath chosen that good part, which shall not be taken away from her" (Luke 10:41,42).

No! Time and fate will take away from us all those things about which we have been so busy. One by one they pass and disappear; but the "good part," our relationship to Christ our Redeemer, the care which we bestow upon our soul—that abides forever.

An old legend relates that once on a cold stormy night Martha was busy in her home preparing for the expected Christ. In the midst of her preparations there was a gentle knock on the door.

Opening the door, Martha saw a ragged beggar standing there in the wet and cold. Immediately she shut the door on the beggar, and saying, as she did so, "I am expecting Jesus, the great prophet of Galilee, tonight. I have no time for beggars. Come again."

After a little there was another gentle knock on the door. This time, when Martha opened the door she saw a frail, ill child standing on the threshold. To this child also Martha said, "I am expecting Jesus tonight. I have no time to give to you." But before she could close the door, suddenly Jesus, in all His majesty, stood before her!

Martha had been too busy to recognize her Lord. How is it with us? Are we so busy that we cannot recognize Christ when He comes? Are we so engaged with the world that we cannot recognize and hear the voice of God when He speaks to our soul?

SCENE 2: A FUNERAL

The next scene is also at Bethany; but it is not a banquet this time, but the house of sorrow. Lazarus, whom Jesus loved, lay dead and buried. When his sickness had become serious, the sisters sent word to Jesus, who was across the Jordan, saying, "He whom thou lovest is sick" (John 11:3). They thought that would bring Him at once. But the hours and the days slipped by, and Jesus did not come. But death came, as it will come to all.

Finally, Jesus also came. The house at Bethany was filled with friends of the family, who had come to show their sympathy by wailing. When word came that Jesus was at hand, Martha arose and ran to meet Him, crying out, with gentle expostulation, "Lord, if thou hadst been here, my brother had not died" (John 11:21). But that was immediately followed by one of the most beautiful confessions of faith in Christ that mortal lips ever expressed: "But I know, that even now, whatsoever thou wilt ask of God, God will give it thee" (John 11:22). There we have the ground of Christian prayer. We pray in the Name of Christ; and God will do great things for Christ's sake.

Then Jesus spoke to Martha about the resurrection. When Martha replied that she knew her brother would rise at the last day, Jesus answered with His great grave-shaking affirmation, "I am the resurrection, and the life!" (John 11:25). Awed by that utterance, Martha returned to the house, and going to the room where Mary was weeping by herself, said to her, "The Master is come, and calleth for thee." When Mary heard that, she hurried to meet Jesus and fell at His feet, saying just what Martha had said before her: "Lord, if thou hadst been here, my brother had not died" (John 11:32). When Jesus saw her weeping, and heard the Jews weeping, He Himself wept. There you have it—the shortest, and in some ways the greatest, sentence of the Gospels: "Jesus wept" (John 11:35). Then followed the great scene at the sepulcher when Lazarus came forth, bound hand and foot with the graveclothes, and Jesus said, "Loose him, and let him go!" (John 11:44). We leave to your imagination the happy reunion that night in the home at Bethany.

Heaven, I think, will be just like that—just as simple and just as real—father there; mother there; brothers there; sisters there; and all the dear old memories about us.

SCENE 3: A BANQUET

The last scene in which the two sisters appear is the banquet which was served for Christ at Bethany, no doubt a feast of commemoration and thanksgiving for the resurrection of Lazarus. This is the same banquet of which Matthew tells us, only he says it was in the house of Simon the Leper, and does not give the name of the woman who poured out the ointment. But it is clear that it is the same supper John speaks of when he says, "They made him a supper; and Martha served" (John 12:2).

This is the same capable Martha, taking full charge of the important banquet. All the disciples were there; Martha was there; Lazarus was there; and, best of all, Jesus was there. How wonderful to them to sit by the side of a man who had been among the dead, and by the side of Him who brought him back. What were the thoughts of Lazarus?

> When Lazarus left his charnel-cave—[1]
> And home to Mary's house return'd,
> Was this demanded—if he yearn'd
> To hear her weeping by his grave?

---

1. Tennyson, *In Memoriam*, xxxi.

"Where wert thou, brother, those four days?"
    There lives no record of reply,
    Which telling what it is to die
Had surely added praise to praise.

From every house the neighbors met,
    The streets were fill'd with joyful sound,
    A solemn gladness even crown'd
The purple brows of Olivet.

Behold a man raised up by Christ!
    The rest remaineth unreveal'd;
    He told it not; or something seal'd
The lips of that Evangelist.

And Mary was there, although not in evidence at first. But there is no doubt as to what her thoughts were.

Her eyes are homes of silent prayer,
    Nor other thought her mind admits
    But, he was dead, and there he sits,
And He that brought him back is there.

Then one deep love doth supersede
    All other, when her ardent gaze
    Roves from the living brother's face,
and rests upon the Life indeed.[2]

It was a notable banquet, I am sure. Martha would see to that. The best the market of Jerusalem could supply was there. But that was not enough for Mary. Something more was due her Lord than baked meats and costly drinks. She had purchased a pound of ointment, very costly, the most expensive she could buy. Waiting her opportunity, she broke the vessel and poured the dark, luxurious ointment over the feet of Jesus as He reclined at the table. Then with the tresses of her hair she wiped his feet. "And the

---

2. *Ibid*, xxxii.

house was filled with the odor of the ointment" (John 12:3)—and the world has been filled with it ever since.

Some of the disciples, led by Judas, complained about this waste. But Jesus answered their indignation by telling them that Mary had anointed him against the day of His death and burial. Then came that great sentence, which endowed Mary's deed with fadeless immortality: "Verily I say unto you, Wheresoever the gospel shall be preached throughout the whole world, this also that she hath done shall be spoken of for a memorial of her" (Mark 14:9).

Men did other acts of kindness for Christ. One lent Him his boat, another his beast, another his strength, another his cup, and another his grave. Men were to witness for Him and suffer for Him and die for Him; but the only deed done to Christ upon which He pronounced an immortality of fame was what Mary of Bethany did that night at the supper when she poured the ointment on His feet and dried them with her hair. Yes, Mary chose the better part, the good part. She chose to give her heart to Christ, and therefore she lives forever.

Woman, you are a sister to Mary; that is what Christ asks of you. He desires your love. He asks for your heart. Has no man ever asked for your hand? But here is the One altogether lovely, and chiefest among ten thousand. He comes and asks for your heart. Will you give it to Him?

THE ONE THING NEEDFUL

Mary chose that good part, the one thing needful which could not be taken from her. Have you done the one thing needful? Have you chosen that good part, which is salvation through faith in Christ? That is the one thing and the only thing, that is needful. Other things may be helpful, convenient, desirable, useful; but only one thing is needful, one thing without which you cannot do; that is saving faith in the Lord Jesus Christ.

Sometimes you read the obituaries of men in the newspapers, telling of what they have done in life, institutions they have founded, books they have written, factories they have built, money they have had to leave behind them; but what about the one thing needful? Did they have that?

Saving faith in Christ is the "good part," which cannot be taken from you. All other things will be taken from you—health, money, beauty, fame, pleasure, friends. Time and death will remove all these things, but not that better part. Have you chosen it, definitely, finally, irrevocably, and gladly—that better part? If not, will you choose it today? If you do, I can see Martha and Mary and Lazarus standing before the Throne, and I can hear them mention your name as they say to their Lord, "Lord, another soul has chosen that good part."

QUESTIONS FOR DISCUSSION:

1. As you read about Martha and Mary in Luke 10:38-42 and John 12:1-11, try to picture them and their contrasting personalities. Which one can you most identify with?

2. Macartney says, "Martha seems to have been the head of the house." What does that tell you about Martha? About Mary? About Lazarus?

3. If you were a man looking for a wife, which sister would you prefer—Martha or Mary?

4. As you look at yourself and your life, which of these sisters would you "like to be like"?

5. Note that both sisters spoke the same words about their brother's death. What does that tell you about their faith?

6. Martha "served" and Mary "worshiped." Which action do you think most pleased Jesus?

Editor's Note: For the biblical background to
this story, read Judges 14 through 16.

6

THE WOMAN WHO SHEARED HIM

And she made him sleep upon her knees   (Judges 16:19).

S amson is the great humorist of the Bible. He was the perpetrator
of huge practical jokes, as when he carried off the gates of
Gaza and stacked them up on top of the hill near Hebron. In the
horse-and-buggy days, when people still had gates about their
homes, that was always the chief Halloween prank, to carry off the
gates and set them up on top of a high building. All this, I suppose,
was an echo of Samson's ancient joke.

Another bit of horseplay of Samson's was to choose for his
weapon the jawbone of an ass, and with that weapon smite the
Philistines, hip and thigh, with a great slaughter. But perhaps the
most famous of his exploits and practical jokes was to catch 300
foxes, tie them tail to tail, and, setting a firebrand between the
tails, turn them loose in the barley fields of the Philistines. Joker,
riddle propounder, doer of great exploits—it was not until the
very last hour of his life that Samson began to take life seriously,
and then it was almost too late. Like Samson, a great many people
never wake up to the earnestness and seriousness of life until life is
almost over.

But Samson is more than the great joker of the Bible. He is one
of its supreme tragedies, one of its saddest shipwrecks, one of its
outstanding exhibitions of the deep, deep pathos of life—of powers prostituted, talent debased, and genius soiled. The secret of

that shipwreck was a woman—to be correct, several women, but one in particular—that Delilah upon whose knees Samson slept when his head was sheared of its golden locks and his divinely bestowed strength departed from him.

This was a dangerous place to sleep, for out of that sleep none ever wakes but to weep. Out of that slumber men awake to find it is not morning, but midnight. And how dark that night!

Delilah is one of several temptresses who appear in the Bible. The other notorious ones are Potiphar's wife, who tempted Joseph; Jezebel, who stirred up Ahab; and Herodias, who tempted Herod. No series of sermons on the great women of the Bible would be complete without a sermon on Delilah; for, if the other women in this series illustrate woman's higher nature, her beautiful and beneficent influence over men, her power to stir the ambitions, to incite to deeds of heroism and valor and power, to launch a thousand ships, Delilah illustrates another power in woman just as real, her influence over man for the power of evil, turning him back from his high undertaking, obscuring the dawn of his ambition, putting out the stars of his hope, and stripping him of his strength and his honor. That frequently happens in life. The Bible is a Book that holds the mirror up to life. Therefore, in the Bible we find the story of this beautiful temptress, Delilah.

Every life represents a purpose of God. Unfortunately, sin thwarts and mars and destroys that divine purpose in many a life. Nevertheless, it is important, and it is inspiring, to remember that you and your life represent a plan and purpose of God. Are you living up to that purpose? That was the way Samson came into the world. He was born for a purpose; and that purpose was to deliver Israel out of the hand of its oppressors, the cruel and blasphemous Philistines. Yet even in the angel's announcement of Samson's birth there was a prediction of the sorrow and tragedy of his life, for the angel said to Samson's mother, "He shall *begin* to deliver Israel" (Judges 13:5). That was all that Samson did. He only *began* to save Israel. The morning of his life was bright; but soon that brightness was overclouded with gloom.

They called him Samson, "Sunshine," when he was born into that home in Israel. That is a good name for every child. How God, from hour to hour, from day to day, from week to week and month to month, from year to year and age to age, alleviates the sorrow and gloom of the world and penetrates its darkness with sunshine by the birth of little children!

Manoah and his wife asked the angel how they should bring this child up: "How shall we order the child, and how shall we do unto him?" (Judges 13:12). The angel answered that the child was to be a Nazarite from his mother's womb, which meant that he was to drink no wine nor strong drink, and that no razor was to come upon his head. It is worth noting that the strongest man of the Old Testament, Samson, and the greatest man, according to Jesus, of the New Testament, John the Baptist, were both total abstainers.

There was a law in Israel that no tool or instrument of iron was to be lifted over an altar, for the altar was dedicated to God. The Nazarite was a dedicated, consecrated man, and for that reason no shears or metal razor was to be lifted over his head. His unshorn locks were not the *source* of his strength, but the *sign* of his devotion to the will of God.

That is an uplifting and sublime view of man's life. Man is an altar man. He ought to live for God. Keep that in mind! You are an altar man, an altar woman. Revere yourself! If you want the respect and reverence of others, revere and respect your own life. Have for yourself what John Milton tells us in his college days was a wall of defense about him against the vice and temptations of the college—"a just and pious reverence for my own person."

Now arrived at full manhood, Samson began to do exploits. After he made his first successful assault upon the oppressors of his country, his own people, stricken with an inferiority complex, and in dread of the Philistines, came to him and said, "Knowest thou not that the Philistines are rulers over us? what is this that thou hast done unto us?" (Judges 15:11). Much that Samson did was wicked and sinful, according to our standards today; but give him credit for this—he had a hero in his soul. When all his countrymen cowered before the Philistines, he smote out at them in the name of God. Boldly he answered his accusers: "As they did unto me, so have I done unto them" (Judges 15:11).

But a thing happened that happens to most young men. Samson fell in love. This was the first of three love affairs in Samson's life, the first of the three women who betrayed him and did him injury. Samson was a giant in strength and a hero in courage; but, as we shall presently see, he had his weak side. He was not able to say "No" to a woman. History abounds with men who, in certain respects, tower like giants above their fellow men—men like Lord Nelson, the hero of Trafalgar, and like Napoleon, who nevertheless were themselves easily conquered on one side of their life.

WOMAN NO. 1

This woman down in Timnath was a Philistine. You can imagine their consternation when Samson, returning from there, announced to his father and mother that he had fallen in love with a Philistine maiden and that he intended to marry her! All their entreaties and prayers and protests and warnings against such an ill-advised alliance with a woman who belonged to the deadly enemies of Samson's country fell, as they often do, upon deaf ears. Samson wanted her. "I like her," he says; "I'll look after the future. Don't worry about that. Get her for me to wife" (see Judges 14).

One would have thought that Samson was big enough and strong enough to get a wife for himself, but that was the way they did things in those days. His parents agreed to arrange the betrothal, and Samson in high feather went down to visit his beloved. On the way down a lion roared against him, but in the exultation of his spirits at that time a lion was nothing to Samson. Seizing the lion he tore him asunder as one would a piece of paper. When he made his next visit to Timnath, bees had swarmed in the carcass of the lion; and, dipping in his rod, Samson tasted of the honey. That suggested to him a joke and riddle for the feast which he gave to the Philistine young men before his marriage, like the dinner a man about to be married gives to his male friends.

When they asked him to entertain them with some story or joke, Samson said, "All right, I will lay a wager with you. If you can guess my riddle within seven days, I will give you thirty changes of garments. If you cannot, then you give the thirty changes of garments to me" (see Judges 14:12).

They said: "All right, Samson. Put forth thy riddle. Let us hear it." And this was the riddle, which shows that Samson's strength was not all in his body and that he was well endowed above his shoulders: "Out of the eater came forth meat, and out of the strong came forth sweetness" (Judges 14:14).

Day after day the young Philistine blades debated and worked in vain over that riddle. Then they went to Samson's bride and ordered her, upon threat of death, to entice Samson and pry from him the secret of his riddle.

Now we see where Samson was weak. He did not yield at first; but after his bride came at him for seven days, weeping all through those seven days, and telling him that if her loved her he would tell her, Samson yielded and told her the riddle. When the seven days were up the young Philistines appeared before Samson with a look of confidence and said to him: "We know your riddle, Samson. What is sweeter than honey, and what is stronger than a lion?" (see Judges 14:18). Samson kept his promise and gave the thirty changes of garments to the young Philistines; but he turned it into one of his famous jokes by getting the garments from the backs of Philistines whom he had slain. The upshot of that first romance of Samson was that his wife was given to his companion "whom he had used as his friend" (Judges 14:20). Samson was betrayed by his friend and mocked and betrayed by his wife.

WOMAN NO. 2

"We live and learn," the old saying has it. But some men never learn. Samson's next woman friend was a much worse woman, as far as her station was concerned, than the first one. This time it was a harlot in Gaza. The Philistines were told of a visit he made at the home of this woman, and that night they surrounded the house and said, "When it is day, we shall kill him" (Judges 16:2). They were both right and wrong in their prediction. Samson escaped that time, and celebrated his escape by carrying off the gates of Gaza in mockery and setting them up on top of a high hill near the city. Nevertheless, Samson, although unknown to himself, had weakened his character. These indulgences in sin were "softening" him for the final kill.

It has been said that hell is paved with good intentions. It is well to remember, however, that there is always a path that leads to hell before one gets there, and that path is paved with bad intentions and with bad deeds and bad associations. Yes, Philistines, plotting for the death of Samson, you were right when you said, "When it is day, we shall kill him." You did not kill him, however;

but sensuality did. When the night of indulgence and passion and sin is gone, then comes the dawn of judgment and retribution. "When it is day, we shall kill him!"

WOMAN NO. 3

Samson's narrow escape from the Philistines at Gaza had taught him no wisdom. Now comes the third woman—the one who accomplishes the final overthrow of Samson. "And it came to pass afterward, that he loved a woman in the valley of Sorek, whose name was Delilah" (Judges 16:4). This woman was undoubtedly the most beautiful and beguiling of all three.

The Philistines rejoiced when they heard that Samson was waiting upon Delilah. "Now," they said, "we will get him. This time he shall not escape." So they went to her house and offered her a bribe of 1100 pieces of silver—perhaps as much as $25,000—if she would get out of Samson the secret of his great strength.

It was the money that did the business with Delilah. Perhaps when she gave her consent she said to herself, "I can feel that when I do this it is a patriotic deed, for I am delivering into the hands of the Philistines the great enemy of my country." But it was the money that did the business.

She thought of the chariots and horses she could have, the fine villa down by the seashore, the Ethiopian slaves to wait on her, the rich garments dyed with Tyrian dye, the gold of Ophir and the jewels of India.

Then Delilah went to work on Samson. There is no reason to think that these four teasings of Samson, these assaults upon his honor, took place in immediate succession, or on the same day and at the same visit. Very likely there were four successive visits that Samson paid to Delilah, and each time she beset him with her blandishments, her intoxicating beauty, and her guile. The first time, when Samson was in good humor, she said to him, "Samson, I have often admired this wonderful strength of yours. How the fame of it has gone through all this part of the world! There is not a man among the Philistines who could in the least way match you. I would like to know, Samson, the secret of this great strength, and I am sure you will tell me; for, of course, you can count on my confidence. I will never mention it to anyone else" (see Judges 16).

You can see the look in Delilah's eyes and hear the soft tone of her seducing voice as she says this to Samson. It is clear that Samson has no thought whatever of disclosing to Delilah, much as he loves her, the secret of his strength. What it suggests to him is the perpetration of another joke on the Philistines. So he tells Delilah that if she will bind him with seven green withes that have never been dried, he will be weak just as another man. Delilah passed this information on to the Philistines; and the next time Samson came to visit her she produced the green withes and, reminding Samson of what he had told her, bound him tightly with them—one of her slaves, no doubt, assisting her in the task.

You can see Samson smile to himself as the seven green withes are tightly fastened about his arms and his legs. Then, after a while, coming in suddenly upon Samson—superb actress that she was—with a tone of feigned alarm and concern for her huge lover, Delilah shouts, "Samson, the Philistines be upon thee!" (Judges 16:9). With that Samson sprang to his feet, breaking his bonds as a thread of twine is broken when it is touched with fire. The Philistines, dreading the power of the aroused giant, fled before him.

The next time Samson came down, Delilah again set to work on him. She reproached him for mocking her and telling her lies, but in a tone of voice that must have pleased and flattered Samson. Still he has no thought of revealing to her the real secret of his strength, and only thinks of another good joke he can play upon the Philistines. This time he tells her to bind him with new ropes that have never been used.

At a subsequent visit, new ropes were in readiness, and Delilah and her slaves proceeded to bind Samson with those ropes. Again she came hurriedly in on him shouting, "The Philistines be upon thee!" (Judges 16:12). And again Samson leaped to his feet, breaking the new ropes like threads, and rushed out against the fast-retreating Philistines.

Unwarned, and still confident, not only in his strength, but in his ability to keep the secret of it to himself, Samson makes yet another visit to the siren of the valley of Sorek. Delilah again reproaches him with her soft voice for mocking her and deceiving her, and again begs him to tell the secret of his strength. This time Samson tells her to weave the seven locks of his hair with the web and fasten it with the pin, and then he will be weak like other men.

He was coming a little nearer—indeed, dangerously near—to the truth; for the secret of his strength—rather, the sign and symbol of it—was in his hair. Delilah rolled out the spinning wheel with the loom and the beam and, as the shuttle played to and fro, took the seven braids of Samson's hair and wove them to the beam, and then clamped it down with the pin.

Excusing herself for a little while, she returned and in feigned excitement cried out, "Samson, the Philistines be upon thee!" Again Samson, awakened out of his sleep—for he had so enjoyed having his hair woven into the beam by the soft hands of Delilah that he had gone to sleep—rose up in his might carrying web, beam, and loom, wheel, and all with him, and with the whole contraption clattering about his gigantic shoulders, rushed out upon those who lay in wait for him.

Three victories over the Philistines and his threefold resistance to the wiles of Delilah probably made Samson feel invincible. If there was any voice of conscience that warned him, he probably said to himself, "I'll take the chance. I came pretty near to telling Delilah the last time; but this time I'll deceive her altogether. I'll go down to see her just once more." But, as is frequently the case, "just once more" was too often, for when Samson came this last time she assumed wounded feelings, and, with easily produced tears, said to Samson, "You don't really love me. If you did, you would hide nothing from me, but tell me all that is in your heart, and let me know the secret of your strength" (see Judges 16:15-17).

This time, moved by her appeal to his affection, Samson spoke the fatal word, yet never expecting that his strength would go from him. He had been strong for so many years that he never thought that even his shorn locks would deprive him of his strength. Then he "told her all his heart" (Judges 16:17). If his hair were cut he would be weak as other men. He must have had some little self-reproach, I think, as he spoke of his youth and of his mother. The thought of one's mother has often saved a man on the very edge of the pit and the abyss. But not here. Samson told Delilah— and when he did so he must have thought of the difference between this painted beauty and his godly mother—that he had been a Nazarite unto God from his mother's womb.

Delilah felt sure that this time she had the secret of his strength, and sent word to the Philistines to post themselves near her chamber and be ready for action. Then she put him to sleep upon her knees. His great golden locks hung down to the floor. That fatal sleep! Samson, look up at the blue Syrian sky, visible through the window of Delilah's chamber, for you will never see it again! Samson, look upon the golden sun in the heavens, for you will never look upon the sun again! Samson, look upon your brawny arms—those arms which have done such great exploits for God—for you will never see them again! Samson, look upon the beautiful, bewitching countenance of that Delilah who bends over you, for never again will you look upon her face! Out of this sleep, Samson, you will awaken to blindness and degradation.

And that was what happened. While he slept, Delilah's slave sheared off his golden hair. The Philistines came rushing in as Delilah shouted to him, "The Philistines be upon thee!" Samson stirred himself, for "he wist not that the Lord was departed from him" (Judges 16:20), and thought he could easily conquer his enemies as he had done so many times before. But the moment he stood on his feet he realized that something had gone from him. He was weak just like any other *ordinary* man! The Philistines overcame him, bored out his eyes, and carried him off to the dungeon, where they set him to the work of the ass, grinding in the mill.

HOW MEN FALL

"Samson wist not that the Lord was departed from him." There is something infinitely sad about that! Perhaps you have heard a great musician who played after his skill was gone, or a great singer who sang after her voice was gone. Some years ago I heard a preacher who in his prime was able to stir thousands; but now the fire had sunk, his power had departed from him. There was not the least tone in his voice, or flame in his countenance, or flash in his eye, to suggest the great preacher of not so many years before. As it always must, time had taken its deadly toll. There is a pathos about departed physical strength, in that sense; but oh, how much deeper is the pathos of departed moral and spiritual strength!

Samson did not lose his strength all in one day, or in one rash promise to the Philistine courtesan. No; it had been steadily ebbing from him. That is the way men lose their moral and spiritual strength.

A great tree stands yonder in the fields. Its leaves are green; its trunk appears to be solid and strong. Then suddenly, when the great wind blows, the tree goes down with a crash and leaves a lonely place against the sky. But when the tree is fallen you can see that it was rotten within. It was just waiting for the sufficiently strong wind to bring it down in ruins.

So men sink slowly and gradually to their ruin. When the crisis of a strong temptation comes upon them, and the cry goes up, "The Philistines be upon thee!" then they go down.

ENEMIES ALWAYS WAITING

The moment Samson revealed the true secret of his strength to Delilah, those who lay in wait were ready for him. There are always "liers in wait"—enemies of your soul—waiting for you, ready to rush in when you lower the shield of your defense as Samson did. And what was that shield of Samson's defense? It was his consecration to God, of which his hair was only the sign and token. Whoever lets the thought of God pass out of his mind has, as it were, parted with his hair, the secret of his strength; and the enemies of the soul will quickly overcome him.

Therefore, my soul, be on your guard. Live as if in the presence of God. Test daily your consecration to Him. Samson went down when he let go of God. But Joseph, greatly tempted by another wicked woman, won his victory and lives forever an example to young men and young women because he would not let go from him the thought of God and his obligations to Him. In the dreadful moment of his temptation Joseph cried out, "How then can I do this great wickedness and sin against God?" (Gen. 39:9).

Let anyone whose locks are now being toyed with remember Samson and be warned by what happened to him. A moment's consent, and then the degradation, the slavery, and the long darkness.

A Bright Sunset

Sometimes you have seen an autumn or winter day that rose in beauty and splendor and then, before midday had come, was clouded and darkened. But in the late afternoon, just before night came, the sun reappeared and there was a bar of flaming gold across the western horizon. That is what I think of when I read the life of Samson. Just before his death, the sun comes out again.

The Philistines had assembled in the temple of their god Dagon to celebrate their victory over Israel and their conquest of Israel's great champion, the blind Samson. Suddenly a roar goes up from the half-drunken lords and ladies: "Bring in Samson! Let him make sport for us!"

Samson is brought out of his dungeon, a boy leading him by the hand. He is a huge figure of a man with his hair grown again and hanging over his shoulders, but with sad, sightless eyes. At the command of his keepers he makes sport for the Philistines. Among those Philistines who lean over the parapet of the gallery I see a face that poor, blind Samson cannot see. It is the face of Delilah!—the cruel, coldly beautiful, licentious face of Delilah. And in that face there is not a look of pity or compassion! Listen, as she shouts down some taunt or mockery at her erstwhile lover.

Just This Once!

But wait! Samson's hair has grown again. Something more important than that has taken place, however. Samson has repented. He has come back to God. He asks the boy who conducts him to let him feel and lean against the two main pillars that uphold the balustrade and the gallery. As he stands there he puts one great arm about the marble pillar; and then, in a voice which is lost in the hubbub of the drinking and jeering Philistines, but not lost to God, Samson makes his last and beautiful and pathetic prayer: "O Lord God, remember me, I pray thee, and strengthen me, I pray thee, only this once, O God!" (Judges 16:28). With that his powerful arms tighten around those pillars.

In his epic poem, *Samson Agonistes*, John Milton graphically describes the scene:

Straining all his nerves, he bowed:
As with the force of winds and waters pent,
When mountains tremble, those two massy pillars
With horrible convulsion to and fro
He tugged, he shook, till down they came, and drew
The whole roof after them, with burst of thunder
Upon the heads of all who sat beneath—
Lords, ladies, captains, counselors, or priests,
Their choice nobility and flower.

One mighty heave and pull, and the pillars are pulled from their sockets, and down in one red roar of ruin crashes the temple of Dagon, burying in death the blasphemous Philistines—and Samson, too, for he had gladly asked to die that he might strike one last blow for God.

And there by the side of the dead Samson I see another face, and another form, all covered with blood, and blackened with the dust of ruin. Whose is it? It is the face of the temptress Delilah. Now, Delilah, you have had your wish! You have learned what the secret of Samson's strength is, and how dreadful that strength can be in judgment and retribution. It is the strength of repentance and faith in God.

"O Lord, God, remember me, I pray thee, and strengthen me, I pray thee, only this once." That may be your need, your desperate need. You have forgotten God. You have broken His commandments. You have sinned against Him. But God is merciful. He will in no wise cast out that man who comes unto Him. Call on Him now. Pray as Samson did, "O Lord, God, remember me, I pray thee, and strengthen me, I pray thee, only this once." Yes, thanks be unto God, "only this once." Only one heartfelt prayer for forgiveness, only one courageous and sincere choice and decision for the right, and that "only once" can be stretched into a never-ending eternity of happiness and joy.

QUESTIONS FOR DISCUSSION:

1. Marcartney says that Delilah illustrates the evil influence a woman can have in the life of a man. Was she to blame for all that happened to Samson? If not, why not?

2. Discuss Macartney's description of Samson: "His unshorn locks were not the *source* of his strength, but the *sign* of his devotion to the will of God." What does the author mean by this statement?

3. Samson's weakness seems to have been his lack of self-control and his attraction to pagan Philistine women. What are some other weaknesses you see in his personality?

4. Do you think Delilah was the "best" Philistine woman to whom Samson was attracted—or the worst? Try to discover what it was about her that most attracted him.

5. Macartney says, "Samson must have noted the difference between this "painted beauty" and his godly mother. Do you think that thought crossed his mind?

6. What part do you think his repentance played in the return of Samson's strength? Do you feel reprentance is ever needed in the life of a Christian today?

Editor's Note: Read 1 Samuel 25; 27:3; 30:5; 2 Samuel 2:2; 3:2-3.

7

THE WOMAN WHO MARRIED
THE WRONG MAN

*She was a woman of good understanding, and of
a beautiful countenance: but the man was churlish
and evil in his doings* (1 Samuel 25:3).

"It was a mistake," she said as I greeted her, a friend of former years, as she came out of the pew. She had been married since I saw her last, and naturally I made some allusion to her marriage. But that was her only comment, as a look of sadness came into her face—"It was a mistake."

Like many another woman, she had married the wrong man. And she was not the first, nor the last, to do so. There are all kinds of husbands and wives, and all kinds of marriages; and the Bible would not have been the complete Book that it is, and the perfect mirror of life that it is, had it not had a story of a woman who married the wrong man.

There are, indeed, plenty of men who married the wrong woman. Job is a classic example of that; for when things were at their worst for Job, his wife, instead of encouraging him and strengthening him, told him to curse God and die. One of the wisest of men, Socrates, married a scold. Charles Dickens, the man who touches all the chords of the heart in its relationship to the home, married the wrong woman. John Wesley was one of the saintliest of men, but he married the wrong woman, if ever man did. But more numerous and more tragic are the number of women who married the wrong man.

Here in this masterpiece of Old Testament biography we have the story of the Beauty and the Beast. Sometimes you have seen a charming, gracious lady married to a boorish, churlish, cruel, wicked man; and you have wondered how it ever could have happened. But in ancient days you would not have wondered so much, for the woman had comparatively little to say as to whom she would marry. That was arranged for her. Particularly would she have little to say about the matter when the husband was a rich man like Nabal; for "the man was very great, and he had three thousand sheep, and a thousand goats" (1 Sam. 25:3). Then one did not say a man was worth so many thousand dollars or pounds, but so many sheep, oxen, camels, goats.

It was a sad marriage for Abigail, as such marriages often are. In a town in California where I spent a year as a boy, I used to see riding down the avenue every morning near our house a large man mounted on a magnificent sorrel horse, with a great mastiff following after him. But the man's reputation was not good. He had married the daughter of a minister, and one wondered how she could be happy. In the old pagan days men used to deck the oxen devoted for sacrifice with garlands and ribbons. But that did not keep back the gleaming knife of the priest when he slew them at the altar. Neither does wealth, station, or a great name hold back the knife of unhappiness when a woman is married to a man like Nabal.

It was sheepshearing time in Carmel, a still, green and pleasant country south of Hebron. And what a shearing time it was—3,000 of Nabal's sheep to be shorn of their fleecy wool. Everywhere one could hear the bleating of the sheep and the sound of the clippers. From all parts of the nearby country the people had gathered to assist in the ritual of the sheepshearing. Just as in the early days on American farms, the barnraising—or the threshing season—was a time of social activities, of joy as well as labor, when the tables groaned with plenty, and there was singing, and sometimes dancing, so in ancient Palestine—and still today—the sheepshearing season was a time of festive joy and reunion, of feasting and drinking and the giving of gifts.

The news spread through the land that Nabal was shearing his

3,000 sheep. At that time David, pursued by the relentless and sleepless jealousy of Saul, in whose place he had been anointed king, had taken refuge in the south country. He had gathered about him a band of several hundred young men who were willing to share the hardship and excitement of David's life. The kingship must then have seemed far off to David—so much so that Jonathan had to go to David secretly at night in the wood of Ziph and strengthen his hand in God and restore his faith that God would make him king over Israel.

Some of David's followers brought word to him that Nabal was shearing his sheep. That reminded David that no matter what hill they had climbed or what valley they had penetrated Nabal was the man whose flocks they had encountered. They had never molested his flocks, but had protected them against raiding and thieving Bedouins.

It was the fine custom of the ancient shearing season that the man whose sheep were being sheared should give gifts to all as a token of thanks to God and of good will to his neighbors. With this in mind, David dispatched some of his young men to greet Nabal and to receive from him the usual present.

The sheepshearing and the accompanying festivities were well under way when David's messengers arrived. All about the sheepshearing platforms were pitched the black tents of the people who had come with their families and their animals—camels, sheep, goats. The red, yellow, and blue headdresses of the women were brilliant in the Syrian sunlight. In groups of six, ten, twenty, the sheep were driven first into the pools to be washed. Then they were driven up to the shearing place, where they were thrown down on the platforms while the shearers, holding them between their knees, clipped from them their thick and infinitely soft garments that people might be clothed and warmed.

After watching for a time, and perhaps lending a hand themselves, the messengers of David made their way to where Nabal sat drinking under his pavilion. They stated their errand on behalf of David, and also notified Nabal how David had protected his flocks. But when Nabal heard their request, the churlish fool broke out into an angry insult: "Who is David, and who is the son of Jesse? There be many servants that break away nowadays from their masters. For all I know, David, this son of Jesse, may be one of those fugitive slaves, skulking about the country, stealing and poaching. Do you think I am going to take my bread and my water and my flesh that I have killed for my shearers and give it to a set of vagabonds?" (see 1 Sam. 25:10,11).

The coarse insult was all the more offensive because of the Oriental laws of courtesy, which require politeness, under certain circumstances, even to a man's deadly enemy. When the young men brought word back to David how Nabal had received them and what he had said to them, David was beside himself with rage. His ruddy countenance blanched as the wave of anger swept over him. Drawing his sword, and turning to his 600 men, David gave his angry command, "Gird ye on every man his sword!" (1 Sam. 25:13). By nature David was a kind, generous, loving, magnanimous man; but, like all strong characters, he was capable of great indignation, and when once aroused, his anger and rage could carry him to terrible lengths.

It looked as if it was going to be so on this occasion. Marching at the head of his men, David started for Carmel, fierce revenge flaming in his heart. As he marched along, and heard behind him the tread of his armed men, their swords clanking on their thighs, he said to himself, or probably spoke aloud so that his men might hear: "Never heard of David, never heard of the son of Jesse, did he? Thinks we are runaway slaves, vagabonds, eh? Well, we will teach him a lesson. Before the night comes down, Nabal and all his people will find out who David is. God do so to me and more also, if Nabal or any of his household is left alive by morning!" Thus he planned not only revenge on the churlish Nabal, but the destruction of all his people. And with great satisfaction David listened to the tramp, tramp, tramp of his soldiers behind him.

But there was another procession on the march that day. Nabal's frightened servants had brought word to their mistress, Abigail, of their master's coarse insult to David. Abigail knew what was coming. David was not the man to let such an affront go unpunished. She might have taken steps to protect only herself; but in the nobility and kindness of her nature she made haste to save from death and vengeance the innocent household of Nabal, and even that wicked man himself.

Did a voice say to her, "Now, Abigail, is your chance! Now is your chance to be rid of that drunken fool and beast to whom you have been joined all these years. Do not stand in the way of David's vengeance, and all will be well with you"? If such a voice spoke, if such a desire rose up for a moment, the high-minded Abigail quickly suppressed it and turned all her wits and energies and charms to save Nabal and his household from death—and also, as we shall see, to save David from himself.

Summoning her servants, she ordered them to load the animals with presents for David's men—cheese, wine, bread, raisins—and, mounted on her own beast, she led the caravan in the direction from which David was marching. So the two caravans, the two processions—one the procession of anger and revenge, the other of peace and forgiveness and reconciliation—approached each other.

At the covert of one of the hills, just as the morning mists were lifting, the two processions met. Dismounting from her animal, and hurrying to where David stood, his face angry and threatening, his hand on his sword, Abigail bowed before him and commenced her beautiful and immortal plea.

If you leave out the speeches of our Lord, there are two which are the most famous and eloquent speeches and addresses of the Bible. First of all, there is the wonderful speech that Judah made to Joseph in Egypt, when the still-disguised Joseph was threatening to keep Benjamin as a hostage, and Judah pled with him for the sake of their aged father to have mercy, saying that if Benjamin did not return it would bring the gray hairs of their father Jacob down in sorrow to the grave. That speech made Joseph, polished statesman of Egypt, break down in uncontrolled tears; and to read it even today brings a lump to the throat.

The other most eloquent speech of the Bible is this beautiful plea that lovely Abigail made with David to keep back his hand from blood and vengeance. Perhaps in heaven it will be permitted me, when I meet Judah, to ask him to go apart for a little from the company of Jacob and his brethren and sit down with me, under one of the trees of life by the river of water of life. There I will ask him to repeat for me that wonderful speech he made to Joseph. And perhaps, if David can spare her from his side for ten minutes, I can persuade Abigail to go over again, with that lovely voice and lovely face, the speech she made that morning to David by the covert of the hill.

Let me repeat now for you that whole speech, for it is so eloquent that we must not lose a single word of it:

"Upon me, my lord, upon me let this iniquity be: and let thine handmaid, I pray thee, speak in thine audience, and hear the words of thine handmaid. Let not my lord, I pray thee, regard this man of Belial, even Nabal: for as his name is, so is he; Nabal is his name, and folly is with him: but I thine handmaid saw not the young men of my lord, whom thou didst send. Now therefore, my lord, as the Lord liveth, and as thy soul liveth, seeing the Lord hath withholden thee from coming to shed blood and from avenging thyself with thine own hand, now let thine enemies, and they that seek evil to my lord, be as Nabal. And now this blessing which thine handmaid hath brought unto my lord, let it even be given unto the young men that follow my lord. I pray thee, forgive the trespass of thine handmaid: for the Lord will certainly make my lord a sure house; because my lord fighteth the battles of the Lord, and evil hath not been found in thee all thy days. Yet a man is risen to pursue thee, and to seek thy soul: but the soul of my lord shall be bound in the bundle of life with the Lord thy God; and the souls of thine enemies, them shall he sling out, as out of the middle of a sling. And it shall come to pass, when the Lord shall have done to my lord according to all the good that he hath spoken concerning thee, and shall have appointed thee ruler over Israel; that this shall be no grief unto thee, nor offence of heart unto my lord, either that thou hast shed blood causeless, or that my lord hath avenged himself; but when the Lord shall have dealt well with my lord, then remember thine handmaid" (1 Sam. 25:24-31).

It was not strange that David melted before that speech. Not only did he turn back from his errand of blood and revenge, but he blessed God for the providence that had sent Abigail to meet him. Thrusting his sword into its scabbard, David gave the order to his men to march back to their own encampment—which they were willing enough to do, having listened with rapt countenance to the moving words of Nabal's wife.

Nabal had been spared; his household had been spared; and David himself had been saved. When Abigail got home Nabal lay in a drunken stupor. The next day, when he was aroused out of his stupor, she told him what had happened. It is hard to tell whether it was out of anger at his beautiful wife's interference, or the shock of learning how narrowly he had escaped the vengeance of David; but when he heard the news, Nabal had a seizure—a stroke. His heart, it is said, became as stone, and in a few days he was dead.

The story has a pleasant, and not at all surprising, sequel. When David heard that Nabal was dead, he paid his court to the beautiful widow and soon thereafter married her; and never did a man make a happier choice.

We know something of some of the other wives of David— Michal, who mocked him, and Bathsheba, whom he loved well, but not wisely. We are glad that early in his history he had the counsel and affection and companionship of a woman like Abigail. Sometimes I think that Abigail cannot have lived long; for if she had, I feel sure she would have kept David from many of the deeds of folly and sin and cruelty which stained his reign, even as she did there by the covert of the hill when she kept him back from blood and death.

A WOMAN UNSOURED AND NOT MADE BITTER BY ADVERSITY

When we come to sum up the truths which come home to us from the story of lovely Abigail, the first one that strikes us is this: she did not permit the trial and adversity of life to embitter her spirit. For such a woman to be married to such a beast must have been the sorest of trials. What could be greater? How poignant must have been the sorrow of Abigail when she awoke not many days after her marriage with the conviction that she had made a supreme mistake and had married a besotted, stupid fool!

But it is evident that she bore her cross with resignation. She did not become bitter or turn against life. The harder her experience, the sweeter her disposition. As certain trees when struck by the ax will answer only by sending forth sweet-smelling sap, so the keen edge of adversity and trial evoked from the soul of Abigail only peace and beauty. Her affliction, no doubt, seemed grievous to her; but afterward, as the apostle puts it, it yielded the peaceful fruits of righteousness. In your disappointment, your sore trial, your bitter grief, think of this woman and follow in her steps.

GOD'S PROVIDENCE IN OUR LIVES

Another truth that comes home to us from this brief but superb biography of Abigail is the providence of God in daily life. I like that famous speech of Abigail, not only for its surpassing pathos and eloquence, but also because it stirs tender memories in my heart. That was the phrase often upon my father's lips when he prayed in the old home at family worship, asking God that all his children might be bound up "in the bundle of life." Earnest, simple, beautiful prayer, he made for us. Long since, now, his earthly life has ended. But not till they themselves sleep the last sleep will his children forget his accents as he prayed on bended knee for us, and asked God that we might be bound up forever in the bundle of life, safe at last in that everlasting home, where they no longer go in and out!

In her intercession with David, Abigail reassured him that God's hand was not withdrawn from him, and that, however dark and forbidding the present day, he would be king over Israel. What better can one do for another than that? To remind him that God has a purpose and a plan in his life, and that if he will but obey and trust in God, all things will finally work together for good.

Perhaps you are discouraged, or even rebellious. God's way with you seems hard. Your life seems to you useless and all your efforts futile. Be of good cheer! God who created you has high things in store for you. Be faithful! Keep back your hand from evil and your heart from unbelief! Wait, I say, on the Lord, and be of good courage, and He will bring it to pass!

THE REGRETS WE HAVE MISSED, AND THOSE WE CAN MISS

The final truth we hear from the lips of this most eloquent preacher, Abigail, as she pleads with David, is that no one ever regrets the evil he did not do. To David she said, "Now seeing the Lord hath withholden thee from coming to shed blood"—for, you see, she assumes that David is going to heed her plea—"when the Lord shall have appointed thee ruler over Israel, this will be no grief unto thee, that thou hast shed blood causeless."

How true that was! Poor David had many things to regret when later in his life he looked back over its checkered history, many acts of revenge and folly and shame; but there was one thing he did not need to regret, and it was that in an hour of insult and anger he avenged himself against Nabal by slaying, not only the insulter, but his whole family and house. Through the gentle plea of Abigail, and through his wise yielding to her plea, David was spared that one regret and remorse. Bitter as his cup was, that drop of bitterness was never mixed in it.

Think, friend, of the regrets you have missed. When you look at the scroll of yesterday I know there will be much that you will wish had not been written there. But do not forget the things that are not there—the things you might have had occasion to regret, but which are not there, because God, in His grace and providence, kept you back from them. And when you think of those things that are not there, thank God for it.

But think, also, of the regrets that you might miss. Abigail told David of a regret he might miss if he would only listen to her advice. He listened and was spared that regret. Be wise, then, for your future. That noble woman said to David, "When you are king, it will be no regret to you that you kept back your hand from blood and vengeance."

I appeal to you now on the ground of those things, that course of conduct, those choices and decisions, which you will never regret. It will be no regret to you that you did not forget God, but "remembered thy Creator in the days of thy youth," and in middle life, and in old age. It will be no regret to you that you did not neglect God's Word, God's Holy Day, God's House of Worship. It will be no regret to you that you did not forget the poor and the oppressed and the afflicted. It will be no regret to you that you did not yield to your angry passions. It will be no regret to you that you did not take a mean advantage for the sake of gain; but, rather, suffered loss. It will be no regret to you that, when insulted or persecuted or shamefully treated, you did not do as you had been done unto; but overlooked the wrong and forgave the wrong-doer.

No! These things will never cause your soul regret. Answer me, enthroned and blessed saints in heaven, and tell me if any of these things caused you a moment's regret! I know that you will answer that those deeds, those choices or decisions, those good things that you did, those evil things you did not, have rather brought you peace of mind and added to your cup of joy in the heavenly places!

And one thing more I know you will never regret. You will never regret that, as David heeded the pleading of this beautiful woman, you heeded the pleading of God's Holy Spirit, and, repenting of all your sins, beholding Jesus Christ, the Son of God, wounded for your transgressions and bruised for your iniquities, gave your heart to Him for time and for eternity—your Savior, Guide, and Friend—and asked Him to bind you up with Him in the bundle of Eternal Life. Have you done that? Are you bound up in the bundle of Eternal Life? If you are not, then God's Holy Spirit pleads with you now and asks you to choose Eternal Life, not tomorrow, not next year, but now.

QUESTIONS FOR DISCUSSION:

1. The name "Abigail" means "father of the dance" or "of joy." Did that definition fit Abigail's marriage to Nabal? Do you think her marriage to David was any different?

2. Can you think of examples of "mismarriages" such as that of Nabal and Abigail elsewhere in Scripture? In history? Among your own acquaintances?

3. How would you have handled Nabal if you had been his wife?

4. Re-read Abigail's speech to David. What does it reveal about her character? About her spiritual maturity?

5. What would Abigail have gained by being bitter toward Nabal?

6. What kind of marriage do you think Abigail and David had?

7. Macartney says, "David had many things to regret when later in his life he looked back over its checkered history, many acts of revenge and folly and shame; but there was one thing he did not need to regret, and it was that in an hour of insult and anger he avenged himself against Nabal . . . ." Can you think of any experience in your own life (or in your own family) where a similar lesson was learned?

Editor's Note: Read Genesis 24–27 to acquaint yourself with the biblical background of this character.

8

THE WOMAN WHO DECEIVED HER HUSBAND

And Rebekah took goodly raiment of her eldest son Esau . . . .
and put them upon Jacob her younger son (Genesis 27:15).

Rebekah was the woman who deceived her husband. She was not the first to do that, nor the last. But that is not what one thinks of when one hears her name. More than any other woman in the Bible, Rebekah spelled romance; and her romance, beginning at the well in Mesopotamia, is all the more engaging because she was in love with a man she had never seen.

Sometimes people secure a reputation and fame not altogether in keeping with their real history and conduct. That is certainly so, to a degree, in the case of Rebekah; for the marriage service, in its concluding prayer, asks that "as Isaac and Rebekah lived faithfully together, so these persons may surely perform and keep the vow and covenant between them made." That was true, perhaps, in the early life of Isaac and Rebekah. But later on, as we shall see, there was a breach of faith on the part of both Isaac and Rebekah.

The closing chapter of their relationship was anything but ideal. There the beautiful girl of Mesopotamia's well, who became Isaac's wife and comforted him after the death of his mother Sarah, has been transformed into a scheming old woman who cruelly deceives her blind and dying husband.

Isaac, too, has changed for the worse. He is no longer the winsome youth, the child of Abraham's and Sarah's old age, the central figure in the scene on Mount Moriah when Abraham was about to offer him up as a sacrifice. No longer is he the gentle dreaming youth who went out into the fields to meditate at the eventide, and was so engaged when the veiled Rebekah came with her camels. Nor is he now the nonstriving, nonresisting Isaac who, when the herdsmen of Gerar stole the wells he had dug, did not strive with them, but moved elsewhere and called the place a name still borne by so many old-time country churches—"Rehoboth," there is room.

Ah, if only the nations today would follow that policy of Isaac's, they would realize that there is room for all; then the lips of the cannon would grow still, and the seas of blood would be dried up! No; it is not that winsome and attractive Isaac whom we see in this closing scene, but a gluttonous old man, who wants a dish of venison before he dies.

Rebekah deceived her husband, for she was the chief architect in the whole miserable business. But that does not tell the story of Rebekah. There is no doubt that, despite her deception, Rebekah is one of the great women of the Bible—beautiful and romantic in her youth, strong and decided in her character. Even in this act of duplicity, where the curtain drops on her history, she is animated by a noble ambition and desire.

The story of Rebekah begins at an eastern well. Take out of the Bible the scenes at the well, and you have robbed it of much of its charm and beauty. It was at the well of Midian that the exiled Moses drove off the rude shepherds and drew water for the flocks of Zipporah, who turned out to be his future wife. It was at another Mesopotamian well that Jacob first kissed Rachel and waited fourteen years for another chance. It was near the well of Bethlehem that the fugitive David, his heart stirred with the tender memories of youth, sighed and said, "Oh that one would give me a drink of the water of the well of Bethlehem, that is at the gate." And it was by the well of Jacob that Jesus sat down and talked with the woman of Samaria about the Water of Life.

Although it is always dangerous to try to retell the perfect tale, let us go back to that old well in Mesopotamia where the story of Rebekah had its beginning. The sun is sinking over the desert near the city of Nahor. Yonder, winding down from the south-west, comes a small caravan of camels. Seated on one of the camels is Eliezer, the chief servant of Abraham.

Having had intimations that his end was not far off, Abraham had called his steward to him and made him swear that he would not permit Isaac to marry a woman of Canaan. He charged him to go down into the far east whence Abraham had come, and find a wife for Isaac among his own kindred and people. There was only one restraint laid upon the steward—he was not to let Isaac dwell in the eastern land, for God had promised to Abraham and his descendants the land of Canaan.

Faithful to his vow and oath, Eliezer is on his way east to find Isaac a wife, for Isaac was a reticent, retiring young man who probably would never have been able to find one for himself. Here they come, swaying along the desert highway, the ten soft-footed camels of the chief steward laden with presents for the family of the as-yet-unkown bride-to-be. In obedience to the command of Eliezer, the ten camels kneel down at the well outside the town of Nahor. It is at the eventide; and, according to the customs, the women come out from the gate of Nahor, their vessels on their heads, to draw water at the well.

When the steward saw them coming, he offered up a devout petition, asking God to grant him good fortune that day and give him a sign that he might know which of the young women he saw approaching the well was to be the bride of Isaac. What he asked was that the one to whom he should say, "Let down thy pitcher, I pray thee, that I may drink," and who should immediately respond, "Drink, and I will give thy camels drink also," would be the one God had appointed as Isaac's wife (read Gen. 24).

He had hardly concluded his prayer, when Rebekah, a niece of Abraham, and cousin to Isaac, came to the well with her pitcher upon her shoulder. She lowered her pitcher into the well and came up with it on her shoulder. As she did so, the servant of Abraham said to her, "Let me, I pray thee, drink a little water of thy pitcher" (Gen. 24:17). Rebekah at once answered, "Drink, my lord," and gave him a drink. Then she ran back to the well, and drawing water with her pitcher, poured it into the trough for the camels of the stranger.

WILT THOU GO?

Certain now that Rebekah was the chosen wife for Isaac, the steward presented her with a golden earring and golden bracelets, and inquired of her her name and family (see Gen. 24:22,23). When he learned that her family was related to that of Abraham, he was all the more satisfied in his mind, for Rebekah had good family background. She had grace and beauty, for it is said that she was "very fair to look upon"; she had courtesy, too, and hospitality, and vital vivacity, for everything she did, she did quickly. The old matchmaker bowed his head and gave thanks to God who had thus led and directed him to this beautiful girl.

When he made his proposal to Rebekah's brother, Laban—for the father seems to have been dead—Laban gave his consent, but said that Rebekah must make the final decision herself. When they had called Rebekah and explained to her why the man had come and what the proposal was, they said to her, "Wilt thou go with this man?" Without a moment's hesitation, Rebekah answered, "I will go!" (Gen. 24:58).

Down through the ages, over and over again, have echoed that question and that answer: "Wilt thou go?" "I will go!" Rebekah, Rachel, Sarah, Mary, ancient, medieval, and modern young woman, sought by the young man—all of you have answered that fundamental and momentous question, "Wilt thou go with this man?" Had you not, the world long ago would have ceased to move, and men would have ceased to praise God their Creator and Redeemer.

With the servant of Abraham and his caravan, Rebekah, trusting in God, traveled from Mesopotamia down to Canaan, where Isaac lived. She was deeply in love, as many young women have been, with a man she had never seen. It was not long after the death of Sarah, Isaac's loved mother; and at the eventide Isaac was out in the fields meditating—grieving, no doubt, for his mother, as many a man after him has done, and wishing he could have her back, if only for an hour.

Riding on her camel, Rebekah saw Isaac in the distance and

said to the servant, "What man is this that walketh in the field to meet us?" When she learned that it was Isaac, her future husband, she alighted from her camel and modestly covered her face with a veil. Thus Isaac first met his wife. The rest of the meeting the Bible tells best of all: "And Isaac brought her into his mother Sarah's tent, and took Rebekah, and she became his wife; and he loved her: and Isaac was comforted after his mother's death" (Gen. 24:67).

That was the beginning. Would that the rest of the story were as fair and charming as the first chapter. But I suppose that is rarely so in this world. Even this marriage, made in heaven, directed of God, had its less lustrous side. In the course of time two sons were born to Rebekah—Esau and Jacob. Isaac loved Esau, because he was a hunter and brought him wild game to eat; but Rebekah—discerning, wise Rebekah—seeing the difference in the sons, and remembering how the Lord had said to her, "The elder shall serve the younger" (Gen. 25:23), loved Jacob.

By and by Esau married Judith, a Hittite woman. To the ambitious, proud, and pious Rebekah that was a bitter blow, that her son should have married a heathen woman. It seemed to Rebekah that, by this union with the Hittite woman, Esau had renounced and repudiated all the promises which had come down through Abraham concerning a great future, and a great mission for God, and a great blessing for mankind; and she was determined that Jacob should not follow in his brother's steps. To Isaac, Rebekah said, "I am weary of my life because of the daughters of Heth: if Jacob take a wife of the daughters of Heth . . . what good shall my life do me?" (Gen. 27:46). Thus it is an old custom among proud, loving mothers to think sometimes that the woman her son has chosen for a wife is not worthy of him.

Rebekah noted that Isaac was getting weaker every day. At first he went just a little distance from the black tents on his daily walk. Then it was shortened and shortened, until he no longer stirred from the tent. One day she overheard him say to Esau that his end was not far off, and that he wanted him to take his bow and arrow and bring in a deer, so that he might eat the venison, and then bless him before he died. At once a cunning idea came into Rebekah's mind.

The patriarchal blessing meant a great deal in those times. Isaac was blind and weak. Why not deceive him by substituting Jacob, and thus get the blessing for Jacob? Had not Esau proved himself unworthy of it, first by his marriage to a heathen woman, and then by selling the birthright to Jacob for a mess of pottage? And as for Isaac himself, probably Rebekah had ceased to respect him. How could she ever forget Isaac's despicable cowardice when they were traveling through the land of the Philistines? Isaac, fearful lest the Philistines, taken with the rare beauty of Rebekah, would kill him so that they might take her for a wife, passed Rebekah off as his sister. Recently a woman wrote to me, "I have married a man ten years older than myself whom I love and respect." It is always sad when those two do not go together—love and respect. Love sometimes lingers on, I suppose, even when respect is gone. But the ideal relationship is where the wife both loves and respects her husband and the husband loves and respects his wife.

With Rebekah, quick in old age as she had been at the well in her youth, to think was to act. Calling Jacob, she laid before him her plan. He was to kill two kids of the goats, and Rebekah would prepare them so that Isaac would not know the difference between the meat of the kid and venison. That would be easy. But Jacob was not sure about the rest.

Jacob was a smooth man; Esau was hairy. What if blind Isaac should put out his hands to feel Jacob when he brought his father the meat and asked for the blessing! But Rebekah said she would see to that. Whatever blame or curse there might be for such a deception, she would bear it. "Upon me be thy curse, my son; only obey my voice" (Gen. 27:13). Then she put the skins of the kids upon his hands and upon the back of his neck; and thus disguised, Jacob went in to his father.

When Jacob saluted his father and gave him the meat Rebekah had prepared, Isaac, whose ear was not as dull as his eye, thought the voice sounded like that of Jacob. Wondering how Esau had shot and prepared a deer in so short a time, he said to Jacob, "Come near, I pray thee, that I may feel thee, my son, whether thou be my very son Esau or not" (Gen. 27:21). With his trembling hands Isaac felt of Jacob's arms, and then the back of his neck, but wherever his hand touched he felt the hairy skin of the kids. Perplexed, the old man said, "The voice is Jacob's voice, but the hands are the hands of Esau" (Gen. 27:22). Still unconvinced, he made one more pathetic appeal to Jacob: "Art thou my very son Esau?" And Jacob said, "I am" (v. 24).

Then, having partaken of the meat, Isaac lifted his hands over the kneeling Jacob and bestowed upon him the blessing. "God give thee of the dew of heaven, and the fatness of the earth, and plenty of corn and wine: let people serve thee, and nations bow down to thee" (Gen. 27:28,29).

LIFE'S IRREVOCABLE

Thus Jacob cheated Esau of the blessing. And there, looking out from behind the fold of the tent, stands Rebekah, anxiously watching and listening to see if her plot succeeds, and if Jacob will get the blessing.

The first scene was hardly over, however, and Rebekah had hardly spoken her whispered congratulations to Jacob, when Esau made his appearance, and coming to his father with the venison he had prepared, asked him to eat it and then bless him. The startled old man cried out, "Who art thou?" "I am Esau, thy first-born son," answered the surprised Esau. "Who?" cried the father. "If so, then who was it that brought me venison a little while ago, and upon whom I laid my hands in blessing?" (see Gen. 27:30-40).

Then they both knew what had happened. Jacob had stolen the blessing! Lifting up his voice with an exceeding bitter cry, Esau, realizing what it meant, said, "Bless me, even me also, O my father!" But Isaac could not now recall the blessing. Esau found no place for repentance, though he sought it carefully and with tears.

The irrevocable had been done—yet, cheated and robbed and wronged though he was, Esau was but reaping the harvest of his own sin when he sold the birthright for a mess of pottage. Ah, those tears of Esau! Those tears of Esau! Those bitter, bitter tears! Those tears of unavailing remorse and regret!

I hear that bitter cry of Esau echoed in David's cry, "I have sinned." I hear it echoed in the cry of Judas as he flings down the thirty pieces of silver at the feet of the high priest, saying, "I have sinned!" I hear it echoed in the remorse of the son who has neglected his parents, in the remorse of the husband who has wronged and outraged his wife. I hear the echo of that lament in the cry of the man who has sullied his soul in youth, and now cannot wash out the stains. I hear it echoed in the cry of that great number who, like Esau, put the appetite of the moment above the eternal satisfactions of the soul, and start a sequence of events which no power can ever stop. I hear the echo of that cry in the lament of one who has, in a passion, spoken fearful words which now can never be recalled.

Turn back, then, before you cry that bitter, bitter cry of Esau, and discover that there are some things which are irrevocable. Beware of the irrevocable on the wrong side of life—in your decision for Christ, in your resistance to the tempter, in your choice of Eternal Life. These are the acts and decisions which are blessedly irrevocable and the influence of which will abide till moons shall wax and wane no more.

PARTED FOREVER

To save Jacob from the vengeance of Esau, Rebekah urged her son to flee to Mesopotamia and take refuge in her old home—the home of her brother Laban. There he would be safe from Esau's rage, and safe also from another calamity which Rebekah nobly prayed might be spared her—that he should marry a Canaanite as Esau had done. "Flee thou," said Rebekah, "to Laban my brother to Haran; and tarry with him a few days, until thy brother's fury turn away; until thy brother's anger turn away from thee, and he forget that which thou hast done to him: then I will send, and fetch thee from thence: why should I be deprived also of you both in one day?" (Gen. 27:43-45).

Yonder is Jacob, starting on his long journey to Mesopotamia with his staff and his bundle over his shoulder. Take a last, long look, Rebekah, for it is not for "a few days" only, as you fondly suppose, but for thirty years and more. Never again, Rebekah, will you see the face of that beloved son. Yonder he goes. Now he stops, and turning, looks back at the encampment of Isaac, and waves to his mother, who waves back to him. His form is lost as he moves on over the distant horizon.

Morning will dawn again about your black tents, Rebekah. The tinkle of the goats' bell and the bleating of the sheep will be heard tomorrow as of old. The sun will rise in splendor and in splendor go down again, and when night comes down Orion will stretch his golden band across the heavens and the Pleiades will look down upon the earth; but you will never see Jacob again, for when Jacob returns, Rebekah, you will be sleeping by the side of Isaac and by the side of Abraham and Sarah in Machpelah's lonely cavern.

NEVERTHELESS, A GREAT MOTHER

With all her faults, Rebekah was a superb woman and a great mother. Her consuming ambition was that Jacob should fulfill the destiny that was marked out for him at his birth when the Lord said the elder should serve the younger. It was not for herself, but for him, for his future and for the glory of the promise given to Abraham, that Rebekah acted. If she fell into guile and deception, her motive was high.

Like Salome, the mother of James and John, who asked for seats at the right hand and left hand of Christ in glory for her two sons, Rebekah asked a high spiritual destiny for her many children, but always that they might stand high with God.

Mothers, what kind of blessings do you ask for your sons and daughters? Do you pray first of all, above all else, that they should be redeemed men and women, the children of God?

"WILT THOU GO?"

Always, when we think of Rebekah, this is the refrain that comes back to us: "Wilt thou go with this man?" That was what Eliezer and her family said to her—"Wilt thou go with this man?" But I think now of another messenger who comes—none other than God's Holy Spirit—and of another Man with whom you are invited to go—the Man of Galilee, the One altogether lovely. The Holy Spirit asks you, "Wilt thou go with this man?" "His left hand is under your head, and his right hand doth embrace you."

Hear the voice of your Beloved. You need His affection. You need His protection. You need His kindness and His strength. Are you going through life without Christ? If you choose Him He will never leave you nor forsake you. Sorrows, failures, trials, and tribulations will come upon you. Youth and its beauty and its transient charms will pass. But He will love you with an everlasting love. In every condition and circumstance and every hour of life, and in the rolling years of eternity you will prove His sovereign, eternal, unchangeable love. Wilt thou go with this Man?

QUESTIONS FOR DISCUSSION:

1. Genesis 25:28 says, "And Isaac loved Esau, because he did eat of his venison: but Rebekah loved Jacob." Consider this verse in the light of Genesis 27:15 which appears at the beginning of this chapter. What do these verses reveal about Rebekah's character?

2. Why do you think the young and idealistic Rebekah became the devious mother of Jacob?

3. Both Isaac and Rebekah "played favorites" between their twin sons. Why does this happen in families even today? What steps can parents take not to fall into this trap of favoritism (not only between twins, but between siblings)?

4. In the beginning, Rebekah seems to have been an answer to prayer, but in the end she was a schemer who took advantage of her blind husband. How do you account for this seeming decline in her character?

5. Put yourself in the place of Esau. How would you feel if you had thus been deceived—either out of your birthright or in any other way?

6. Macartney concludes: "With all her faults, Rebekah was a superb woman and a great mother." Do you agree with that assessment? What would have made her even greater?

9

THE WOMAN WHO MARRIED THE RIGHT MAN

And they seemed unto him but a few days,
for the love he had to her   (Genesis 29:20).

Where is there a record that surpasses that? For the love which he bore to Rachel, seven years seemed to Jacob but a few days. Other men would have become discouraged and given up. Others would have been taken with another face, fallen in love with another woman. Others would have said, "There are as good fish in the sea as ever came out of it," and would have fished elsewhere. But not Jacob. He was not that kind.

Strange co-mixture of the heavenly and the earthly, the spiritual and the sensual, yet Jacob had that quality which lifted him above ordinary men. He had a divine persistence and perseverance. We see it that night by the fords of the Jabbok, when he wrestled with his mysterious adversary until the breaking of the day, and would not let him go until he blessed him. Here Jacob wrestles for seven years with the Angel of Love and will not let him go until he blesses him.

The Bible is first in everything: first in history, first in biography, first in philosophy, first in poetry, first in prophecy. Therefore, it is not strange that it is first also in love. And here is the greatest lover of the Bible. Jacob soars above all the great lovers of history—Hero and Leander, Dante and Beatrice, Abe'lard and He'loise. Seven years seemed to him but a few days while he waited for

Rachel. Two thousand five hundred and fifty-five days seemed like little more than a day with Jacob for the love he had to Rachel!

If Thomas Moore's beautiful song had been written at that time, when Jacob kissed Rachel by that old well of Mesopotamia—or at any other time in their long association, clear down to their parting for this life, not far from the gates of Bethlehem—I am sure that is the song Jacob would have sung to Rachel:

> Believe me, if all those endearing young charms,
>   Which I gaze on so fondly today,
> Were to change by tomorrow, and fleet in my arms,
>   Like fairy-gifts fading away.
> Thou wouldst still be ador'd, as this moment thou art,
>   Let thy loveliness fade as it will,
> And around the dear ruin each wish of my heart
>   Wound entwine itself verdantly still.

Coleridge once remarked of Jacob, "No one could love like that and be wholly bad." When Rachel married Jacob she married the right man.

THE WOMAN AT THE WELL

This, too, is a story which commences at a Mesopotamian well. Yonder comes Jacob, with his bundle and staff over his shoulder. He had fled from the wrath of his brother Esau, whom he had basely cheated out of Isaac's blessing. On the way he had a visit with the angels at Bethel, when he saw the ladder which stretched from heaven to earth with the angels of God ascending and descending, and heard the promise that God would be with him wherever he went and would bring him again unto his father's house.

When he reached the well, Jacob revealed the aggressiveness of his character—and, indeed, of his race—by proceeding to give orders and instructions to the shepherds, telling them to water the sheep and then feed them. They told him they would not water the sheep or feed them until the stone was rolled away from the mouth of the well. While he was talking with them, Rachel came to the well with her father's sheep. That was the turning point in

Jacob's life and in hers. Providence brought them together at that well, where they drank of one single cup and never separated again until death parted them.

Stirred and animated by Rachel's beauty, Jacob hurried to roll away the stone from the mouth of the well. The women who came to the sepulcher on the morning of the Resurrection wondered who would roll away the stone from the door of the sepulcher for them, but an angel had already done that. As Rachel came to that well on that summer day, and saw the shepherds and others standing about it, no doubt she too wondered who would roll away the stone from the mouth of the well for her. But Jacob was there, appointed of God from all eternity to do that very work for Rachel. And when he had rolled away the stone, he "kissed Rachel, and lifted up his voice, and wept" (Gen. 29:11).

Why did he weep? If he wept, why did he kiss her? And if he kissed her, why did he weep? Jacob himself would have to tell you that. Yet how true it is in life; kisses and tears come close together. The tears of dew are on the flower at morning, when the sun kisses its face. Kisses and tears, tears and kisses, sorrow and joy, joy and sorrow, the brightness of life and the mystery of life—these follow one another in swift, unchanging succession.

Laban, Rachel's father, who had let Rebekah go to be the wife of Isaac without making anything out of it, was determined this time to profit out of the love that Jacob had for his beautiful daughter Rachel. So he made the hard bargain that Jacob was to serve him seven years for the hand of Rachel.

Seven years was a long time—what they call a complete cycle of life, in which all the particles of our bodies change; so that physically, as they tell us, a new man, a new woman, emerges. Think of all the things that have happened to you in seven years—changes in your family, changes in the world, changes in your body, changes in your heart.

But it did not seem a long time to Jacob. It seemed but a few days because of the love he had for her. Perhaps they met sometimes, without the grasping Laban's knowing it, at that old well. There they sat together and looked down into the water and, seeing the star reflected there, read together their common destiny. But, whether they did or not, the seven years passed quickly for the infatuated Jacob.

There is the first reason why Rachel married the right man. She married a man who was capable of deep and tender and abiding romance and affection.

At length the marriage day comes around. The seven years' labor and apprenticeship are over. Now Jacob, before all the people of the village, who have gathered from far and near for the festivities, comes to claim his bride. The words of mutual avowal are spoken, the gifts are exchanged, and then Jacob leads Rachel to his tent. But when she unveils herself, lo, it is not Rachel—not the woman he loved, and for whom he had waited seven years—but the ill-favored and cross-eyed Leah! Laban had played a wretched trick on Jacob and had palmed off on him the older and less attractive daughter.

THE MULTIPLE MARRIAGE

It is hard to tell from the narrative whether, after a week had passed, Jacob was permitted to marry Rachel also, and then serve another seven years for her, or whether he had to wait the full fourteen years. But whether he married her then, or at the end of the second period, he served and labored for her fourteen years; and I doubt not that at the end of the second seven years he would have said what he said at the end of the first—that they seemed to him but a few days.

Yes, love shortens the day. Love shortens the journey. Love lifts the burden. Love lights up the pathway. With love all things are possible; and long waiting passes quickly where love holds the torch and shows the way.

Why did Jacob not resent the gross fraud of Laban? Why did he not strike Laban to the ground with his shepherd's staff? I suppose one reason was that Jacob felt he was being punished for his own deception. It is written that "he that doeth his own wrong shall receive for the wrong that he hath done." We reap what we sow.

Sometimes sin is not only punished, but punished in kind. Here we have an instance of that. Jacob had deceived and cheated his father and his brother. Now he in turn is deceived and cheated by Laban. That, no doubt, was one reason why Jacob made no protest. His conscience said to him, "Thou art the man."

Rachel's home life was at first unhappy. It was unhappy, too,

for Leah—wretchedly unhappy, for she knew that Rachel had
Jacob's love. Leah had six children, but Rachel had none. There is
deep pathos in that utterance of Leah when her first child was
born. She called his name Reuben, "for," she said, "surely the
Lord hath looked on my affliction. Now, therefore, my husband
will love me" (Gen. 29:32). Many a young wife and mother has
fondly, but vainly, uttered that same hope and prayer. "Now that
our child is born, now will my husband love me." "Now that we
have a child, my husband will treat me kindly." "Now that we
have a child he will stop drinking." "Now that we have a child he
will go to church with me." Beautiful, but sad, because oftentimes
it is a fruitless hope and prayer.

Leah had six children, but Rachel had none. Every time she
heard one of Leah's children cry in the neighboring tent it cut her
to the heart with envy and grief and self-reproach. The only time
that even the shadow of a cloud came between Jacob and Rachel
was when Rachel said to him, in her distress, "Give me children, or
else I die" (Gen. 30:1). And Jacob exclaimed, "Am I in God's stead,
who hath withheld thee the fruit of the womb?" (Gen. 30:2).

At length the prayer and the cry of Rachel were answered, and
Joseph was born to her. That was a child worth waiting for! Then
the long years that Rachel had waited for Joseph seemed to her
but a few days, as did the years that Jacob had waited for Rachel.
In the mystery of maternity and childhood, all the sorrows and
disappointments of her life were forgotten. Only such lovers could
have produced such a child—that wonderful Joseph, in many respects the prince of all the characters of the Old Testament, and
certainly the most Christlike among them; Christian in spirit and
forgiveness beyond his time.

THE RETURN HOME

One day Jacob's black tents were struck. He was migrating
westward again and separating himself from Laban. His two wives,
Leah and Rachel, with the seven children, and the other children
whom he had by their maids, and all their attendants, started with
him on the long trek back to the land of Canaan; for God had
spoken to Jacob and told him to return to his father's country.

On the way Jacob received an alarming message. Esau his brother was marching to meet him with 400 armed men! Esau! That was the man of all men whom Jacob wished to forget—Esau whom he had cheated, Esau whom he had wronged. Twenty years had passed since that base deception; but now the infamy and sin of Jacob came back to him with unchanged freshness.

How mysterious and how strange is the vitality of sin. Twenty years have come and gone, but Jacob's heart sinks within him as he hears that Esau his brother is marching toward him with an army of men! Those tidings stirred the pool of conscience within the breast of Jacob. Sin is one traveler who never changes and never grows old.

That night, after he passed his families and flocks and herds over ahead of him, Jacob, held by some mysterious power, tarried on the other side of the Jabbok. "And Jacob was left alone; and there wrestled a man with him until the breaking of the day" (Gen. 32:24). Mysterious, unaccountable, indescribable conflict! The angel wrestling with Jacob! Jacob wrestling with the angel! Who, until we meet that angel and Jacob himself in heaven, will be able to tell us what this struggle meant? But as to the results, there is nothing mysterious. Jacob emerged from that battle with the angel a changed man with a new name. He was no longer Jacob, the Supplanter; but Israel, one who had power with God.

TOUCHED BY GOD

And there is another reason why Rachel married the right man. She married a man upon whose life was the touch of God. At least once in his life every man has one close encounter with God, and in that night and in that encounter great things are possible for the soul. Out of the midnight struggle men learn that God is love and that He smites only to bless. How beautifully that is put in Charles Wesley's great hymn, one of the best commentaries on that mysterious battle:

> Come, O thou Traveler unknown,
>   Whom still I hold, but cannot see;
> My company before is gone,
>   And I am left alone with Thee.
> With Thee all night I mean to stay,
> And wrestle till the break of day.

I need not tell Thee who I am,
    My sin and misery declare;
Thyself hast called me by my name—
    Look on Thy hands, and read it there:
But who, I ask Thee, who art Thou?
Tell me Thy name, and tell me now.

Yield to me now, for I am weak,
    But confident in self-despair;
Speak to my heart, in blessing speak;
    Be conquered by my instant prayer:
Speak, or Thou never hence shalt move,
And tell me if Thy name be Love.

'Tis Love! 'Tis Love! Thou diedst for me!
    I hear Thy whisper in my heart;
The morning breaks, the shadows flee;
    Pure, universal Love Thou art:
To me, to all, Thy mercies move;
Thy nature and Thy name is Love.

On that critical night, when his whole future seemed at stake, Jacob took great precautions for the safety of His beloved Rachel. Both Jacob's father and his grandfather, Isaac and Abraham, when they felt that their lives were in danger, had practiced a cowardly deception, passing their wives off as their sisters in order that they might protect themselves, and not caring what happened to the honor of Rebekah and Sarah.

But not so Jacob! With all his many gross faults, and occasional sensuality, Jacob would never have done that. No! Rachel was the apple of his eye. To protect her, he sent the servants with their flocks and herds in advance; and after them Leah and her maids, and their children and servants; and then, furthest in the rear—furthest away from the point of danger—he placed his beloved Rachel and Joseph. There is thus another reason why Rachel married the right man: he was a man who had deep and tender and affectionate solicitude for her welfare.

A MESSAGE FROM GOD

When Jacob returned to Canaan, instead of going to Bethel to worship, as there twenty years before he had vowed to do, he settled down in the lush pastures of Shechem, where his family sank into idolatry. There Jacob forgot all about Bethel, and if at times there came a fleeting vision of a youth dreaming at Bethel, of a ladder reaching up to heaven, and the angels ascending and descending, he quickly dismissed such unearthly things and fell to counting his sheep and cattle. But one day God spoke to him and said, "Arise, go up to Bethel, and dwell there; and make there an altar unto God, that appeared unto thee when thou fleddest from the face of Esau thy brother" (Gen. 35:1).

So God calls men back to their better selves. So God calls men back to the early dreams and the holy aspirations of their lives. The first thing that Jacob did was to bury the idols his family had accumulated; for he knew that he could not take them with him to Bethel and find God again. Then, with Rachel and Joseph, and all his family, he set out once more for Bethel. He found the stone upon which his head had rested that night, set it up for a pillar, and knelt down and worshiped the God who had appeared unto him there. And God appeared again unto Jacob and blessed him. I can imagine how, as they sat together there on the starlit desert, Jacob told Rachel of the events of that wonderful night.

And there is another reason why Rachel married the right man: he was a man who, in his best moments, could see more than sheep and cattle, and black tents, and the things of the world. He was a man who could see ladders reaching to heaven and the angels of God ascending and descending, a man who was spiritually sensitive.

At length, the fairest and most sacred friendships and associations of life come to the parting of the ways. Yes; that was prophesied at the very beginning—there at the well in Mesopotamia, when, after he had drawn water for her sheep, Jacob kissed Rachel and lifted up his voice and wept. Kisses and tears! Prophetic kisses! Prophetic tears! And here we find them—kisses and tears—close together again, when Jacob and Rachel are parted. They were journeying together from Bethel; and, like another mother of Joseph's own line and descent centuries afterward, when they got almost to Bethlehem, Rachel's great hour came upon her and she went down again into the valley of motherhood.

This time she did not emerge from the valley; and, in her plaintive grief, the son whom she was leaving behind her she called "Benoni"—"the son of my sorrow." But brokenhearted Jacob could not bear to think of that, and called him "Benjamin"—"the son of my right hand." For the last time Jacob looked on that beautiful face—the face that had won him there at the well when first he saw her. With Jacob it had been love at first sight—and second sight, third sight, and all through the years, down to the very end.

To memorialize and perpetuate his grief, Jacob reared a tomb and monument to the memory of Rachel; and there you can still see it, not far from the gates of Bethlehem. But Rachel's real tomb was in Jacob's heart. She lived again, too, in those two sons, Joseph and Benjamin.

Jacob thought he had drunk deep enough of sorrow's cup; but there was another bitter draught for him when his sons came home one day and told him that Joseph was dead—Joseph, whose every look and whose beautiful life mirrored for Jacob the face and the life of the mother Rachel. But out of the sorrow Jacob was at length delivered, when he saw the chariots of Pharaoh and knew that Joseph still lived.

Now the old patriarch is dying down in Egypt. He gathers his sons and grandsons about him, and with that energy of soul which never forsook him, pronounces a blessing upon them one by one. Just before Joseph's children, Ephraim and Manasseh, are brought unto him, and the old man's mind wanders back to Rachel, and this is what he says: "Rachel died by me in the land of Canaan in the way when yet there was but little way to come unto Ephrath; and I buried her there in the way of Ephrath; the same is Bethlehem" (Gen. 48:7).

So with his last breath Jacob speaks of Rachel. It makes one think of that stern old American soldier and president, Andrew Jackson, sitting in his beautiful home, the Hermitage, near Nashville. The storms of his turbulent life lie behind him, and the harbor lights of eternity are beginning to flash for him. In one hand he holds the Bible, and in the other the miniature of his own Rachel—the beloved Rachel who for him was next to the Bible itself.

And there is another reason why Rachel married the right man: she married a man who tenderly and reverently cherished her memory long after she was in her grave.

So life goes on—its pilgrimages, flights, fears, angelic visions, ladders reaching to heaven, altars, apostasies, illusions—made tolerable by the light of love. And what is this love that Jacob had for Rachel but the shadow of a greater and deeper love? With a word about that love, I now conclude.

Jacob became Israel, a prince of God; and it was this prince of God who loved Rachel to the end. But the One who loves you is none other than the Prince of Heaven Himself. Jacob loved Rachel for seven years before he took her as his wife, and then loved her clear down to the end of her life. But Christ has loved you from before the foundation of the world. "I have loved thee," He says, "with an everlasting love." Jacob toiled hard for Rachel seven years; but this Lover toiled and suffered for you on the Cross. Jacob endured the heat of the day and the cool of the night through all those seven years for the love which he had for Rachel. But your Eternal Lover endured the pain and despised the shame on the cursed Tree for you. They taunted Him on the Cross, and said to Him, "If thou be the Son of God, come down from the cross." But He would not come down, for He was thinking of you and the salvation of your soul. Therefore, He could not, and would not, come down from the Cross.

Will you take now His redeeming love? You will need that wonderful love for life—for all its trials and sorrows, and battles, and temptations, and hard and lonely places. You will need that love in the hour of death. You will need it for the Day of Judgment. He will never leave you nor ever forsake you. Jacob had to part from Rachel, there near the gates of Bethlehem; but your Eternal Lover will never leave you and never forsake you. Will you take Him now, and rejoice forever and ever in His sovereign, unchangeable, unspeakable Love?

QUESTIONS FOR DISCUSSION:

1. The author classifies Jacob as the greatest lover of history—biblical or otherwise. Do you agree? Can you think of other couples in the Bible whose devotion to each other equaled that of Jacob and Rachel?

2. Jacob seems to have been happy to "serve" Rachel herself as well as to "serve" *for* her. What does this tell you about his love?

3. The author says that "Kisses and tears come close together . . . . in swift and unchanging succession." Do you agree? Is this always the case?

4. Why do you think Rachel's son Joseph turned out to be the most outstanding of all Jacob's children?

5. In a time when "arranged marriages" were the order of the day, why do you think Jacob had the luxury of marrying for love?

6. Macartney says that Jacob was the right man for Rachel for several reasons (i.e., he was "a man upon whose life was the touch of God," etc.). Pick out the reasons he gives and discuss.

7. Jacob's name means "supplanter," yet he became Israel, "a prince with God." What part did his love for Rachel play in that transformation?

Editor's Note: Read John 4 in its entirety to acquaint yourself with this Samaritan woman.

10

THE WOMAN WHO HAD FIVE HUSBANDS—AND ONE WHO WAS NOT

Thou hast had five husbands; and he whom thou now hast is not thy husband (John 4:18).

This is another of those beautiful and memorable scenes at the wells of the Bible. Only this time it is not Moses wooing Zipporah at her father's well in the desert, nor Eliezer wooing Rebekah for Isaac at the well of Mesopotamia, nor Jacob wooing Rachel by the well of Haran; but Christ Himself, the Eternal Lover, wooing the soul of a woman who was a sinner.

This is one of the greatest scenes in the Bible. So clearly and fully is it related by John—who must have been greatly impressed by it, since he gives so much space to it—that it is easy to follow and envisage even after the lapse of all these centuries. It came early in the ministry of our Lord; and yet here are some of the sublimest profundities of His teachings.

The Pharisees were saying that Jesus was baptizing more people than John. Not wishing to reflect in any way upon His great forerunner, Jesus—who, Himself was not baptizing at all, but His disciples—left Judea to go to Galilee. "And," John says, "he must needs go through Samaria" (John 4:4). Because of the ancient feud

111

between the Jews and the Samaritans, no orthodox Jew would pass through Samaria if he could help it.

The Samaritans were not real Jews, but descendants of Assyrians who had been colonized in Samaria after the conquest of that kingdom by the Assyrians. These colonists had been instructed by a priest of Israel sent to them from the captives of Assyria. The result was a dual worship which combined the heathen idolatries with the worship of the true God, a kind of "mongrel" religion. Their sacred mountain was Gerizim, where they built a temple. This was why the Jews had no dealings with the Samaritans.

But John says that Jesus "must needs go through Samaria" on His way to Galilee. The orthodox Jew, rather than do that, would cross the Jordan twice—into Perea and then back again—and reach Galilee by that roundabout journey. But Jesus went through Samaria. It is evident from what follows that He did so because He was convinced that there were those in Samaria to whom He could minister. Somewhere in that land and among those ostracized people, a seeking soul was waiting for Him. Thus it was that on His journey He came to Sychar, the ancient Shechem where Abraham had dwelt, and Jacob also.

In the summer some years ago, traveling in the other direction—that is, coming from Galilee to Judea and Jerusalem—I left Tiberias, passed along the eastern shore of the Lake of Galilee to Capernaum, and then, leaving the Sea of Galilee, went to Cana, where Jesus turned water into wine; from there to Nazareth; then across the plain of Esdraelon to the ruins of Jezreel, where the apostate Ahab and the ferocious Jezebel had their palace. From there I crossed the plains of Dothan, where the sons of Jacob were tending their flocks that morning when they lifted up their eyes and saw Joseph in the distance with his coat of many colors. From Dothan I continued to Sebaste, high up on the top of a mountain, and the site of Samaria, the capital of the northern kingdom of Israel, with the supposed graves of Elisha, Obadiah, and John the Baptist. There you can see the ruins of Herod's palace, where Salome danced before Herod and his lords. Continuing my journey, I came to Nablus, one of the most fanatical of the Arab towns, on the site of the ancient Shechem.

THE WELL

It was to this same place that Jesus came on His journey to Galilee. You can see, rising on either side of the valley, Mount Gerizim, where Joshua stationed half the people to pronounce the blessings, and across from it, Mount Ebal, where he stationed half the people to pronounce the curses. Down in the valley, surrounded by a square wall, is the ancient well of Jacob. When a man plants a tree or digs a well he blesses mankind for generations to come. When the awards and honorable mentions are given out in heaven, I expect to see well-diggers and tree-planters stand much higher on the list than many a poet and painter and speaker and inventor and soldier. The well is one hundred and five feet deep and nine feet in diameter. The priest of the little Greek church lowered the vessel far down into the well, where we heard it strike the water, and presently he drew it up again, "dripping with coolness." As I drank of that pure water, the centuries vanished, and I saw Christ sitting on the very curb of the well where I was sitting, and asking the woman of Samaria for a drink of water.

John says that Jesus, "being wearied with his journey, sat thus on the well" (John 4:6). The sun was just as hot then and the roads were just as hard then as they are today in that part of the world. Jesus was tired; just as I was tired, when I sat thus on the well and asked for a drink. Only He was much more tired, because He had come all the way from Judea on foot.

Here we have the Weary Christ. That makes you understand how often Jesus must have been weary on those long journeys of His. But from what followed we see that, weary as He was, He was not too weary to work for God, and not too weary to forget His own fatigue and His own hunger and thirst that He might have a soul.

How easily we excuse ourselves from labor for the church and for Christ on the ground that we are tired and weary. But Christ was never too weary to help a soul. I think it was Wesley—or was it Whitefield?—who said, "Lord, I am weary in Thy work, but not of it."

Jesus dismissed the disciples to go to the village of Sychar and buy bread. The fact that He sent all the disciples away arouses our interest. Was there something in His mind that John did not tell us here—the conviction, the premonition, that He was to meet this woman? There Christ sits alone by the well. It is one of the few times that we see Christ by Himself. He was alone at the beginning of His ministry, when He was tempted of the devil in the wilderness; and alone when He prayed on the mountain top; and alone in the Garden of Gethsemane. There is something very moving and appealing about this incident in the life of our Lord, as we see Him sitting there all by Himself, looking down into that deep well.

THE WOMAN

Presently Jesus hears the sound of sandals on the stony pathway. Looking up, He sees a woman who has come out from Sychar with a waterpot on her shoulder. Why had she come at that hot hour of the day—the sixth hour? Why had she come alone? In that land you can still see the women going out in groups to draw water at the early morning hour, or at the evening hour, talking gaily with one another. But this woman came alone, and at the hottest hour of the day. Perhaps it was that she might avoid the sneers and taunts of the other women, who knew her past, and her present.

From what is said, we gather that this woman was not old, and yet was not young—somewhere in that border land between youth and middle age. In her face are lingering traces of a departed beauty, and from her conversation it is evident that she has a quick, engaging, and pleasing personality. It is not hard to understand how she charmed so many lovers. But now all that is past. She had given herself to passion, and now the fires of passion have burned themselves out in her. Despised by her neighbors, she comes to the well alone, not weary in body like Christ, but weary and depressed in spirit.

Seeing her, Jesus said, "Give me to drink." There is nothing in John's story to indicate that the woman was in any way discourteous to Christ, or that she intended to refuse Him a drink. But she knew at once, by His appearance, that He was a Jew; and she expressed her surprise that He should deign to talk with a Samaritan woman—and still more, to make a request of her. There was perhaps more in that request of Christ's than the woman understood. In His agony on the cross Christ cried, "I thirst!" And it was more than a thirst for water. It was a thirst for souls. So when He asked this woman for a drink, it was drink divine, too, that He wanted. He was athirst for a soul.

The Water

The woman, whose way of talking catches and pleases us today just as it must have pleased Jesus, said to Him, "How is it that thou, being a Jew, askest drink of me, which am a woman of Samaria?" (John 4:9). Jesus did not enter into the merits of that ancient dispute between the Jews and the Samaritans, or say why He had disregarded the prejudice of His race. Instead of that, He told her of a real and present opportunity. How eagerly He reached out after this woman's soul! He said to her: "If thou knewest the gift of God, and who it is that saith unto thee, Give me to drink; thou wouldest have asked of him, and he would have given thee living water" (John 4:10). It is as if He had said, "Woman, I have asked you for a drink of water; but if you only knew who I am, and what I can do for you, you would ask of Me, and I would give you living water."

Living water! How much of His meaning did the woman grasp? Probably very little of what you and I understand today. And yet it is clear that in the soul of this woman—as, conscious or unconscious, in the soul of everyone—there was a thirst after something higher and better. Christ had at least aroused her curiosity. *Who is this, she wondered—this stranger who tells me that I ought to ask a drink of Him; and that if I did, He would give me living water? And what is living water?* So in her perplexity, and now with the greatest respect she said, "Sir, thou hast nothing to draw with, and the well is deep: from whence then hast thou that living water? Art thou greater than our father Jacob, which gave us the well, and drank thereof himself, and his children, and his cattle?" (John 4:11,12). In other words, "Have you better water than Jacob had, better water than this well where the generations of men and women have slaked their thirst?"

Then came that great answer of Jesus. His was not only a deeper well, and the water in it better than any other water, but so much better that one drink of it quenches thirst forever; and that water, once tasted, becomes a well of water springing up unto Eternal Life. Jesus said, "Whosoever drinketh of this water shall thirst again: but whosoever drinketh of the water that I shall give him shall never thirst; but the water that I shall give him shall be in him a well of water springing up into everlasting life" (John 4:13,14).

THE WONDERING

Here again we cannot say how much the woman understood of what Christ was saying. Certainly, he had stirred her soul with a desire for something more than just water. The interview had started by Jesus making a request of the woman. Now she makes a request of Him. *Whatever He means*, she thought to herself, *He looks and speaks as if He could make good what He says. At least He can relieve me of this long, hard journey; toiling from here up to the village on the hillside with this waterpot on my shoulder.* So she said, "Sir, give me this water, that I thirst not, neither come hither to draw."

Then came the startling and, to her, amazing reply of Jesus, "Go, call thy husband."

My husband! What has that to do with it? she must have thought to herself. And likewise, at the first reading, we think today, for it seems altogether irrelevant, an inappropriate inconsequence. But the purpose of Christ was to appeal to the woman's sense of sin, and show her that she could not drink—as no one can—of the Living Water until she had repented. Not imagining that Jesus had any real knowledge about her history and her life, and wondering why He had asked about her husband, she said—what was not true in the sense that she meant it—"I have no husband."

Then Jesus, who had complete knowledge of the woman's past and her history, said to her, "Thou hast well said, I have no husband: for thou hast had five husbands; and he whom thou now hast is not thy husband; in that saidst thou truly" (John 4:17,18). She had had five husbands, now either dead or separated from her, and at present was living in sin with a man who was not her husband.

Silent for a moment, subdued and awed by this marvelous insight into her life, the woman said, "Sir, I perceive that thou art a prophet." She was certain now of what she had felt all through this remarkable interview—that she was dealing with no ordinary man.

THE WORSHIP

But she now had such reverence and respect for Him that she felt ashamed and abashed that He should know of her unworthy life, and in the most natural way sought to turn the discussion away from herself to a matter of race and theological dispute. From where she was sitting she could see the grim outlines of Mount Gerizim. That suggested to her a way of escape from the probing of Jesus. So she said, pointing to the mount where the Samaritans had their temple, "Our fathers worshiped in this mountain; and ye say, that in Jerusalem is the place where men ought to worship" (John 4:20). In other words, "The theologians and doctors differ. I should like to know what you think on the subject."

And Jesus, accommodating Himself for the moment to this subject, and indulging the woman, did turn aside to discuss that question. He said the Jews were right. They had the true religion. The Samaritans worshiped they knew not what. Salvation is of the Jews. "But," He added, "the hour cometh, and now is, when the true worshipers shall worship the Father in spirit and in truth: for the Father seeketh such to worship him. God is a Spirit: and they that worship him must worship him in spirit and in truth" (John 4:22,23). Thus He tells her that the true approach to God is not now by way of Mount Gerizim, nor Mount Zion, but by repentance and faith, and a heart cleansed of sin.

To this the woman answered, no doubt with something of a sigh, and greatly stirred in her heart, and still perplexed in her mind, "I know that Messias cometh, which is called Christ: when he is come, he will tell us all things" (v. 25); that is, He will settle all these disputes and we shall all worship Him. Then said Jesus, "I that speak unto thee am he!" Now the woman understood His power to search her heart. Now she understood why He could offer her the Water of Life. The stranger who sat on the curb of the well of Jacob, looking into her face, was the Messiah of Israel!

The Witness

Just at that moment the disciples returned from Sychar, where they had gone to buy bread. They looked with astonishment upon their Master engaged in conversation with this solitary woman. Yet there was a light in His face—and, I am sure, a light in her face—which silenced every question that was in their minds. Seeing them, the woman hastily withdrew, forgetting her waterpot and leaving it behind her as she went back to the city. There she said to the men of Sychar, "Come, see a man, which told me all things that ever I did: is not this the Christ?" (John 4:29). Then they went out—probably with her again—to the well and talked with Jesus. Many of them believed on Jesus because of what the woman had told them about Him, and what she testified, saying, "He told me all that ever I did." They besought Him to remain in their city, and He accepted their invitation and stayed for two days. During that period many more believed on Him because of His own word. They said to the woman of Samaria, "Now we believe, not because of thy saying: for we have heard him ourselves, and know that this is indeed the Christ, the Savior of the world" (John 4:42).

But before Jesus accepted their invitation and came to the city with them, He spoke a great word there to His disciples at the well. They brought out their bread and said, "Master, eat." But Jesus had forgotten all about His hunger and His thirst. He said, "I have meat to eat that ye know not of" (v. 32). And following that came this great word: "Lift up your eyes, and look on the fields; for they are white already to harvest. And he that reapeth receiveth wages, and gathereth fruit unto life eternal" (John 4:34,36). What He meant was that all about them, even there in despised Samaria, there were souls ready to be won for the Kingdom of God.

There are three great truths that we taste here at this well of Samaria, as we drink of its waters.

1. Only Christ Can Satisfy the Soul

The first is, that Christ alone can satisfy the thirst of an immortal soul. Jesus said, "Whosoever drinketh of this water shall thirst again." Men have experimented with every well of this world. They have drunk of the water of power, fame, knowledge, riches, and sensual pleasures—but only to thirst again. When you think of it, how few faces there are, as you see them on the street, or anywhere else, that show complete content and satisfaction. No; they are all thirsting, consciously or unconsciously, for something higher. God has put eternity in our hearts, and He alone can satisfy that thirst.

Jesus said, "The water that I shall give him shall be in him a well of water"; that is, henceforth, he does not depend upon external things, but depends upon that well of water within himself. All parts of the world have their fables and myths about fountains and wells which had the power to bestow eternal youth and to satisfy man's every desire. But here is the only well and the only water which can do that.

Some years ago, driving up the Syrian coast between Tripoli and Antioch, I came to the enormous Crusader's stronghold, the Krak des Chevaliers, an immense world of stone where the Crusaders defended themselves against the Moslems. In the very heart and center of that colossal citadel and fortress was the ancient well into which the caretaker let down his vessel and drew water for us. All the old castles had their own well upon which they could depend when cut off from the rest of the world. When the world fails you, or turns against you, have you a well within you—a well of faith in Christ, springing up into Eternal Life?

2. THE DIVINE IN EVERY SOUL

The second truth that we drink out of this well of Jacob is this: There is a beauty and priceless value in every soul. How the Bible likes to declare and illustrate that, and never more beautifully than here. Here was this woman with her shady past, her five husbands, and her present companion in sin; and yet of all the women in Samaria at that time, this is the one for whom Christ was looking. In her He found the pearl of great price. Fanny J. Crosby's hymn expresses it beautifully:

> Down in the human heart
> Crushed by the tempter;
> Feelings lie buried that grace can restore:
> Touched by a loving heart,
> Wakened by kindness,
> Chords that were broken will vibrate once more.

3. THE PASSING OPPORTUNITY

The third and last important truth that we taste in the water out of this old well is the importance and the value of the moment. This was a wayside chance. The woman almost missed it; but through the goodness of Christ she did ask for and receive the Water of Life. When, in answer to Jesus' request for a drink, she said, "How is it that thou, being a Jew, askest drink of me, who am a woman of Samaria?" Jesus replied, in all the eagerness of His soul, "If thou knewest the gift of God, and who it is that saith to thee, Give me to drink; thou wouldest have asked of him, and he would have given thee living water" (John 4:10). She did know before that interview was over; and she did ask of him, and did receive the Living Water.

Yet how solemn are those words of Christ, "If thou knewest the gift of God"! Oh, how oblivious we often are to our opportunity! The Great Traveler passes our way; and too often as He goes by the soul does not ask of Him and does not receive. How nearly this woman missed the gift of Eternal Life. Lord, open our eyes to the sacredness of the divine opportunity.

Christ said to this woman, "If thou knewest." He used the present tense, for He meant, "If you will, you can know who I am and what I can give to you, and you can ask of me, and I will give it to you." But there was another and sadder occasion when Jesus used this same phrase, but this time in the past tense; not, "If *thou knewest*," but, alas, "If thou *hadst* known!" That is what He said to the people of Jerusalem when He saw the city and wept over it. "If thou *hadst* known, even thou, at least in this thy day, the things which belong unto thy peace! but now they are hid from thine eyes . . . . because thou knewest not the time of thy visitation" (Luke 19:34).

The time of thy visitation! God give you grace to know that. The Holy Spirit is speaking to you, I am sure. Oh, do not turn away! If you know the gift of God, and who it is for whom God's Holy Spirit speaks, you would ask of Him. You may be even now on the edge of the supreme moment of your life. If you *knew*! Before Christ must say, "If thou *hadst* known," ask now, and you shall receive Eternal Life.

QUESTIONS FOR DISCUSSION:

1. What does the weariness of Christ at the well tell you about His humanity?

2. Does this "human" side of Jesus seem incongruous to you as you contemplate His person and His mission? Discuss.

3. On page 114 Macartney says, "Despised by her neighbors, she comes to the well alone, not weary in body like Christ, but weary and depressed in spirit." Can you identify with her feelings of rejection and isolation? Have you ever felt that way?

4. Can you put Jesus' phrase, "living water" (John 4:10), in your own words? What other way could you express the same concept? Compare John 4:13,14.

5. Notice the gracious way Jesus rebukes the woman in John 4:17,18. Can we as Christians learn something from this about "loving the sinner, but hating the sin"?

6. Study the woman's witness in John 4:29. What can we learn from the way she testified?

7. Review and discuss the three great truths summarized at the end of this chapter.

Editor's Note: Read 2 Kings 4:8-37 for the full story of this woman and her son.

11

THE WOMAN WHO LOST AND FOUND LIFE'S GREATEST TREASURE

Thou shalt embrace a son   (2 Kings 4:16).
He sat on her knees till noon, and then died   (2 Kings 4:20).
Take up thy son   (2 Kings 4:36)

There you have it! There is the woman who received, lost, and received again, life's greatest gift. What greater gift is there than a son? What greater loss than to lose a son, and what greater joy than to have him back again?

Between the getting, the losing, and the finding again of that son, lies one of the great stories of the Bible, and the history of one of the Bible's greatest women.

Near the present ruins of Jezreel, in the valley of Esdraelon, is a little village called Sulem, standing on the site of the ancient town of Shunem. In this town there once lived one who was spoken of as "a great woman." As we shall see, she was great in other ways—great in her faith, great in her courage, great in her kindness and hospitality; but what is meant here, when she is called a great woman, is that she as a woman of prominence, of high standing, and of wealth.

Little is said of her husband, for the woman seems to have been the chief partner in this marriage. All persons of note who came through that town were entertained at her home.

Elisha happened to pass that way on one of his journeys through the land, and he was invited to eat bread in this woman's house. They were taken with Elisha and he with them, and thus it came about that whenever he passed that way he stayed in their home. One day, after Elisha had been their guest and had departed on his journey, the woman said to her husband, "Behold now, I perceive that this is an holy man of God, which passeth by us continually" (2 Kings 4:9). A splendid description that, of a godly, consecrated, and industrious minister of the Gospel—"an holy man of God, which passeth by us continually." "Let us," the woman said to her husband, "make a little chamber on the wall; and let us set for him there a bed, and a table, and a stool, and a candlestick: and it shall be, when he cometh to us, that he shall turn in thither" (2 Kings 4:9,10).

The woman's husband gave ready consent to her proposal. The stonemasons and the carpenters were called in, and before many months had passed the addition to the house was completed; and either on the flat roof of the house, or extending from its wall, there was a separate apartment for Elisha, with a private entrance. It was spoken of as "the prophet's chamber"; and down to this day that phrase is used to describe the room in the house where the visiting minister is entertained. In old Alexander Hall at Princeton that is what they call the guest chamber—the "Prophet's Chamber."

ELISHA'S OFFER

One day, while Elisha was resting from his journeys in this prophet's chamber, he was moved to do something which would show his gratitude for this woman's kindness and hospitality. He told his servant, Gehazi, to call the woman to his apartment. When she stood before him, he said, "Behold, thou hast been careful for us with all this care; what is to be done for thee? wouldest thou be spoken for to the king, or to the captain of the host?" (2 Kings 4:13). Elisha was a man of power in the kingdom, and his word went a long way with the king and with the captain of the host. But here was a woman who was satisfied with her lot.

She told Elisha that there was nothing she desired him to do for her, saying, "I dwell among mine own people."

In consultation with Gehazi afterward, Elisha wondered what could be done as a token of gratitude to this woman. Then Gehazi told him—what the prophet, singularly enough, had not thought of—that since the woman had no child she must greatly desire one. That was true. The woman had wealth; she had social position; she had health; she had high standing in all that part of the country. But she had no child. She would gladly have exchanged her great house which was childless for a peasant's cottage, if only she could hear the ring of a child's voice.

ELISHA'S PROMISE

Elisha then told Gehazi to summon the woman. When she came again to his apartment, Elisha said to her, "About this time of the year thou shalt embrace a son" (v. 16). The woman thought that hardly possible, and said, "Nay; thou art a man of God. Thou must not deceive me that way" (v. 16). Elisha answered nothing, but dismissed her.

And so it came to pass. When the year had gone by she gave birth to a child. You can imagine the change the child made in that home. The great woman now became what was greater. The child was tenderly nourished and brought up. By and by he was able to walk a little, and then to talk; and I am sure that, after the name of Jehovah, the first word they taught him to speak was the name of Elisha. When Elisha stopped at the house on his frequent journeys he would call the lad to his chamber and play with him and talk with him. So the happy years went by, full of sunshine and hope and expectation, until the boy was grown; that is, about twelve years of age.

It is harvest time in the fertile valley of Esdraelon. Before the sun is up, from every little village clustering along the sides of the mountains which guard that great valley the men, women, and children are going forth to the fields. In the distance looms the majestic dome of Mount Tabor, rising high above the plain. Every foot of this fertile valley is historic ground. Over yonder is Gilboa, where Saul and his sons fell in battle with the Philistines. Toward Carmel is the battlefield of Kishon, where Deborah and Barak overcame Sisera and the armies of Canaan. And yonder is where Gideon and his 300 men, with their pitchers and their trumpets and their swords, routed the vast host of the Midianites.

But men cannot live on history. Men must have bread; and year after year, century after century, the fertile fields of Esdraelon have been plowed and sowed and reaped, and so they will be plowed and sowed and reaped until the last great battle—the Battle of Armageddon—is fought there.

A FATHER AND SON

Now the sun has risen and the men and women and children are hard at work. Grain standing, grain falling like a receding wave of the sea, grain lying flat on the ground, grain gathered by the binders, grain tied together in bundles, grain tossed into the stack. First of all go the reapers with their sharp and gleaming sickles; then the binders; and last of all the widow and the orphan and the stranger, who gather up some of the grain that has been allowed to remain on the ground, according to the old law, "Thou shalt not wholly reap the corners of thy field." What a picture it is!—the stalwart men bending rhythmically to their task, the women picturesque in their blue skirts, yellow waists, and red headdresses.

In this part of the vast harvest field at which we are looking, the head man and master is the well-to-do farmer of the town of Shunem. He is a fine, upright figure, with his dark features and his gray beard. And following him about over the field is his little son.

When the Shunammite landlord started for his field that morning his little boy begged to be taken along. The father consented, but only after the boy's mother had charged him to see that the boy was not allowed to be too long in the sun, for the sun burns fiercely in August in that part of the world. It was a big day for the lad when his father consented to take him to the field. He was put astride a donkey; and, full of pride and joy, he followed the reapers and the gleaners into the field.

Busy with his task of supervision in every part of the broad fields, the boy's father forgot about him for a little, and the lad exposed himself too long to the sun as he ran hither and yonder over the fields, and now and then tried to take a hand himself and gather a little bundle of the grain and tie it into a sheaf. But presently he came running to his father, all the joy and pleasure vanished from his countenance, and cried out, "My head! My head!"

His father anxiously took him up in his arms and carried him into the shade of the tent that had been pitched for the comfort of the reapers, and he called for one of the women to do what she could for the lad. One ran for water; another opened his tunic and rubbed his chest and his throat. But he didn't grow better. All that they heard him murmur as he lapsed into unconsciousness was, "My head! My head!"

The anxious father then said to one of his servants, "Carry him to his mother! She will know what to do." So the servant carried him back to the village, where his mother held him on her lap and watched over him and prayed over him until noon, when the child died.

The child was dead. No mother's clasp, no mother's cry, no mother's prayer, could reanimate his body. The child for whom she had waited so long, and who for twelve years had filled her life with heaven on earth, was dead. I know how that woman felt. I never saw her, but I often heard my mother speak of her first-born child. My father went aboard as a student to study divinity in Scotland. There he fell in love with the daughter of a Glasgow manufacturer. He brought his bride to a little community in what was then the frontier in Ohio. In the course of time a child was born—a daughter who filled that home, and filled the parents' hearts, with joy and sunshine. After a year or two, my mother took the child on a visit to her parents in Scotland.

The brothers and sisters in that home had now married and had homes of their own, and the grandfather and grandmother had their hearts so warmed by the advent of this little grand-daughter that they persuaded my mother to leave the child with them, with the promise that in the springtime they would come out to America and bring the child with them. Willing to cheer them in their loneliness, my mother left her with them and re-turned to America. But she never saw the child again. From what she sometimes said, and from sentences in her diary of that year, I know how she felt. Her little daughter died in Scotland. And so I know how this great woman of Shunem felt when her son died on her knees. She felt that the light of her life had gone out and that she was living in a dark and empty and hollow cavern.

A WOMAN'S FAITH

But the woman did not lose her courage and did not lose her faith. This was a child given of God; perhaps the same God who gave the child would give the lad back to her again. It was natural that she should have thought of Elisha. Taking the child in her arms, she went up to Elisha's chamber and laid him on the prophet's bed and closed the door. Then, returning to her own apartment, she called her husband and asked him to have one of the servants prepare a beast for her to ride, and go with her to Mount Carmel, where the man of God, Elisha, was.

Her husband does not seem to have been told that the child was dead. He probably thought it was just some mild summer complaint, for he expressed great surprise when his wife wanted to start off on such a long journey at that time in the afternoon. His wife gave him no explanation except to say that all would be well. Mounting her beast, she told her servant to drive, and go forward, and not to slow up in the riding.

Elisha was sitting in his retreat on the slopes on Mount Carmel, when he saw in the distance the woman riding her beast along the highway. Looking more carefully, he said to Gehazi, "Yonder is that Shunammite woman. Run to her now, Gehazi, and say to her, Is it well with thee? Is it well with thy husband? Is it well with the child?" When Gehazi met her that was the salutation he gave her. The woman answered briefly, "It is well" (2 Kings 4:26). Either she did not want Gehazi to know what her trouble was, or she had great faith that in the end all would be well.

Not tarrying to talk with Gehazi, she pressed on toward Elisha, and when she came to where he was standing, fell down and clasped him about the feet. To the coarse-grained and insensitive Gehazi this seemed an unwarranted familiarity on the part of the woman with his master; and, laying a rough hand upon her, he started to push her aside. But Elisha rebuked him, and said, "Let her alone; for her soul is vexed within her: and the Lord hath hid it from me, and hath not told me" (2 Kings 4:27).

Then Elisha asked her what her desire was and what her trouble was. The woman said, "Did I desire a son of my lord? did I not say, Do not deceive me?" (2 Kings 4:28). That was as far as she went. But from the tone of her voice and the distress in her face, Elisha knew what had happened. Either the child was dead or he was desperately ill. For some reason Elisha did not propose to go himself, at first; but, giving his staff of authority to Gehazi he told him to go in all haste back to Shunem and lay the staff upon the face of the boy. He was not to stop to salute anyone by the way, for in the East then, and down to this day, a salutation was a much more lengthy thing than it is with us.

Gehazi did as he was bidden. He rode in all haste to Shunem, and, going up into the chamber, laid the staff upon the face of the child. But there was no response. The child did not awaken. This is perhaps the only account in the Bible of an attempt to work a miracle which was frustrated, unless we consider as such the attempt of the disciples of Christ to heal the boy possessed of the demon, while Christ and the three disciples were on the Mount of Transfiguration. Why did Elisha's staff fail in this instance? Perhaps because it was in the hand of an unworthy man, a latent hypocrite. Perhaps because Elisha ought not to have attempted to restore one to life again through another person, or to substitute the activity of Gehazi for his own. But whatever the reason, the staff failed.

A BOY RESTORED

When he arrived at the house Elisha went immediately up to the chamber where the lad lay, and going in shut the door and prayed earnestly unto God. Then he lay down upon the child and stretched himself upon him. After a little he arose and opened the door and walked up and down in the hall, or passageway, saying nothing, and over yonder stood the distraught and anxious, and yet believing, mother. Then Elisha went into the chamber again and shut the door and again stretched himself upon the child. This time the child sneezed and opened his eyes. Life had come back! Opening the door, Elisha called Gehazi and said, "Call the Shunammite woman." When she had come he said to her the sweetest words she had ever heard, "Take up thy son" (2 Kings. 4:36). The woman first fell at his feet and bowed herself to the ground in silent thanks, and then, taking up her child, went out.

This great and unforgettable miracle—perhaps the greatest miracle of the Old Testament—because of the beautiful and pathetic circumstances which attended it, is to us a prediction of the power of Christ to restore the dead to life. Eight hundred and eighty years after that woman took up her child, at the village of Nain, just around the shoulder of the hill from this village of Shunem, Jesus stopped the funeral procession and, laying His hand on the coffin, said to the dead, "Young man, arise!" And the young man arose, and Jesus delivered him to his mother. That great miracle at Shunem must have been a prophecy of the power of Christ one day to heal all broken hearts and to restore to every mother her lost child.

But what I wish to center upon in this noble narrative about the great woman of Shunem and the child whom she got, lost, and got again, is that word which the child's father spoke to the reapers when the child suffered a sunstroke that morning in the fields—"Carry him to his mother."

"Carry him to his mother!" Who is there now, a grown man, who does not have some recollection of being carried to his mother? When you stubbed your toe, when the dog bit you, or you fell out of the haymow, or you had a sunstroke, they carried you to your mother. She knew best how to comfort and soothe and bind up. It was good to be carried to mother.

Some speak rather lightly of Mother's Day as just a bath of emotionalism and sentimentalism, as if all mothers were good and godly like this Shunammite mother whose boy fell sick in the harvest fields. It may indeed be sentiment, but it is a mighty wholesome sentiment. It will do everyone good to be carried to his mother.

CARRY HIM TO HIS MOTHER WHEN HIS FAITH IN GOD IS HURT

The world makes war on a man's faith and conspires to steal it away from him. The loss of faith is the most serious of all losses, and the deepest of all hurts. Therefore, when a man's faith is hurt or shaken, carry him to his mother. This Shunammite woman was a woman of great faith before she was a mother. When trouble came she knew where to go. When this child came into the world, miraculously given to her and her husband, he found waiting for him that greatest advantage which can fall to an immortal soul when it comes first into this world—a godly, believing mother.

If a man's faith is shaken, that is the thing to do—carry him to his mother. What is said about a mother's prayer and a mother's Bible is far more than sentiment; it is a deep and powerful reality. One of the greatest and most gifted of the defenders of Christianity was Chateaubriand, the author of the famous book, *The Genius of Christianity*. This tribute of Chateaubriand to Christianity is all the more striking because he himself was a man who lapsed from the Christian faith and afterward returned to it.

He had written a book in which he had expressed the most skeptical ideas. He had said that reason would not permit him to believe in the immortality of the soul, and that we should have no desire to outlive our ashes. But about that time he received word of the death, on May 31, 1798, of his mother. This mother was a woman who had renounced the vanities and shows of her high social position and had devoted herself to religion. In the letter from his sister which informed him of his mother's death, Chateaubriand was reminded of the many tears his beloved mother had shed over his errors, and how she had prayed that his eyes might be opened, and that he would give up his writings against the Christian faith.

This affliction, and the subsequent death of his devout sister also, wrought a complete change in the heart and mind of Chateaubriand. Describing this change, Chateaubriand said in a celebrated praise, "I wept and I believed." The result of his change of heart was that he now devoted the pen which had been used to write against Christianity to defend it and to praise it. The result was his superb work, *The Genius of Christianity*. What had happened to Chateaubriand? Affliction had carried him to his mother, and to his mother's God. "I wept and I believed."

There was a man who once was assailed by an atheist. He plied him with argument after argument, and many of them apparently unanswerable, as he sought to undermine the foundations of his faith. After a brilliant and effective argument, the atheist exclaimed to the man, "Now what have you left?" He answered, "My mother's life." Yes, that is a great and unanswerable answer! "Carry him to his mother."

CARRY A MAN TO HIS MOTHER IN THE HOUR OF TEMPTATION

In the hour of temptation there is no stronger barrier between a man and sin than the memory of a godly mother or father. A great preacher and evangelist of a decade or two ago related how one night he was going out with evil companions to a place of disrepute. It would have been his first departure from the path of innocence; but on the way he had a sudden vision of his father's face—the godly father who had put his arm around him and said, "My boy, it would kill me if you went wrong." The recollection of his father saved him from his temptation, and from marring his soul with a scar which time could never erase.

Every man and woman knows that this is not sentiment, but real and beautiful and profound truth—the saving influence of the memory of a godly father or mother. Harriet Beecher Stowe, writing of the mother of the Beechers—that extraordinary family—said:

"I think it will be the testimony of all her sons that her image stood between them and the temptations of youth, as a sacred shield, and that the hope of meeting her in heaven has sometimes been the last strand which did not part during the hours of temptation, and that the remembrance of her holy life and death was a solemn witness to the truth of religion, which repelled every assault of skepticism and drew back the soul from ever wandering from the faith in which she lived and died."

The great actor Edwin Forrest, when asked how he had come unscathed through the temptations of the theater, said: "True, I have had temptations; nor have I always resisted them on the instant. The moment, however, when I was on the point of becoming the inebriate, or the gambler, and disgracing my profession, the words of my mother came up angel-like and checked me in my career."

Yes, in the time of temptation, carry a man to his mother. "Three times," wrote a man to me, "the memory of my mother has kept me from crime."

WHEN A MAN HAS BEEN HURT BY SIN, CARRY HIM TO HIS MOTHER

When a man has wandered from God and virtue, then carry him to his mother. Lay his scarred and stained soul in her arms for she will never despair of him. She will have faith in his spiritual recovery, as the Shunammite woman did in the physical recovery of that sick child, now dead, whom she laid on Elisha's bed.

Sometimes about the only place we can carry a sin-stained soul is to his mother. Others may scorn him or refuse him or abandon him; but not his mother. The warden of one of our great penitentiaries says that the mother is the one who holds on to a prisoner to the last. First his friends fall away; then his brothers and his sisters; then his children, if he has any; and then the wife, if the prisoner is a man, or the husband, if the prisoner is a woman. All of them fall away and cease to write letters and cease to visit. But the mother holds on to the last. In that respect she illustrates the infinite patience and mercy of God.

Carry the sinning man to his mother. The very thought of her righteous life, or her unfailing prayers, may bring him back to God. It may bring him back to God, if it is the influence of a living mother; and still more—mysteriously and beautifully so—if the mother's influence is an influence which shines like a star from the other world. "Carry him to his mother."

This is a word not only to sons and daughters, but also to mothers—the mothers of today, the young women who are to be mothers tomorrow. Are you living so that when your child comes he will find a woman of faith waiting for him? And mothers of today, are you living so that when your son is losing his faith, or is tempted to sin, or has fallen into sin, the recollection of you and your character, and your faith, will strengthen him and deliver him and save him? Are you the sort of mother of whom they can say, "Carry him to his mother"?

And this is a word, too, for all sons and daughters, both young and old. God's Holy Spirit is speaking to you. Do you remember what the greatest of all mothers said of the greatest of all sons— "Whatsoever he saith unto you, do it"? That is the word that we speak and repeat now. It is the word that your godly mother would say unto you. "Whatsoever *He* saith unto you"—that is, the

Lord Jesus Christ—"Whatsoever *He* saith unto you, do it." "Carry him to his mother."

If God has been speaking to any son or daughter through these words, then do what He says.

> O Mother, when I think of thee,
> 'Tis but a step to Calvary;
> Thy gentle hand upon my brow
> Is leading me to Jesus now.

QUESTIONS FOR DISCUSSION:

1. The wealthy woman in this account had everything but a child—and she seems to have adjusted herself to a life of childlessness. What does her acceptance of her lot tell you about her? Contrast her with Hannah, Samuel's mother. Why the difference—and what was the difference?

2. What kind of parents were the woman and her husband?

3. What do you think happened to the boy? What illness did he probably have?

4. Macartney says, "The woman did not lose her courage . . . (or) her faith." What does this say about the quality of her faith?

5. Do you agree that the father probably didn't know about the seriousness of the boy's illness?

6. What was the matter with Gehazi's faith?

7. What do you think of Elisha's method of reviving the boy? Does it appear to be an early form of mouth-to-mouth resuscitation?

8. Review and discuss the summary points at the end of the chapter.

Editor's Note: Read Luke 8 and Matthew 9: 18-26.

12

THE WOMAN WHO TOUCHED HIM

And Jesus said, Who touched me?   (Luke 8:45).

In the gospels we have the record of six persons whom Jesus touched, and who were healed by that touch of divine power and compassion. But here we have it the other way. Here is one who touched Jesus and was healed.

Like the play within the play in Hamlet, what we have here is a miracle within a miracle. You might call it a wayside miracle—just an episode in the raising from death of the daughter of the ruler of the synagogue at Capernaum. And yet the more one contemplates this episode, the more wonderful and beautiful it seems, until one almost loses sight of that other, and greater, miracle.

Jairus, a ruler of the synagogue, had gone to Jesus to ask Him to heal his little daughter, who was "at the point of death." Since the scribes and Pharisees and the rulers of the synagogue were, as a class, hostile to Jesus, it must have taken considerable courage and humility for this prominent citizen of Capernaum to go to Jesus and ask Him to heal his daughter. But he loved this child, who was an only child; not an only son this time, as so often in the Bible stories, but an only daughter.

He had called in the most reputable and famous physicians; but none of them could do anything for his little daughter, and it was

135

plain that she was going to die unless a miracle took place. So he put aside his pride and went to Jesus. Falling at His feet—which shows how greatly distressed he was—he begged Jesus to come to his house and save the life of his little girl. "Come," he said, "and lay Thy hand upon her, and she shall live."

This was an urgent case, and one that required immediate action; so Jesus rose up at once and followed him. When He got word of the sickness of Lazarus, He waited three days before He went to Bethany. But now He rises up immediately to go to the ruler's home. The word quickly spread that Jesus was going to the ruler's house to heal his sick daughter. Some had heard that the daughter was already dead, and they were all excited to see if Jesus could work so stupendous a miracle as to raise one from the dead. Everywhere people left their houses and shops and joined in the procession that was marching toward the mansion of the chief ruler of the synagogue.

Among those who heard that Jesus was on the way to the house of Jairus was an unfortunate woman. Since Jesus called her "daughter," she must still have been a young woman; but hard labor and sorrow and the drain of her disease had withered the flower of her youth. For twelve years she had suffered from a hemorrhage. This grievous disease not only weakened her body and depressed her spirits, but made her a social outcast. If she was a married woman she was compelled to leave her husband. She could not go up to the Temple and the place of sacrifices. If she touched any object or any person, that object and that person were defiled. If any other person touched her, that person was thereby made unclean.

Such was the sad and terrible plight of this unfortunate woman. She had gone to one physician after another, who took her money but could effect no cure. Mark says that she "had spent all that she had, and was nothing bettered, but rather grew worse" (Mark 5:26). Twelve years had passed. Think of all the things you have done, the places you have gone, the sights you have seen, and the joys you have had in twelve years! But the only experience of this poor woman was to see her strength and health wasting away and her fortune completely consumed in vain efforts to be healed.

But this day she was on the street there in the midst of the crowd at Capernaum, for she had heard that Jesus was on His way to heal the daughter of Jairus. There you can see her, crouching against the wall, trying to make herself as inconspicuous as possible, lest someone should recognize her and order her away. She had heard many things concerning Jesus. We have to hear about Christ before we can go to Him and be healed. That was Paul's meaning when he said, "Whosoever shall call upon the name of the Lord shall be saved. How then shall they call on him in whom they have not believed? and how shall they believe in him of whom they have not heard? and how shall they hear without a preacher?" (Rom. 10:14).

The preachers in this case had been the neighbors and friends whom this woman had heard speak about Jesus. Through them she had heard that He had raised up Peter's mother-in-law, that He had healed a nobleman's son, and the slave of the Roman centurion; and now she heard that He was on his way to raise up the daughter of Jairus. Now a flicker of hope lights up her soul.

If you and I had been there, and had seen her crouching against the wall with downcast countenance, we might have seen in her face and in her eyes at least a faint reflection of that hope and that light. And there she stands, waiting, waiting, and hoping that Jesus might pass that way. How many there are like this woman—just waiting, just hoping. Move carefully, speak gently, act kindly; for someone there where you are passing is just waiting and hoping.

But now she hears the stir of the multitude and the trampling of many feet; the boys, as usual, running ahead of the crowd, and crying shrilly one to another. Presently she sees Jesus approaching. He is walking beside Jairus, who is arrayed in his rich robes of the ruler, and other elders of the synagogue and prominent people are about him. The crowd presses close behind, and on either side, and walks in front of Jesus. He and the ruler are walking rapidly, for time is valuable because the little girl is at the point of death.

Now watch this woman against the wall, as she lifts her head and looks eagerly in the direction of Jesus. She is talking to herself, and this is what she is saying: "If I do but touch His garment, I shall be made whole. And yet, do I dare to try it? How can I get through this great crowd, when I am so weak and frail, and hardly able to stand? If the rulers see me, will they let me approach Him? After all, I am only an outcast; but so were the lepers; they were unclean too, and yet I hear that He healed them. He is on His way, also, to the house of a rich man. Perhaps He will not care to heal a poor woman like me, for I have spent all I had on the physicians, and have nothing with which to pay Him. And yet I have heard that He takes pity on the poor."

Thus alternate waves of hope and despair rolled over her soul. But Jesus was passing, passing, passing! Soon He would be gone, and her chance would be gone too. Summoning her courage, she resolves to try to touch Him. She steps out into the crowd on the street and works her way through the throng, fearful every moment lest someone will rebuke her and send her back. But at length she gets close behind Jesus. Every loyal Jew wore four tassels on his garment, bound in blue. These hung from the four corners of the robe—one at each side, one in front, and one behind. This was the hem of the garment. Now the woman puts out her hand quickly and touches that tassel which hangs down behind. Instantly, the feeling of weakness and sickness to which she has awakened every day for the last twelve years leaves her, and in its place comes the delightful, indescribable surge of health. She knows immediately that she has been healed.

When Christ healed the woman, she knew it. When great changes come over your body, you know it. And when great changes come over the heart and the soul, you know it.

With a great joy in her heart the woman hastily turns away to lose herself in the crowd, and is on her way back to the wall again when the crowd around her suddenly stands still, and she with them, for Jesus has stopped. She trembles in her heart as she hears Jesus ask that question, as He looks about him over the crowd, *"Who touched me?" Will He find out,* she thinks to herself, *that I touched Him? Will He think that my touch has made him unclean, and will He punish me because of that?*

Then, in a moment, she feels a degree of relief as she hears the people around Jesus say, "Lord, none of us touched Thee," and then Peter's loud ringing voice, saying, "Master, the multitude throng Thee and press Thee, and sayest Thou, Who touched Me?" But Jesus answers, "No; that is not it. I was not thinking of the press of the multitude. It was a different kind of touch. Someone has touched Me. Who touched Me?"

All the time you can imagine the distress of Jairus; you can see the look of anxiety on his face, as he thinks of his little daughter at the point of death. Perhaps he said to Jesus, "Master, why do You stand here arguing about some invisible person who touched You, when my little daughter is at the point of death? Oh, Master, come quickly with me, else my daughter die!" But wait, anxious Jairus, wait! What Christ does here for this woman will give you faith in His power to heal, to raise from the dead, when presently that terrible word comes to you that your daughter is dead and your neighbors say to you, "Trouble the Master no more."

The poor woman, certain that she cannot be hid and that Jesus will know who touched Him, and that she will be exposed, comes trembling and falls down before Him, and tells Him why she has touched Him and how she has been healed. After she has told the story of her sickness and her faith and her healing touch, Jesus says to her, "Daughter." As far as we know, she is the only woman who was thus addressed by Jesus. He calls her "daughter"—the same tender word which the rich ruler, Jairus, used when he asked Jesus to come and heal his little daughter. It was a word of encouragement and of affection. "Daughter, be of good comfort: thy faith hath made thee whole; go in peace" (Luke 9:48). That, you know, was what Jesus said to the unknown woman who washed His feet with her tears and dried them with the hairs of her head—"Go in peace." "It was not the hem of My garment that you touched that healed you; but your faith in Me has made you whole. Go in peace."

Christ and the Individual

This beautiful story shows, first of all, the interest that Jesus took in the individual. His public ministry was brief, and great was the work that He had to do and the truths He had to declare; yet He always had time for the individual, for the one who was in need, and for the one who sought Him. He saw Zacchaeus the publican there in the top of the sycamore tree, outside the gate at Jericho, and told him to come down. Although so many other voices were calling and shouting that day by the gate at Jericho, He heard the cry of the blind beggar, Bartimaeus, "Have mercy on me," and stopped and called him to Him and opened his eyes.

Yes, Christ was always on the lookout for the individual. At the very last, when He hung on the cross, He stopped dying for mankind long enough to talk with a thief and take him to heaven with Him. You may feel that no one is interested in you, that no one cares for your soul; there is One who is deeply interested in you, and that is He who died for you on the Cross.

Once more, this miracle shows us how faith heals. Was it superstition—this touching of the hem of His garment? Was her act like that of the people in Jerusalem who laid their sick along the street, so that when Peter passed by at least his shadow might fall over them? Was it like those people at Ephesus who brought to their sick friends handkerchiefs and aprons which Paul had touched with the hope that thus they might be healed? She did not try to touch the hem of the garment of Jairus, or any of the rulers or notables who were in the procession that day; but only the hem of the garment of Jesus.

Prayer, the Bible, worship, the sacrament of the church—all these are, as it were, the hem of His garment; and if you have faith, if you are seeking the Christ who is back of them, your touch on these things will have healing and cleansing power.

Again, this woman, when she had been healed, told the whole story and confessed to the healing power of Jesus. Not only Christ and Jairus, but all the people heard it. If some touch on the hem of Christ's garment has blessed you and helped you, then tell it; for your telling of it may encourage some other to come from behind in the press of the crowd and touch His garment. I have not the slightest doubt that this woman's story had great influence upon Jairus. Jesus had no sooner finished speaking with the woman than the messengers came from the house of Jairus and said to the ruler, "Thy daughter is dead; trouble not the Master" (Luke 9:49). But Jesus, hearing that, said to Jairus, "Fear not; believe only, and she shall be made whole" (Luke 9:50). I am sure that it was easier for Jairus to believe and trust that Jesus could raise his daughter, even from the grave, because of what that woman had told about the healing touch on the hem of Christ's garment.

Who touched me? Many today are thronging the churches. Many today are thronging Christ. But who will touch Him with the touch of faith? Yes, I am sure there are those at this very moment who greatly need to touch Him. Someone has an old sorrow that has been draining his strength—for a month, for a year, for twelve years, perhaps longer. In another's heart is some dread or fear that has hung over him like a dark cloud. In some other heart is dislike, or enmity, or hatred, which tears at his or her soul. Someone is beset by an ugly appetite that defiles body and soul. Someone is troubled and haunted by the memory of the transgressions of yesterday.

Yes; there are many today who need Him, many who need to touch Him. I am sure that as we have been considering this woman's story some of you have been saying within yourselves, as she did there against the wall in Capernaum when Jesus was passing by, "If I do but touch His garment, I shall be made whole." And what you say within yourself, to your soul, is true. Christ is still here; the healing of His seamless robe is in our midst.

I sometimes wonder what became of that robe of Jesus, with its four tassels of blue—that one which this woman touched. No doubt it was the very robe over which the Roman soldiers cast lots and threw their dice when Jesus hung dying on the Cross. One of those soldiers threw the lucky number and got the robe of Jesus and carried it off to his home. Perhaps he wore it himself when he was pensioned from the army, or perhaps it was made into garments for his children.

What happened to that robe after the Roman soldier won it, no one can tell. Yes; I can tell you now. That same robe is in our midst.

Crowds have thronged Him; who will touch Him? Who will touch Him now? Would you not like to stretch forth your hand and touch Him now? "Jesus of Nazareth passeth by!" This woman heard the cry that day in Capernaum. It was her first and last chance. In a moment He would have passed by and been lost to her—perhaps forever; but while He was passing, and before He had passed, she overcame her doubts and her fears, and stretched forth her hand and touched Him, and was made whole. She heard Him say, "Daughter, be of good comfort: thy faith hath made thee whole; go in peace." Would you not like to hear Him say that to you at this moment? Will you stretch forth your hand now and touch Him?

QUESTIONS FOR DISCUSSION:

1. This account reveals the power of Jesus over both illness and death. Why do you suppose the response of Jesus to the illness of Lazarus was different from His immediate reaction to the need of Jairus's daughter?

2. What does His reaction to the woman's touch on the hem of His garment tell you about Him?

3. Does the description of the woman's condition give a hint as to her problem? What do you think it was?

4. How do you think Jairus felt as all this was happening?

5. Was the woman's touch on the hem of Jesus' garment an act of superstition?

6. What does the woman's later witness tell us about her experience?

Editor's Note: Read Proverbs 31:10-31 in a modern translation to get an idea of how gifted she was.

13

THE IDEAL WOMAN

Thou excellest them all (Proverbs 31:29).

In the days when the Czars still ruled in Russia, I once paid a visit to Peterhof, the summer home of the Czars, not far from St. Petersburg. At that time it was a beautiful and attractive country palace, with fountains in the gardens rivaling those of Versailles. In one of the chambers of the palace the walls and the ceiling were completely covered with portraits of beautiful women, favorites of the Czars who lived there.

But the Bible is the greatest portrait gallery in the world. The famous galleries such as Dresden, the Rycks Museum at Amsterdam, the Louvre at Paris, the National Gallery at London, and Pitti Gallery at Florence cannot compare for a moment with the gallery of Old Testament and New Testament paintings; and very notable is the Bible's gallery of female portraits.

In this book we have taken our journey through the biblical gallery of women, where we have looked on the faces of Ruth, Esther, Rahab, Martha, Mary, Delilah, Abigail, Rebekah, Rachel, and others whose names are unknown. What a great thing it would be if we could have a composite portrait which would unite the fascination of Delilah, the decision of Ruth, the beauty of Rachel, and the ambition of Rebekah, the faith of Rahab, the eloquence of Abigail, the efficiency of Martha, and the pious meditation of Mary.

Annotations in margins (handwritten):
Important, Intelligence, Kindness, Industry, Spirit, Religious, Provides Food & Clothing, Purchases Property, Engages in trade, Exercises charity

Alphabetical Acrostic, Each line successive letter of alphabet

Fortunately, we have the Ideal Woman painted for us in the last chapter of the Book of Proverbs. Here we have the words that King Lemuel learned from his mother, warning him against strong drink and the wrong kind of women. But the book comes to a close with a hymn in praise of Ideal Womanhood. We cannot be sure, but perhaps King Lemuel was describing his own mother.

Many a man would think of his own mother as he reads this immortal passage. I knew of a minister who used to tell me how his father would sometimes read this chapter at family worship, then close the Bible before kneeling in prayer and, looking around the family circle, say, "Boys, there's your mother."

This king wanted to know where he could find a virtuous woman. Now he has found her, and here is her description and portrait.

HER INDUSTRY

Women who work & children Graduate School

"She looketh well to the ways of her household, and eateth not the bread of idleness" (Prov. 31:27). The bread of idleness, upon which so many women feed, is the source of much weakness and evil in their life. One has defined a popular perversion of Christianity as "imagination working on idleness." But here is a woman whose candle does not go out at night. That burning candle is a symbol of the sacrificial life of a good woman.

> I love to think her like a blessed candle
> Burning through life's long night;
> Greatly useful, simple, gentle, tender,
> Always giving light.

In George Eliot's *Clerical Sketches* there is a fine description of the faithful wife of the rector, Amos Barton, lighting her candle at early morning and attacking the heap of stockings at her side.

Mrs. Barton carried upstairs the remainder of her heap of stockings, and laid them on a table close to her bedside, where also she placed a warm shawl, removing her candle, before she put it out, to a tin socket fixed at the head of the bed. Her body was very weary, but her heart was not heavy, in spite of Mr. Woods the butcher, and the transitory nature of shoe-leather; for her heart so overflowed with love, she felt sure she was near a fountain of love that would care for husband and babes better than she could foresee; so she was soon asleep. But about half-past five in the morning, if there were any angels watching round her bed—and angels might be glad of such an office—they saw Mrs. Barton rise up quietly, careful not to disturb the slumbering Amos, who was snoring the snore of the just, light her candle, prop herself upright with the pillows, throw the warm shawl round her shoulders, and renew her attack on the heap of undarned stockings.

"She riseth while it is yet night." How many sons and daughters will remember that—how their mother rose before it was day and had their breakfast ready for them as they started out on the battle of a new day.

Many years ago I paid a visit in Edinburgh to Alison Cunningham, the faithful nurse of Robert Louis Stevenson—the one to whom he owed such a debt of gratitude for having led him safely through his early years of sickness. She it was who impressed upon his mind great moral and spiritual truths. He dedicated his volume *A Child's Garden of Verses* to her in these lines:

> For the long nights you lay awake
> And watched for my unworthy sake:
> For your most comfortable hand
> That led me through the uneven land:
> For all the story-books you read:
> For all the pains you comforted:
> For all you pitied, all you bore,
> In sad and happy days of yore:—
>
> From the sick child, now well and old,
> Take, nurse, the little book you hold!
> And grant it, Heaven, that all who read
> May find as dear a nurse at need,
> And every child who lists my rhyme,
> In the bright, fireside, nursery clime,
> May hear it in as kind a voice
> As made my childish days rejoice!

HER LOYALTY

[handwritten margin notes: Intelligence / Buys property / Women of world / work]

The Ideal Woman is loyal to her husband and to her children. "The heart of her husband doth safely trust in her. . . . She will do him good and not evil all the days of her life" (Prov. 31:11). Her husband is "known in the gates." She faithfully affirms him in all things good, in contrast with other women and wives, who frequently are a hindrance to the success and advancement of their husbands. Some of the noblest chapters in human relationships are those which relate to fidelity of wives to distinguished husbands. On the grave of Jane Welsh in Haddington Churchyard, Thomas Carlyle, who suffered remorse because he felt that he had not been always mindful of the treasure he had in his wife, put these words:

"For forty years she was the true and loving helpmate of her husband, and by act and word unweariedly forwarded him as none else could in all of worthy that he did or attempted. She died at London, 21st April 1866, suddenly snatched from him, and the light of his life as if gone out."

"She will do him good all the days of her life." Not just a romantic flash at the beginning of their relationship; but, clear down to the very end, a love that never tires.

And that same Stevenson wrote of his wife:

> Trusty, dusky, vivid, true,
> With eyes of gold and bramble-dew,
>   Steel-true and blade-straight,
> The great artificer
>   Made my mate.

What can surpass the loyalty of a good wife or mother? The author of that terrifying book *Out of the Night*, amid all his wanderings and transgressions, cherished the memory of his godly mother. He tells us how his mother sold the family silver and bought for him sea boots, blankets, oilskins, and gave him a small Bible as he was about to go to sea. When they parted at Hamburg he saw her last at the train window, "shabby, frail, sad, and invincibly loyal."

Her Charity *Kindness*

"She stretcheth out her hand to the poor; yea, she reacheth forth her hands to the needy" (Prov. 31:20). Sometimes women are sacrificial and self-denying at home with their families, but outside the home, they may be hard and unfeeling. But this woman stretched forth her hands to the poor and the needy. She was like that Dorcas of whom we read in the Book of Acts, and whom Peter raised from the dead. "This woman was full of good works and almsdeeds which she did" (Acts 9:36). When Peter came to her home at Joppa, he found all the widows mourning over her, and they showed him the coats and garments which Dorcas made "while she was with them." Yes, the tears of the poor are the best epitaph of the dead. *Coats*

One of the clearest memories that I have of Christmas at home is the recollection of how our mother sent me and my brother across the river one Christmas morning to a humble home in a *Christ* poor settlement, where we left a basket of supplies for the family. I *mas* think I learned that morning the truth of the beautiful saying of *for* our Lord, which was saved and recovered for us by Paul in his *poor* farewell address at Miletus to the elders of the church of Ephesus—how it is "more blessed to give than to receive."

The Beauty of Her Speech

"The law of kindness is on her tongue" (Prov. 31:26). On an old tombstone in Egypt was found this epitaph: "Peace was in the words which came from his mouth, and the book of the wise was on his tongue." In his account of the women of Laputa, how they raised an insurrection when it was proposed that henceforth speech be abandoned and that all communication be with signs, Dean Swift takes a jibe at woman's fondness for speech. He might have said the same thing about men. Yet, where the tongue is wrongly used, woman probably has the pre-eminence over man. In his famous description of the tongue, James calls it "a world of iniquity," which "setteth on fire the course of nature; and it is set on fire of hell" (James 3:6). But here is a woman with the law of kindness on her tongue. No ill report gains an inch of territory through her passing it on to another. She does not impute wrong motives to others. She thinks no evil and does not rejoice in iniquity, but rejoices in the truth. Where praise is possible, she praises; and where it is not possible, she keeps silence. Well do I remember my mother's comment on an unworthy person who was being discussed: "Yes, but he is one of those souls for whom Christ died."

HER GODLY CHARACTER *Religious Spirit*

"A woman that feareth the Lord, she shall be praised" (Prov. 31:30). Was she a beautiful woman? Nothing is said about that; but all the better if these lovely traits were framed in a beautiful body, for the charm of womanly beauty wil last as long as the charm of a beautiful sunrise or the morning glory of roses in June. What is emphasized here is another kind of beauty—the beauty of soul. Strength and honor are this woman's clothing. Bodily beauty is vain and deceitful. It may become the ally and agent of evil and temptation; and even where it is united with a beautiful soul it is bound to fade and vanish despite all the artifices of the beauty parlor. But the beauty of the soul never fades, and it never leads astray or deceives.

Before we bid farewell to this Ideal Woman, we might attempt a brief paraphrase of this hymn in her praise in the Book of Proverbs. "A virtuous woman, who can find? But the worldly woman you can find anywhere today. Her name is legion. The virtuous woman rises while it is night to engage in her labors for the family, but the worldly woman rises sometime before noon. The candle of the virtuous woman goes not out by night, but the cigarette of the worldly woman goes not out by day or night. She lays her hand to the cards, and her hands hold the cocktail. Her husband searches for her in the night clubs. She opens her mouth with folly, and on her tongue is the law of gossip."

But here is another kind of woman. "Thou excellest them all." Her influence abides from generation to generation, and her children rise up and call her blessed. The uplifting, preserving, warning, sanctifying, purifying, and comforting influence of a godly mother is one of the most powerful forces that work upon the soul of man. Well could Paul appeal to Timothy by the faith and love of his mother Eunice and his grandmother Lois.

A great preacher of a bygone generation, T. DeWitt Talmadge, used to tell how when his father was absent from the New Jersey farm home, his mother would take his father's place at the family altar, and would always pray that all her children might be the "subjects of converting grace." Name, if you can, a higher, stronger, more uplifting, and more abiding influence than that of a good mother!

This ancient sketch of the Ideal Woman was written before Christ came. Now the Christian artist can add a few strokes of his own with the New Testament brush; and there you have the complete masterpiece. Make her a woman who has bowed at the Cross; make her a woman who loves the church which Christ loved and for which He shed His precious blood; make her a woman whose Eternal Lover is the Lord Jesus Christ, and there you have the Ideal Christian Woman.

Would you women of today know the highest joy in life? Would you repeat and renew yourself, and have yourself go on from generation to generation? Then join the company of those women who followed Christ when He was on earth and ministered unto Him, and who, when He was dead, brought their myrrh and spices to anoint His body. And these same women were among the first to greet and worship the risen Christ!

QUESTIONS FOR DISCUSSION:

1. Do you feel that the woman of Proverbs 31 would better be called "wonder woman"? Is she, in modern parlance, an overachiever?

2. Note the five characteristics Dr. Macartney brings out about her. Using a topical Bible, discuss each with reference to other passages of Scripture dealing with the same subject.

3. Read Proverbs 31:10-12 in the light of Proverbs 12:4 and 19:14. Read these verses in a modern version and/or paraphrase and apply their lessons to the last decade of the twentieth century.

4. What are some ways modern mothers and wives put these principles into practice? Compare this "ideal woman" to Dorcas in the New Testament and list things a single woman could do that approximate what the writer of Proverbs is talking about here.

5. On page 147 Macartney says, "Where the tongue is wrongly used, woman probably has the pre-eminence over man." Do you agree with his premise? What do you feel is your "besetting sin"?

6. The author calls for a servant's heart as he concludes this book and this chapter. Who is the best example of servanthood you can suggest?

ADDITIONAL RESOURCES FOR YOUR STUDY OF BIBLE CHARACTERS

Sermon Outlines on
Bible Characters (Old Testament)   Compiled by Al Bryant

This collection includes sermon outlines on Old Testament characters from Adam to Samson and Sarah, selected from the writings of such pulpit giants as Jabez Burns, James Hastings and Robert Murray M'Cheyne. They have been selected for their strong scriptural support and solid expository structure. Indexed by subject (Bible Character) and Scriptural references, they will enhance the pulpit ministry and enrich those in the pew.

ISBN 0-8254-2297-3   64 pp.   paperback

Sermon Outlines on
Bible Characters (New Testament)   Compiled by Al Bryant

From the prophetess Anna through the Wise Men who came to worship Jesus, the subjects of these sermon outlines become living, breathing people to preacher and hearer alike. Included are series on the people Jesus profiled in the parables, a unique series on the various facets of the life of Christ, and the life of the Apostle Paul. Included are sermons from pulpit giants like F. E. Marsh, Jabez Burns and other sources.

New insights into how Jesus dealt with individuals will guide preacher and people alike into new understandings of biblical truth.

ISBN 0-8254-2298-1   64 pp.   paperback

Designed for Conquest   Roy L. Laurin

This unique book offers practical help for life's problems. Through the experience of these biblical models, you will discover the secrets which will enable you to be an overcomer, whether enjoying times of plenty or struggling through adversity.

ISBN 0-8254-3139-5   192 pp.   paperback

BIBLE PORTRAITS SERIES   **George Matheson**

Believers looking for fresh insights into Bible characters will find a rich treasure in Matheson's series on Bible portraits. Warren W. Wiersbe says of this blind author, "No evangelical writer . . . surpasses George Matheson in this whole area of Bible biography . .. . God has closed [his] eyes— only to open other eyes, which have made [him] one of the guides of men."

Portraits of Bible Women
ISBN 0-8254-3250-2   264 pp.   paperback

Portraits of Bible Men **(1st Series)**
ISBN 0-8254-3251-0   384 pp.   paperback

Portraits of Bible Men **(2nd Series)**
ISBN 0-8254-3252-9   368 pp.   paperback

Portraits of Bible Men **(3rd Series)**
ISBN 0-8254-3253-7   368 pp.   paperback

Women of the Bible   **Frances VanderVelde**

Character Studies of over 30 women with lively discussion questions included. Excellent for women's Bible study groups.

ISBN 0-8254-3951-5   260 pp.   paperback

Bible Characters from the
Old and New Testaments   **Alexander Whyte**

The most famous writing from this Scottish clergyman complete in one volume! Includes sketches of men and women from the Old and New Testaments. The author was uniquely skilled and through his sanctified imagination, brings to life the times and circumstances of these Bible characters.

ISBN 0-8254-3980-9   928 pp.   paperback
ISBN 0-8254-3981-7   928 pp.   deluxe hardcover

Available at Christian bookstores, or

KREGEL Publications

P. O. Box 2607 • Grand Rapids, MI 49501